SIR JOHN VANBRUGH AND THE VITRUVIAN LANDSCAPE

Sir John Vanbrugh (1664–1726) is one of the most important figures in English garden history, although he is rarely recognised as such. An eclectic early career as a merchant, a soldier and a dramatist preceded Vanbrugh's acceptance of the role of architect to the 3rd Earl of Carlisle in 1699. His impact on architecture was mirrored by a revolution in landscape design as Vanbrugh shifted the place of the architect from the house to the grounds. He used the ancient rules of proportion combined with an empathetic approach to Nature to create innovative layouts that were geometric, but bore no relation to the formal gardens of the seventeenth century.

In *Sir John Vanbrugh and the Vitruvian Landscape* Caroline Dalton seeks to explain Vanbrugh's distinctive style of landscape architecture. The natural and moral philosophy of Marcus Vitruvius Pollio (Vitruvius), Euclid, Plato and Epicurus is traced through the Arabic scientists of the Middle Ages into the Italian Renaissance. The book examines the impact of science and humanism on the landscape ethos of Leon Battista Alberti in the *Quattrocento* and of Andrea Palladio a century later, and looks for parallels with the early Enlightenment in England from 1660 onwards. It becomes clear that the scientific advances and the political, social and economic changes associated with the Enlightenment created an atmosphere in which Vanbrugh could thrive. By reference to the writing of Vitruvius, Alberti and Palladio and by utilising his innate skills as an artist, Vanbrugh combined the science of Vitruvian geometry with the philosophy of the Ancients to create a new English landscape.

The text is illustrated throughout with 100 images, including eighteenth-century maps and plans that have not previously been published, alongside geometrical analysis and computer-generated reconstructions of Vanbrugh's landscapes. The author has combined her extensive knowledge of information technology with her experience as a landscape historian to produce an innovative work that questions our previous understanding of the first English landscape architect. The book is essential reading for students of the history of the eighteenth-century landscape, as well as appealing to those with a general interest in garden history.

Caroline Dalton was educated at the universities of Oxford and Bristol and is currently an Honorary Research Fellow in the School of Geographical Sciences at Bristol. She worked for several years as a programmer and project manager in the computer industry before returning to academia to study the history of designed landscapes. During research for her doctorate on Sir John Vanbrugh she used her experience in IT to establish new and valuable insights into the development of historic gardens and parks, and she has since applied computer technology to many aspects of her work. She is a Tutor of Landscape History on the Continuing Education programme and a Fellow of the Royal Geographical Society.

SIR JOHN VANBRUGH AND THE VITRUVIAN LANDSCAPE

Caroline Dalton

Routledge
Taylor & Francis Group

LONDON AND NEW YORK

First published 2012
by Routledge
2 Park Square, Milton Park, Abingdon, Oxon OX14 4RN

Simultaneously published in the USA and Canada
by Routledge
711 Third Avenue, New York, NY 10017

Routledge is an imprint of the Taylor & Francis Group, an informa business

British Library Cataloguing in Publication Data
A catalogue record for this book is available from the British Library

Library of Congress Cataloging in Publication Data
Dalton, Caroline.
Sir John Vanbrugh and the Vitruvian landscape/Caroline Dalton.—1st ed.
p. cm.
Includes bibliographical references and index.
1. Vanbrugh, John, Sir, 1664–1726. 2. Landscape architects—England—Biography.
3. Landscape architecture—England. 4. Gardens, English—History—18th century.
I. Title.
SB470.V3D35 2012
712.092—dc23
2011019822

ISBN: 978-0-415-61163-3 (hbk)
ISBN: 978-0-415-61164-0 (pbk)

Typeset in Bembo by Prepress Projects Ltd, Perth, UK

Printed and bound in India by Replika Press Pvt. Ltd.

CONTENTS

FIGURES

ACKNOWLEDGEMENTS

I am grateful to Mr Simon Howard for permission to use items from the Castle Howard archives and to Chris Ridgway and Anna Louise Mason for their assistance during my visits. My thanks also go to Karen Wiseman and John Forster at the Blenheim Palace archive; the 1709 and 1719 plans of Blenheim are reproduced by kind permission of His Grace the Duke of Marlborough. Philip Winterbottom at the Royal Bank of Scotland, and Pamela Hunter at Hoare's Bank, have allowed me to access the private accounts of the Dukes of Ancaster, Stephen Switzer and John Vanbrugh, and have responded promptly to my several requests. Kerry Downes was kind enough to answer my enquiry regarding his 1987 book on Vanbrugh and Tim Connor was helpful in resolving a question about Switzer's accounts. I would like to thank Jim Farquharson and Ronnie Farquharson for allowing me to visit the private Eastbury Estate, and the staff at Claremont School for permitting two visits to the school grounds. Michael Richardson in the University of Bristol Special Collections, Roxanne Peters at the Victoria & Albert Museum, Auste Mickunaite at the British Library, Samantha Townsend, Tricia Buckingham and Colin Harris at the Bodleian Library and Barbara Kellum have all been helpful with the images and permissions. I am grateful to Sir Andrew Morritt and the staff at Rokeby Park for a copy of the painting of the West Front of Castle Howard and to the Earl of Scarbrough, who took the photographs of the coloured plan of Lumley Castle. The following historians have accompanied me on tours of Vanbrugh's houses and grounds, or have provided useful information: Nora Butler at Kimbolton Castle, Harry Beamish and Martin Green at Seaton Delaval and Steffie Shields at Grimsthorpe; Valerie Joynt introduced me to Charles Bridgeman's Spring Wood in Hampshire. Finally, my thanks to Robert Mayhew, Tim Mowl and Tom Williamson; this book is founded on a doctoral thesis and has significantly benefitted from their comments and suggestions.

INTRODUCTION

The aim of the seventeenth-century garden designer was to demonstrate man's control over Nature. Where possible, gardens were laid out on a horizontal plain and natural undulations in the ground were removed. Only carefully placed representations of topography appeared in the form of mounts, and stepped terraces were built where it was physically impossible to level the ground. Whether large or small, gardens were close to the house; they were enclosed by walls and divided into separate areas of embroidered parterres, clipped box or groves criss-crossed with paths. On more extensive estates long avenues cut great swathes through the surrounding countryside, signifying the power and wealth of the owner. In 1700 Timothy Nourse wrote that the best choice of site for a house was 'on the side of a Ground gently rising, not amongst *Enclosures*, but in a champaign, open Country'[1]; but his endorsement of a classical setting was not evident in the pages of Johannes Kip and Leonard Knyff's *Britannia Illustrata,* a lavish tribute to the formal gardens of the 1690s (Figure 0.1).

In the summer of 1699, before he commenced work as Lord Carlisle's architect at Castle Howard in Yorkshire, John Vanbrugh had made a tour of 'most of the great houses in the North'.[2] He was about to replace the architect William Talman and the garden designer George London; both men were eminent practitioners of the day but the inexperienced Vanbrugh was not to be intimidated. He could only have seen houses and gardens of the formal style such as those in the pages of Kip's book, and yet from this very earliest commission Vanbrugh's house and landscape architecture was going to be different. His first decision was to redesign and move Talman's proposed house to the south, allowing a clear access route into an existing plantation of beech and oak trees set on a hill, known as Ray Wood. London's landscape plan (Figure 0.2) depicts a formal symmetrical arrangement of parterre and canals about the house, and we can assume that the intention was to level the ground in Ray Wood to create the prominent star of avenues, in accordance with the prevailing taste. But the mixture of clay, limestone and sandstone on which the present house stands had created a rolling topography that presented only scenic opportunities to Vanbrugh. His aim was not to flatten, but to place the access roads to Lord Carlisle's new castle so that the rise and fall of the landscape was used to dramatic effect. He built two

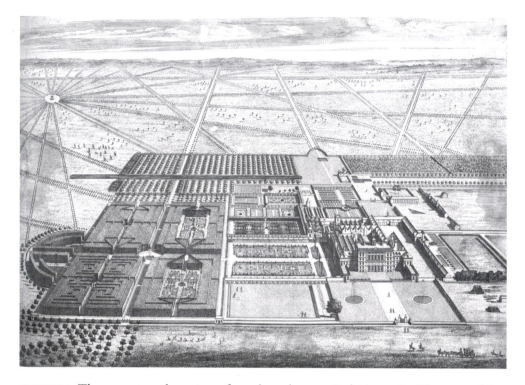

FIGURE 0.1 The seventeenth-century formal gardens at Badminton in Gloucestershire, *c.* 1700. J. Kip and L. Knyff, *Britannia Illustrata* (London: D. Mortier, 1707). Special Collections, University of Bristol.

monumental gateways over the road to the north of the house, framing a statue of Apollo at the top of the hill in Ray Wood to the east, and an obelisk to the west. Visitors arriving at Castle Howard would see these objects appear and disappear from view, as their carriages bowled over the hills and vales of the straight approach roads that were a reference to the Ancient Roman source of the design (Figure 0.3). The completed scheme was distinctive and unusual, and nothing like the formal estates of the seventeenth century.

Vanbrugh would go on to create some of the most important parkscapes of the early eighteenth century. At each project he applied an innovative geometric framework that united all of the disparate elements of his design into a single composition, but he never lost his sensitivity to the topography of the site or his passion for landscape. Vanbrugh's designs demonstrated the Enlightenment understanding of both the beauty and the order of Nature: this was not the hegemony of topography over geometry, it was an imaginative way of using the existing geography *with* geometry in a style that had not previously been seen in England.

The early eighteenth-century garden has been the subject of considerable modern debate and authors have focused on the influence of travel, philosophy, politics or neo-classicism on its design and development; this book examines all of these aspects as part of the socio-political maelstrom that was the early English Enlightenment, and considers how they influenced the work of a talented dramatist who reinvented himself as an exceptional landscape architect. English garden history from the seventeenth to the late

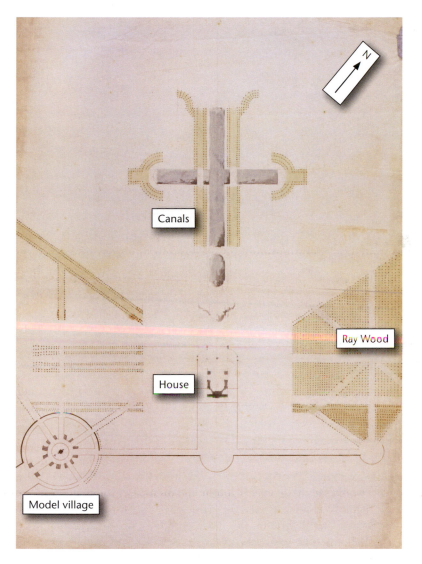

FIGURE 0.2 Plan of the landscape at Castle Howard, attributed to George London, early 1700. © V&A Images, Victoria & Albert Museum, London E433.1951.

eighteenth century has been viewed as a slow transition from formality to informality, as the predictable contiguous garden rooms depicted by Kip and Knyff slowly metamorphosed into Lancelot 'Capability' Brown's landscape garden, where the reign of Nature over Art was firmly established and the lawn ran up to the walls of the house.[3] As a result, scholars have sought the author of 'transition', that period when the overt geometry of the formal garden started to give way to this unstructured style; Peter Willis has identified Charles Bridgeman as the most important transitional gardener, believing that he began to break with the tradition of geometry in the 1720s before the arrival of William Kent, who 'leaped the fence' and softened and romanticised the English landscape from the 1730s onwards.[4] There has been no detailed analysis to date of the period 1700–30 as a distinct

FIGURE 0.3   The tip of Vanbrugh's obelisk framed by the Pyramid Gate on the approach to Castle Howard from the south. Photo: author, 2008.

period of design rather than as a step towards the landscape garden; yet garden makers of the time were not striving to achieve a future informality that they knew nothing about. The interest in winding paths as indicators of incipient naturalism or discussions of the demise of topiary have only emphasised the confusion over the persistence of geometry in a world in which the contemporary literature apparently called for something more natural. This treatise is an attempt to re-read garden history in the context of the Enlightenment rather than that of the twenty-first century.[5] In studying Enlightenment garden design it becomes clear that the eighteenth-century understanding of the word 'natural' was different from ours, and that the presence of Nature in the garden was encoded on paper whilst it was obvious on the ground, and in the mind of the Enlightenment connoisseur.

Twentieth-century studies of Vanbrugh start with Geoffrey Webb's edition of his letters and plays of 1928. In his introduction to the letters, Webb explores the influences on Vanbrugh's house architecture and he concludes a short section on his garden design with the observation that it is in his 'love for wide prospects and romantic vistas, that Vanbrugh appears as the precursor of the landscape gardeners'.[6] Laurence Whistler wrote a biography of Vanbrugh in 1938 but followed it in 1954 with the most extensively researched and scholarly work on his landscape architecture to date.[7] He was the first to consider in detail the gardens and parks around Vanbrugh's buildings, and although more recent work has uncovered new and important information on the architect, and some of Whistler's conclusions are questioned in this book, his study remains a significant contribution to Vanbrughian scholarship. Kerry Downes's two biographies of Vanbrugh of 1977 and 1987 provide the most comprehensive account of the life of the man as well as his architectural projects but add little to the understanding of his gardens, and Frank McCormick focuses on the influence of the theatre on Vanbrugh's work.[8] The papers from a conference at Castle Howard that were published under the title *Sir John Vanbrugh and Landscape Architecture in*

Baroque England include several essays on more general aspects of early eighteenth-century garden design.[9] The conference began the reinstatement of Vanbrugh as an important figure in garden history, but did not attempt an analysis of all of his projects or consider in any detail the causal factors behind his designs. In the most recent biography of 2008, Vaughan Hart develops McCormick's line of reasoning on the influence of the theatre and proposes that both mediaevalism and heraldry had a significant impact on Vanbrugh's buildings. Although he includes short sections on landscape, Hart's focus is again on the house architecture.[10] Other works that have added to Vanbrughian study include Charles Saumarez Smith's (1997) *The Building of Castle Howard* and Tim Mowl's (2004) chapter on Vanbrugh in *Gentlemen and Players*. Willis's study of Bridgeman was the first to catalogue and publish the important collection of early eighteenth-century garden designs in the Gough Collection in the Bodleian Library in Oxford; consequently, the collection has become associated with Bridgeman more than any other. It is time to redress the balance, and consider again whether some of these landscapes can now be credited to Vanbrugh.

The opening chapter of this book traces the form of the classical landscape from its origins in Ancient Rome and Greece through to the Italian Renaissance. The landscape aesthetic of Pliny the Younger in the first century AD was the product of the science of the architect Marcus Vitruvius Pollio (hereafter, Vitruvius) and the mathematician Euclid, and the philosophy of Epicurus and Plato; it valued the order of geometry alongside the untamed wilderness of the countryside. As the culture and science of the Ancients was recovered by Italian humanists 1,300 years later, both geometry and an empathy for Nature became evident in the work of the Renaissance architects Leon Battista Alberti in the *Quattrocento*, and Andrea Palladio in the *Cinquecento*. Chapter 2 examines the equivalences between the Italian Renaissance and the early Enlightenment in England and considers how the environment of neo-classicism and modern progress may have produced Vanbrugh's distinctive landscape architecture.

Chapter 3 is a short biography of Vanbrugh and is followed by a detailed examination of the many influences on his landscape style in Chapter 4. Subsequent chapters present new research on Vanbrugh's major landscapes in chronological order. Between 1699 and 1726 there is evidence that Vanbrugh built eight new houses and altered six others but his name is associated with many other projects. Whistler gives the most complete account: he attributes Duncombe in Yorkshire to Vanbrugh, and also sees the architect's influence at the dockyards at Chatham and Portsmouth, and at Woolwich Arsenal.[11] Downes describes Gun Wharfe Terrace in Plymouth as 'unmistakably Vanbrughian' although the shape of the dockyard itself is more characteristic.[12] In the chapters on Grimsthorpe in Lincolnshire and Heythrop in Oxfordshire I propose that Vanbrugh may also have influenced these designs. The Vanbrugh sites discussed in this text are listed in Appendix A, with their locations plotted on a map (Figure A.1).

Throughout the text original research is presented in the form of annotated maps, photographs and diagrams of Vanbrugh's landscape designs. Overlay mapping and geo-referencing has been used to analyse the geometry and the proportional divisions of historic plans and to understand how the landscapes have evolved; this has been achieved through the use of various computer packages including Adobe Photoshop and ArcGIS. Three-dimensional computer modelling has provided valuable insights into how the landscape at Castle Howard would have looked in the early 1700s and how it might have been understood by those who walked around it. A combination of modern technology with detailed investigation of contemporary material and visits to each of the sites discussed in the following chapters has enabled this new evaluation of Vanbrugh's work as a landscape architect.

A note on 'Enlightenment'

The English Renaissance was a period of cultural development that started in the late Middle Ages and continued into the Tudor dynasty. The term 'Enlightenment' has a wider reach – it encompasses the profound social and economic changes that are usually associated with Europe and America in the second half of the eighteenth century. The idea of an English Enlightenment that had its foundation in the Renaissance but gathered momentum in the second half of the seventeenth century is a relatively recent phenomenon. This book is not meant to be a treatise on the English Enlightenment; for comprehensive works on the subject I refer the reader to the writing of John Pocock, Jonathan Clark and Roy Porter.[13] My intention here is to clarify the similarities between the English Enlightenment and the Italian Renaissance, and to trace the roots of some of the ideologies back to the Ancient Greeks and Romans. It is then to consider how Enlightenment ideas impacted English garden design in the early eighteenth century and, in particular, how they influenced Sir John Vanbrugh's work as a landscape architect. I have used the term 'early Enlightenment' throughout as referring to the period from 1660 up until about 1730, but, again, the dates may not be precise.

Dates, monetary value and spelling

Before 1752 New Year's Day was on 25 March and dates between 1 January and 24 March were usually referenced by the previous year and the current year. Dates in this book take 1 January as the start of the new year and have been converted accordingly.

Early eighteenth-century monetary values have been converted to present-day values using the Retail Price Index figure at http://measuringworth.com/calculators/ppoweruk/. Such calculations will always be challenging, and they are included only to give some idea of relative value.

Spelling and punctuation in the eighteenth century were variable and contemporary authors frequently used different spellings and abbreviations for the same word. Quotations from eighteenth-century published material and personal correspondence reproduced in this book retain the original spelling, punctuation and capitalisation.

1

'ON YE SHOULDERS OF GIANTS'

Philosophy, science and landscape from the Ancients to the Moderns

The Roman author Cato's *De agricultura* written around 160 BC gave advice to the absentee owner of a farm on how to manage his land, his overseer and his slaves. From Cato's manuscript we know that the farms in the countryside around Florence produced wool and hides from livestock, oil, wine and grain.[1] Cato's treatise reflected the contemporary association of virtue with food production, although it focused on the rigours of running a business that was expected to feed the family and servants as well as provide surplus for sale. Some years later Cicero's *De senectute* (44 BC) hinted at the pleasures of country living, of watching vines growing and wheat ripening,[2] whilst Virgil completed his *Georgics*, a poetic treatise on agriculture, in 29 BC with the story of Corycian's smallholding in which 'limes were first in Flow'rs, his lofty Pines/with friendly shade, secur'd his tender Vines'.[3]

Pliny the Younger's letters about his villas in Laurentum and Tuscany written in the first century AD make reference to figs and vines in an architectural garden, which had been designed as a place not just for agriculture but for rest and contemplation.[4] Pliny talks of the 'peace and quiet' of his Tuscan villa where he 'enjoys the best of health, both mental and physical', and his association of the villa with writing is an allusion to the classical concept of the garden as a place of learning.[5] The Greek philosopher Plato held outdoor meetings with scholars in Akademia north of Athens from 385 BC, giving rise to the idea that the garden could be a place of intellectual development as well as vegetative cultivation. Some eighty years later Epicurus held regular gatherings of academics in the garden of his home in Athens; the school included mathematicians, writers and financiers and was appropriately named 'the Garden'. Epicurus eschewed innate Platonic forms and expounded an empiricist epistemology, believing that knowledge came from the senses, from observation, and that withdrawal from city life to the tranquil surroundings of the garden was essential for reflection and meditation. The mix of skills found in philosophical schools from the Ancients through to the Italian Renaissance was fundamental to the advancement of knowledge; Epicurus not only was a philosopher, but also developed the concept of atomism, building on the idea of Democritus that all things are made up of atoms that cannot be further divided. Pliny refers only twice to Plato and makes no mention of Epicurus, yet his writing suggests that he empathised with the philosophical associations of the garden. He continues his letters with a description of the architectural features of his Tuscan estate: the riding ground (hippodrome) laid out in clipped box hedges, the straight paths, grass lawns, seats and fountains, topiary and 'small obelisks of box'.[6] The villa was in the foothills of the Apennines, it looked down across fields of corn to a river that was used to transport produce to Rome, and it is in Pliny's description of the view that we begin to understand how the ancient Romans understood landscape: 'it is a great pleasure to look down on the countryside from the mountain', he wrote, 'for the view seems to be a painted scene of unusual beauty rather than a real landscape, and the harmony to be found in this variety refreshes the eye wherever it turns'.[7] Pliny goes on to compare his garden with the countryside around it, and appears to enjoy the contrast: 'outside is a meadow, as well worth seeing for its natural beauty as the formal garden I have described'.[8] The meadow was visible over a low dry-stone wall hidden from sight by box hedging, and, although there are no contemporary illustrations of Pliny's estates, the pictures in the garden room of the Villa ad Gallinas in Rome provide an indication of how they might have looked (Figure 1.1).[9] Neat rows of small plants in the foreground are separated from an area of lawn by a wicker fence. Over a low wall, Nature is depicted in a profusion of laurel, myrtle, oak, ivy and pine.[10] In discussing these important remains from the time of the Emperor Augustus, Barbara Kellum draws attention to

FIGURE 1.1 One of the wall paintings in the garden room at the Villa ad Gallinas in Rome. Su concessione del Ministero per i Beni e le Attività Culturali – Soprintendenza Speciale per i Beni Archeologici di Roma.

the juxtaposition of order and disorder, Art and Nature in the paintings and the 'rhythms that exist between the two'.[11]

Pliny concentrates his description on the architectural form of his villa and garden at Laurentum and makes few references to practical horticulture; instead, he associates the peace and quiet of his surroundings with contemplation and writing. There was an element of classical thought that connected non-productive gardens, often the domain of the rich and powerful, with unnecessary luxury and immorality, and this may explain Pliny's focus.[12] The Roman Emperor Hadrian's villa Adriana at Tivoli, built in the second century AD, was one such example of luxury: it was a massive development of gardens, buildings and temples extending originally over 120 hectares (Figure 1.2). The complex was built according to a master plan drawn up before building began, and it displayed a complicated asymmetrical layout along many different planes.[13] The closely confined formal gardens of the 'Piazza d'Oro' and the consciously named 'Garden of the Accademia' were balanced by the West Terrace with its low wall that deliberately exposed all of the south side of the estate to the open countryside. The 'Roccabruna' afforded 360-degree panoramic views of the seven hills and the city of Rome. The similarities with the garden room and with Pliny's much smaller estate are striking: the entire composition at Tivoli was about internal form and external perspective; even now it is obvious that Nature was carefully framed such that even the toilet windows 'provided spectacular views of the surrounding countryside'.[14]

Hadrian had a close connection with architecture and construction; he oversaw the rebuilding of the Pantheon in Rome and he may have influenced the designs for his villa complex.[15] At the end of the first century BC the Roman writer and architect Vitruvius had completed his ten books on architecture, *De architectura*; with its detailed instructions on building *De architectura* would have been known to architects during Hadrian's reign. Vitruvius maintained that all buildings should be 'built with due reference to durability, convenience and beauty', in Latin *firmitas, utilitas, venustas*, and often referred to as the 'Vitruvian Triad'.[16] When he wrote that architecture 'depends on Order, Arrangement, Eurythmy, Symmetry, Propriety and Economy', Vitruvius was specifying the six components that, when incorporated within a building, would give it this essential durability, convenience and beauty.[17] In considering the elements of Order and Symmetry, Vitruvius defined the rules of measurement for the three principal classical orders, Doric, Ionic and Corinthian, and stipulated how they should be symmetrically arranged in buildings. He was specific about when each type of column should be used: Doric columns must ornament temples to Mars and Hercules 'since the virile strength of these gods makes daintiness entirely inappropriate', but 'in temples to Venus [and] Flora . . . the Corinthian order will be found to have peculiar significance, because these are delicate divinities, and so its rather slender outlines, its flowers, leaves and ornamental volutes will lend *Propriety*'.[18] Hadrian's Temple of Venus and Roma (inaugurated in AD 135) was appropriately decorated with Corinthian columns.

Although Vitruvius discussed all aspects of building, from choice of site to managing acoustics in theatres to how to make bricks, his discourse on proportion (Eurythmy) is of particular significance to this book. Eurythmy was present when 'the members of a work are of a height suited to their breadth, [and] of a breadth suited to their length'.[19] Vitruvius went on to note that such correspondence is seen in Nature, especially in the symmetry and correlation of the measurements of limbs and features of the human body:

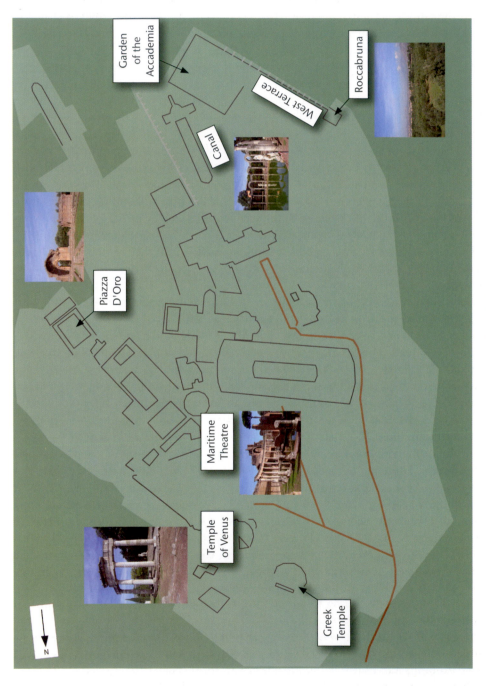

FIGURE 1.2 Plan of Hadrian's villa complex at Tivoli, Italy. Drawing: author, 2011.

For the human body is so designed by nature that the face, from the chin to the top of the forehead . . . is a tenth part of the whole height . . . from the top of the breast to the lowest roots of the hair is a sixth; from the middle of the breast to the summit of the crown is a fourth . . . the other members, too, have their own symmetrical proportions.[20]

Vitruvius contends that the rules of proportion and symmetry as defined by Nature (with their implied perfection) should be applied to buildings, as he observed the Ancients (Egyptians) had already done.[21] There should be a system of proportion for rooms: dining rooms should be twice as long as they are wide and one and a half times the width in height, for example; these simple ratios (2:1 and 3:2) draw from the measurements of the human body. The more complex ratio that Vitruvius suggests for atriums, √2:1, is an irrational number but it could be easily derived from the diagonal of a square.[22] Another irrational number, the Golden Ratio or Phi (Φ), was defined as the 'extream and mean ratio' by the Greek mathematician Euclid around 300 BC, although it was probably discovered two centuries earlier by the Pythagoreans.[23] Euclid's *Elements,* in which he documented many geometric solutions in the form of a number of 'propositions', was to be the most influential text on mathematics for the following 2,000 years. Not all of the content was original but he brought together work by other classical mathematicians into one text and his work on angles, including Pythagoras's theorem, was significant.

The square root of two could be devised simply by using compasses, and therefore had a practical application in classical architecture. The measurement of Phi was more complex and architects were more likely to use ratios from the rational number sequence – 1, 1, 2, 3, 5, 8, 13, 21, 34 and so on – now known as the Fibonacci Sequence. Each number, when divided by the one before it in the sequence, is an approximation of Phi (getting closer as the sequence progresses).[24] The Ancients found irrational numbers to be interesting but the mysticism and speculation around the Golden Ratio or Phi is a more recent phenomenon. Fibonacci numbers appear in naturally occurring growth patterns, including those of the human body as seen by Vitruvius, but the presence of Phi in the proportions of ancient buildings or Renaissance architecture is speculative; George Markowsky argues that the human eye finds it impossible to distinguish the Golden Ratio from other proportions of similar dimensions.[25] The Ancients used Fibonacci numbers in buildings because they were pleasing to the eye. That they associated such proportions with Nature and the divine is evident from Vitruvius, but it should be noted that Vitruvius referred only to rational numbers (as well as √2:1) in his writing; he did not use the 'extream' or Golden Ratio.

Euclid also applied mathematics to the study of optics, building on the work of the Platonists. He documented the rules of perspective in his discourse *Optics*, which were later used by Vitruvius.[26] The mathematician Claudius Ptolemaeus's (Ptolemy) second century AD treatise the *Almagest* advanced Aristotle's model of geocentric planetary motion as well as defining a law for the refraction of light; he also wrote *Geography,* in which he constructed maps based on a square coordinate system, and *Harmonica* on music theory. Anthony Grafton references the Arab scientist Thabit ibn Qurat in discussing the flow of knowledge from the Ancients through to the Italian Renaissance, but it is only relatively recently that the real contribution of the scientists of the Arabic golden age has been recognised and documented.[27] In following the path of Ancient Roman and

Greek innovations Ibn al-Haytham's eleventh-century treatise on optics and perspective is an essential step. Al-Haytham retained Ptolemy's geocentric planetary model but he advanced Ptolemy's work on refraction by his own experiments and by reference to Ibn Sahl's work, *On the Burning Instruments*, written in the ninth century.[28] It was Nasr al-Din al-Tusi's thesis on astronomy of 1261 that finally provided the foundation for a revision of Ptolemy's model: what is now known as the 'Tusi Couple' allowed Copernicus to devise his heliocentric theory of planetary motion in 1543; it is possible that Copernicus referred to Latin translations of al-Tusi and Ibn al'Shatir by contemporary Arabists working at Bologna.[29] Although Copernicus is credited with this groundbreaking innovation, the first heliocentric model was in fact proposed by Aristarchus of Samos in the third century BC, but was later discounted as Aristotle's ideas on geo-centricity gained acceptance. Al-Tusi also revised an earlier translation into Arabic of Euclid's *Elements* and Jim Al-Khalili suggests that it was Arabic that was the link between the two most important Greek texts of the Ancient world by Euclid and Ptolemy and the empiricists of the Italian Renaissance. There can be little doubt that the Arabic treatises of the golden age were an essential element in the advancement of science, yet the flow of knowledge was by many different routes: the English philosopher Roger Bacon's *Opus Maius* (1267) was directly influenced by Latin translations of al-Haytham's work on optics but the Italian Poggio Bracciolini rediscovered Vitruvius's *De architectura* in its original Latin in St Gallen in 1414.

In 1676 Isaac Newton acknowledged to Robert Hooke that he saw further by 'standing on ye shoulders of Giants'; he was specifically referring to René Descartes and to Hooke's own writing on optics although he recognised that the work of the Ancients was the real foundation of the new science.[30] Fifty years earlier Galileo Galilei had observed that the universe is 'written in the language of mathematics and its characters are triangles, circles, and other geometrical figures, without which it is humanly impossible to understand a single word of it'.[31] Vitruvius had already seen mathematics in the dimensions of the human body; it was the source of the earliest measures, the finger, the palm, the foot and the cubit, and of the Ancients' perfect number, ten. Mathematics was therefore bound up with Nature and consequently it embraced spiritual or divine qualities. Although the Ancients worshipped many different gods, the spiritual association with mathematics, and in particular optics, translated into the Christian era unchanged. In his thirteenth-century text *De Luce* (*On Light*) an English bishop named Robert Grosseteste combined theology with his interest in geometry and the natural world and concluded that light was the foundation of all matter.[32] Grosseteste's later work concerning lines and angles discussed the reflection and refraction of light and was to inspire his pupil Roger Bacon. As Martin Kemp explains, the science of optics was revered because 'light, travelling in straight lines, appeared to obey geometrical laws in such a way as to reflect the divine order of God's creation'.[33] By observation and experimentation the empiricists from Ptolemy to Bacon prepared the way for the great Renaissance scholars, but it is notable that empiricism did not preclude religion; the search for knowledge was considered a means of proving their faith for both Muslims and Christians.

After 1434 the Republic of Florence was under the control of the Medici family; together with Venice it was one of eight republics in Italy. The Medici were wealthy bankers at a time when making money without physical work was considered to be sinful, and perhaps as a form of atonement Cosimo de Medici invested in large architectural projects all over the city. To distract attention from their powerful position the Medici deliberately invoked Roman republican ideology to redefine Florence as a second Rome, and themselves as the natural inheritors of classical learning. A similar need for classical validation has been noted amongst the Venetian plutocracy at this time.[34] The Medici became great collectors of literature and art as a means of legitimising their position, but this political stimulus coincided with the more generalised desire for knowledge associated with the Renaissance. The *Quattrocento* engendered a passion for all things Roman in Florentine society, and, although the scholars of the Renaissance used Roman coins as references, the wealthy sought out these imperial portraits as additions to their collections. These were displayed in special cabinets in the houses of the *cognoscenti*, drawing attention to the learning and status of their owners, who also cast their own images or those of modern luminaries in gold and silver medals.[35]

In the *Quattrocento* political stability and a capitalist economy released the country houses surrounding Florence from their castle walls and their ties to agriculture. This gave rise to a new type of villa sustained by the wealth of the city and used solely for retreat and leisure. The first Medici country house to express this change of form was Careggi, where Cosimo de' Medici transformed a castle into a villa in the early fifteenth century. Lorenzo de' Medici was an intellectual who encouraged the philosopher Marsilio Ficino to use Careggi in the late 1400s as a meeting place for his Academia Platonica, a clear reference to its Platonic antecedent. Lorenzo's villa, Poggio a Caiano, was directly influenced by the work of his erstwhile friend and protégé, the humanist and architect Leon Battista Alberti. Alberti's highly influential revision of Vitruvius's ten books, *De re aedificatoria*, was being prepared for posthumous printing when Lorenzo started building in 1485, and Alberti's authority could be seen in the precise use of the rules of proportion that linked the house and garden at Poggio into one harmonious whole.[36]

De re aedificatoria was the first modern edition of an architectural treatise; it was a simplification of Vitruvius's work incorporating other Ancient Roman writers such as Pliny the Younger, Virgil and Ovid, as well as references to Greek texts. This was not a purist translation; it reflected the Renaissance humanist aim of broadening education through the revival of all forms of classical literature including philosophy, poetry and history.[37] What became known as the battle of the Ancients and Moderns had its roots in the *Quattrocento*; in their concern for the recovery of classical culture the humanists were accused of replacing scholasticism with the 'tyranny of antiquity'.[38] However, this pessimistic standpoint was quickly replaced by an understanding that the Moderns of each generation could advance human achievement by standing on the shoulders of the giants of the past, leading Alberti to comment that the creative talents of Filippo Brunelleschi and of Donato Donatello 'cannot be valued less in these arts than those of the famous ancients'.[39] Renaissance humanism was not secular, but the role of the church was questioned as Italian academics became more focused on the place of humans in the world, and they consequently strove to redefine their understanding of how humans related to the divine. Although they believed that the perfect proportions in the human body documented by Vitruvius could engender beauty in objects created by man, the humanist stance was not only a matter of geometry; the concept of beauty was also informed by the senses, by the way that objects were perceived by the onlooker. When Alberti wrote 'when we gaze at the wondrous works of the heavenly gods, we admire the beauty we see, rather than the utility we recognise', he was expressing the belief that the experience of Nature exercised the imagination.[40] The humanists had perceived that the true nature of knowledge was a combination of innate ideas and an understanding gained from experience; their philosophy derived from both Plato and Epicurus. The aspect of humanist thinking that came from Epicurean empiricist philosophy informed an experimental approach to science and an aesthetic movement that had been originally articulated by Pliny when he described the beauties of the natural landscape around his garden. The principles of geometry and moral philosophy began to be exhibited in the design of Italian landscapes: the cultivated fields and hills outside were brought into the villa garden or even into cityscapes, by blurring the division between the two; thus, the gardens of the Renaissance started to take the form of ancient Roman gardens.

Alberti's interest in architecture was a natural progression from his concern with light and perspective that inspired his treatise *De pictura* (1435). In it he laid out the geometrical rules that would successfully encode a three-dimensional landscape in a two-dimensional painting by defining a vanishing point.[41] It is not surprising that Renaissance scholars considered painting, through its associations with light, perspective and Nature, to be a science.[42] Alberti's perspectival system was used to control the relative situation and size of the buildings in the *Città Ideale* (*c.* 1470), a painting that is credited to Luciano Laurana who worked with Alberti in Mantua, and it appeared again in the woodcuts of *Hypnerotomachia Poliphili*, which is sometimes attributed to Alberti, but is probably not of his devising.[43] Alberti was a polymath; he had revived and advanced the work of Vitruvius in *De pictura*, and in the 1440s he turned to the manuscripts of Ptolemy when he created the first map of Rome founded on a revised version of Ptolemy's system of coordinates. He placed features on his map using a horizontal version of the astrolabe to measure angles on a circular rather than a square grid, and a network of triangulation based upon Euclid's mathematics. The astrolabe was not new; it was invented by the Ancient Greeks, had been familiar to the Arabic scientists and was mentioned by Geoffrey Chaucer in *The Miller's Tale* in the late fourteenth century. In his study of astronomy Alberti had used the astrolabe to observe the maximum declination of the sun; now he used it to map the earth. This innovative technique became the basis of modern surveying in which the plan was to replace the bird's-eye view.[44] Alberti's methods inspired Leonardo da Vinci as he surveyed the town of Imola in 1502; da Vinci's own contribution to the advancement of cartography was the use of the colour pink to denote walls and buildings, a new designation that was to be copied over the following centuries.

In his final treatise, *De re aedificatoria*, Alberti combined Vitruvius's ideas on geometric proportion with those of Ptolemy on musical harmonies, when he observed that 'the very same numbers that cause sounds to have that *concinnitas*, pleasing to the ears, can also fill the eyes and mind with wondrous delight'.[45] Thus, the harmonic proportions in music could be applied to architecture; diapente (3:2) and diapason (2:1) are also found in the Fibonacci Sequence.[46] Donnata Mazzini and Simone Martini have postulated that the Villa Medici at Fiesole outside Florence may have been designed by Alberti, after identifying harmonic proportions in the plan of the house that are repeated in the layout of the garden.[47] Alberti was the master of many things and he was the first to apply architectural rules to external design; he made gardens 'the province of the architect'.[48] His architecture was seen as paralleling the work of the Renaissance literary humanists in reviving the classical style of building, but as his contemporary Antonio Averlino recognised: 'in a better way than it was in the past'.[49] Alberti died in 1472, leaving da Vinci and his contemporaries to continue the advancement of understanding of natural philosophy and the arts. Da

Vinci was also fascinated by Vitruvius's writing on proportion and the human body, and famously drew his 'figure of a man in the manner of Vitruvius' in one of his notebooks (Figure 1.3).[50] Seventy years later Michelangelo wrote of architecture: 'he that hath not mastered, or doth not master the human figure, and in especial its anatomy, may never comprehend it'.[51] Geometry pervaded all aspects of Renaissance culture; da Vinci was quite clear about this in one of his manuscripts: 'proportion is not only to be found in number and measure, but also in sound, weights, times and places and every potency which exists'.[52]

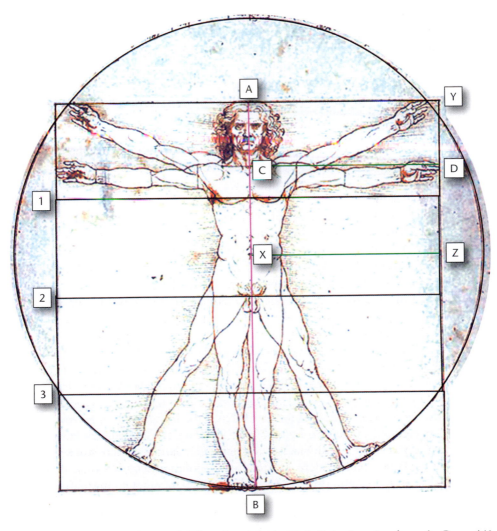

FIGURE 1.3 The proportions of 'Vitruvian Man'. If A–B is 1 unit, then A–C = 1/6, A–X = 2/5, X–B = 3/5, C–D = 1/2. The point X at the navel divides the line A–B into two sections in the ratio 2:3. The lines 1,2,3 are each 1/4. The angle D–C–Y is 20°, Z–X–Y is 40° and Z–X–A is 90°. Annotations: author, 2009.

Alberti successfully combined architectural theory with a sense of place in a book that was to become a source of inspiration for sixteenth-century architects, including Sebastiano Serlio and Palladio.[53] Although Alberti had written a mixture of myth and sound practical advice on building, he had deliberately excluded diagrams fearing that they might be misinterpreted; he advised the construction of wooden models using his instructions before building commenced. Illustrated versions of *De re aedificatoria* originate from the woodcuts of Cosimo Bartoli's Italian translation of 1550. By contrast, Serlio's first book *Rules for Masonry* was published in Venice in 1537 and was comprehensively illustrated. It was followed by Palladio's *I Quattro Libri dell'Architettura* (1570), also published in Venice, which included measured drawings of basic building methods and details of his own projects. With each new text, the rules of proportion associated with Nature, and in particular with human anatomy, became further embedded in architecture. But Serlio missed a crucial feature of Alberti's work; it was Palladio who retained Alberti's response to location and in the opening chapter of his second book he included advice on choice of site and the importance of vista. In describing his Villa Almerico-Capra outside Vicenza, Palladio highlights its elevated situation: 'on one side it is bathed by the Bacchiglione, a navigable river, and on the other it is surrounded by other pleasant hills which resemble a vast theater'.[54]

Palladio acknowledged his debt to Alberti and to Vitruvius in the foreword to his first book of the *Quattro Libri*, in which he laid down rules of proportion to be used in building that were derived directly from the work of both men.[55] Palladio had a preference for harmonic proportions in his designs, although other whole number proportions were used.[56] His insistence that rooms 'on the right correspond and are equal to those on the left' was for practical reasons (to spread the load of the roof evenly), but it resulted in a pleasing symmetry about a central axis that ran through the house. Both Alberti and Palladio invoked the Vitruvian Triad to describe the three most important characteristics of a building and both were sympathetic to site. Echoing Pliny, Alberti advocated that the house of a gentleman should have a view 'of some city, town, stretch of coast or plain, or . . . the peaks of some notable hills or mountains, delightful gardens and attractive haunts for fishing and hunting'.[57] But Alberti was more instructive about gardens and it is in his writing that the rules of design are laid down. Not only were the proportions of the house to be mirrored in the garden but the form of the house was also to be referenced; Alberti tells us that 'circles, semicircles and other geometric shapes that are *favoured in the plans of buildings* can be modelled out of laurel citrus and juniper', and that 'rows of trees should be laid out in the form of quincunx as the expression is, at equal intervals with matching angles'.[58] Palladio's plan for the Villa Mocenigo shows just such a formal garden of squares and rectangles; however, his villas were both social and functional buildings – most were working farms in the Veneto and this is one of only two surviving plans for gardens known to be in his hand.[59] Whilst Alberti was concerned with gardens, Palladio had the opportunity to demonstrate a new form of landscape architecture, in his choice of site and the way that he embedded his villas in their surroundings. His central axis through the house extended into the countryside, tying the buildings to the landscape. Palladio's methodology is exemplified by the Villa Emo at Fanzolo (1558, Figure 1.4) where the approach avenue appears to run through the house as far as the foothills of the Alps to the north, and the trees frame the mountains like a picture (Figure 1.5). As Johann Goethe wrote in 1786, 'there is something divine about his talent, something comparable to the power of a great poet'.[60]

FIGURE 1.4 *Villa Emo-Capodilista a Fanzolo*, Anon., second half of the eighteenth century. Author's copy.

The rich Venetians who employed Palladio had moved from the city to grow corn, diversifying their investments away from the traditional Venetian industries; but as the hinterland was marshland, much like the lagoon that surrounded the islands of Venice, it had to be drained. Denis Cosgrove's study of the drainage projects of the *Cinquecento* has shown that the Venetian hinterland was grounded in Euclidian geometry as the straight lines of the canals started to criss-cross the landscape.[61] One of the canal surveyors of the time, Christoforo Sorte, was also the author of a book on painting, *Osservazioni nella pittura* (1580); his text on landscape art, like that of Alberti, considered both the science of perspective and the link between Nature and the divine.[62] There were layers of meaning in the geometry of Palladio's villa designs; it was not just about a pleasing symmetry in the house. His work evoked the symbolism of mathematical sequences and their derivation from Nature; it signified both a sensual connection with landscape and the power of his employers to frame and control the countryside around them. Palladio's ethos was reflected in the canals of the Veneto and in the writing of his contemporaries.

There were other forms of fashioned landscape in Renaissance Italy apart from the garden, and Claudia Lazzaro contends that the design principles of the woodland (*bosco*) and parks (*barco*) were distinctly different from those of the villa garden.[63] The *barco* was originally a hunting park created from natural woodland, often close to the villa. During the sixteenth century many of these were turned into decorative parks, including that at the Villa Lante outside Rome (1532). The *barco* at the Villa Lante displayed many distinctive features of this form of landscape: areas thickly planted with trees alternated with reservoirs and ponds and regular-planted orchards of fruit and nut trees (Figure 1.6). The park was both dissected and integrated by long straight avenues; with junctions and cabinets within the wood ornamented with statues, fountains and other references to antiquity.[64] The dichotomy between the symmetry and plan of the gardens, and the apparent irregularity of the *barco* is evident, although an overall geometrical framework is maintained. The garden was meant to be viewed from a fixed position, usually from

FIGURE 1.5 The view of Monte Grappa to the north from the Villa Emo, Fanzolo, Italy. Palladio deliberately framed the foothills of the Alps using the doorway and the avenue of trees, which was an extension of the line of symmetry through the house. Photo: author, 2008.

above, so that the architectural forms could be appreciated. The *barco* was to be seen as the visitor walked around it; it offered a variety of itineraries, with avenues meeting at odd angles and surprising openings amongst the trees. The garden and the *barco* offered a mixture of geometry and representations of Nature; the whole was redolent with iconographic meaning, exercising the mind as well as the body.

During the fifteenth and sixteenth centuries in England amateur gentleman humanists wrote in English, in contrast with the professional Latin notaries of Italy such as

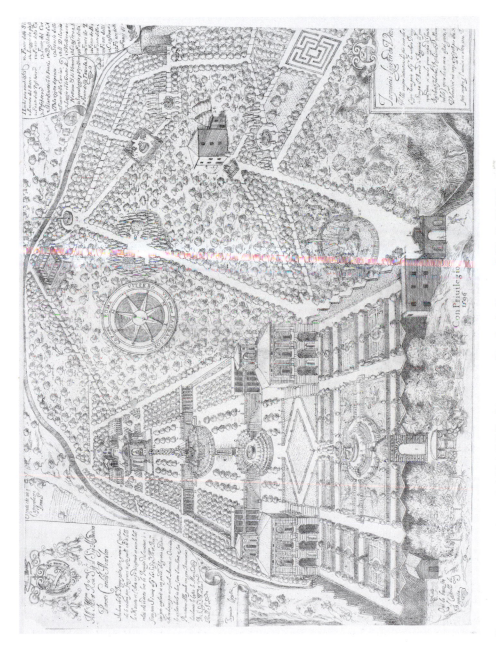

FIGURE 1.6 *Villa Lante*, Tarquino Ligustri, 1596. Bibliothèque nationale de France, NB–C–51006.

Alberti.[65] Early Enlightenment ideas of justice and the common good were evident in William of Worcester's *Boke of Noblesse* (1475), and allusions to empiricist method can be found in Chaucer's fourteenth-century *Canterbury Tales*, in which we find references to Ptolemy's *Almagest* and to the astrolabe. This was to be the first book published in London by William Caxton in 1476, using movable type. At this time most books were printed in Latin, and English books did not sell outside the country, so it appears that Caxton was taking a risk. But Chaucer's text was already popular and there was a market amongst the growing merchant class who bought the book and dispersed the stories in print as they travelled the kingdom; the *Tales* were often read aloud to groups of people who could not read or afford to buy their own copies. Chaucer was, and is still, considered to be a classical poet, 'our English Homer', and his 1391 *Treatise on the Astrolabe* in which he acknowledged his sources as the 'olde astrologiens' who wrote in 'Greke . . . Arabik and . . . Latyn' is often overlooked today.[66] Both texts were accessible because they were in the native language and through them many people were exposed not only to the bawdy anecdotes of the pilgrims' travels and Chaucer's jibes against the Church, but also to references to ancient texts and to the tools of scientific research. The combination of classicism and the vernacular that was evident in the literature of the English Renaissance started to be seen in architecture in the late sixteenth century;[67] the east front of Newark Park in Gloucestershire (completed 1556) with its pedimented doorway is a notable example. Newark's owner, Sir Nicholas Poyntz, held a prominent position in the service of Henry VIII and his hunting lodge was at the forefront of fashion, demonstrating his wealth and influence at Court. In 1563 John Shute published the first book on Vitruvian architecture written in English to be followed seven years later by Sir Henry Billingsley's translation of Euclid (from Latin), with a preface by the Elizabethan polymath John Dee. By the beginning of the seventeenth century the shift in architecture was towards classicism, and this had much to do with the work of Inigo Jones.

When Jones was instructed by James I to make a survey of Stonehenge and to comment on its origins, he promptly concluded that it was Roman.[68] In his assessment Jones quoted Vitruvius's words on the requisite talents of an architect, who must be 'perfect in Designe, expert in Geometry, well seen in the Opticks, [and] skilfull in Arithmetick'.[69] Much of his appraisal of Stonehenge draws on *De architectura* and he also quotes frequently from Alberti. Given his sources, it is perhaps not surprising that Jones designated Stonehenge as a Vitruvian monopteral temple, on the basis of its 'form' and 'order'.[70] He studied the work of Palladio in the Veneto in 1613–14 and it is possible that the English Ambassador to Venice, Sir Henry Wotton, gave Jones some of plates from the *Quattro Libri* whilst he was there.[71] Jones's familiarity with Palladio is confirmed by his design for the Queen's House at Greenwich when he was Surveyor of the King's Works, a few years before Wotton's own treatise, *Elements of Architecture* (1624). As a discourse on the works of several writers including Vitruvius, Alberti and Palladio, *Elements* authorised the classical style of Jones's buildings, and its divergence from the strict focus on the architectural orders in Shute's book made it influential for much of the seventeenth century. In it we find Alberti's dictate on the importance of site and prospects of 'extent and varietie', although Wotton notes that some writers condemn 'vaste and indefinite views'.[72] Wotton admonishes Alberti for being an author rather than a translator, and then proceeds to follow Alberti's example: he considers Alberti's harmonic proportions which transform a 'harmonie of Sounde, to a kinde of harmonie of Sight', but adds his own observation that in the human body, as in architecture, 'Diversitie doth not destroy Uniformitie'.[73] Wotton's often-quoted specification that gardens, unlike buildings, should be irregular has been interpreted as a call for variety of content, a response to the ornamented Italian gardens with which he was so familiar.[74] Central to Quentin Skinner's important article on the reading of history is the argument that, to get closer to what was really intended by the writer, the literary context of a word must be considered alongside other contemporary uses and the prevailing culture; Skinner refers to the 'mythology of prolepsis', in which history is interpreted only in a modern context or as a step towards what is now known.[75] Thomas Blount's *Glossographia* (1661) defines 'irregular' as unequal. Rather than being a contradiction of Alberti's advocacy of mathematics or indeed of the prevailing taste in England for terraced gardens divided into ordered compartments, Wotton could be alluding to an unequal geometry, a 'Variety of Device' as his friend Francis Bacon put it.[76]

Bacon's own essay *Of Gardens* provides fascinating detail of the plants to be used in each section of an early century tripartite garden, but is still prescriptive about proportion in the layout, thus emulating the geometrical theme of *Elements*. All of his essays are directive in style and might even be interpreted as statements of taste; they offer little indication of Bacon's philosophy, or of his pivotal role in the advancement of the new science. Wotton's discourse is of a similar practical nature; in his statement that the classical authors' strictures on the site of buildings were 'rather wishes than Precepts', an understanding of the philosophy of landscape is not evident.[77] Jones employed his talents as an artist in his scene designs for court masques, but his garden backdrops for Thomas Carew's *Coelum Britannicum* (1633), for example, were only interpretations of the given stage directions. There is no evidence that he was a garden designer although he ably demonstrated Vitruvius's list of architectural skills in his backdrops; Jones's precise use of perspective gave depth to the two-dimensional paintings and demonstrated his familiarity with both geometry and optics. It is significant that in considering these three men of the early seventeenth century, a close familiarity with the classical treatises and the Italian Renaissance revivals of them is evident, alongside an understanding of how the principles outlined by Vitruvius were relevant to architecture and to design more generally. There is a brief reference in Jones's work to the effect of Nature on the imagination,[78] but the empirical attitude towards science being ably demonstrated by Bacon was not evident as an empiricist moral philosophy in his or Wotton's writing about landscapes. The humanist aesthetic was missing; that knowledge of the senses which brought about the passion for landscape exhibited by Palladio had not obviously devolved into the new century.

2

THE EARLY ENLIGHTENMENT IN ENGLAND

The year 1660 brought the end of the Interregnum in England, the restoration of King Charles II and the foundation of the Royal Society. The motto of the Society was '*Nullius in verba*', roughly translated as 'take nobody's word for it', a reference to its empiricist ideology that was appropriately quoted from the works of Horace. Despite its association with empirical method and the regular reports of new experimental discoveries in the *Philosophical Transactions* (1665–), Skinner points out that the membership of the early Royal Society was a broad mix of scientists and amateurs, atheists and theists, empiricists and Cartesians.[1] Nevertheless, the scientist Christopher Wren was one of the founding members, whose work on optics and microscopy inspired Robert Hooke, and the Society was to become an important route to publication for scientific works, John Evelyn's *Sylva* and Hooke's *Micrographia* being the first in 1665. Newton's treatise on gravity, *Principia* (1687), was followed by John Ray's classification of plants, *Historia Generalis Plantarum*, written in the final years of the seventeenth century. These innovations and treatises were established by observation and by measurement, and their conclusions started to replace the mythological explanations of the past. As Newton had already acknowledged to Hooke, the exponents of the new science drew on the work of the Ancients and the scholars of the Renaissance, as well as their own contemporaries. Newton's theories of atomism were rooted in the work of Epicurus, his law of inertia owed something to da Vinci's observations of mill-wheel motion, and he recognised Wren's contribution to gravity in *Principia*. From his work on inertia Newton had realised that Descartes's earlier ideas on mechanics were incorrect; Descartes believed that momentum was put into an object by God and was therefore unquestionable and unchanging. Descartes was an outstanding mathematician who created analytic geometry but his philosophy was in opposition to empiricism: he was a rationalist and a theist who thought that knowledge principally came from human reasoning (thereby 'Cartesian'), not from experiment. Thomas Burnett's treatise on the earth, *Telluris Theoria Sacra* (1681), was in a similar vein, arguing that the earth had originally been made in perfect form by God and was disintegrating by the sin of man.

The early Enlightenment scientists were evidently not all atheists; Skinner's views are supported by the more recent observation of Peter Millican that many believed that their experiments revealed the presence of God in an underlying order or 'design'.[2] A strong advocate of this view was Robert Boyle, a brilliant empirical scientist who was also deeply religious; he realised that the new science was seen by some as a potential threat to religion and sought to minimise the repercussions by promoting the design idea. Even Newton theorised that his inability to explain some functions of gravity made them the work of God. Newton and Boyle displayed the humanistic characteristics of their Italian forebears; as they refined the treatises of the Ancients their world became more human-centric and they started to recognise man's potential to decode Nature and re-evaluate the divine. The advancement of science originated from an innate human need to understand the natural world and was underpinned by Euclid's mathematics, as da Vinci had understood some 200 years before. Even the use of the term 'natural philosophy' during the Enlightenment demonstrated the close association of science with nature. Today scientists still use mathematics to suggest how the universe might function, but empirical method remains vital and nothing is believed until it is proved by observation. The difference, as we grapple with string theory and multiple universes, is that now we know that in science there is no incontrovertible truth.

During the Italian Renaissance empiricist science was complemented by empiricist philosophy, evidenced in the work of Alberti, da Vinci and their contemporaries. Hence, the Epicurean belief that knowledge came from observation and experience was mirrored by an appreciation of the importance of the senses in the acquisition of that knowledge, and, as an extension of these ideas, the importance of Nature in sensual reception. Sir William Temple's essays *On Ancient and Modern Learning* and *Upon the Gardens of Epicurus*, written in the late seventeenth century, convey an English perspective on Epicurean philosophy. The first is a treatise on the old argument of Ancient versus Modern; Temple argues for the superiority of the Ancients and is unimpressed by the 'Productions of Gresham College', a negative reference to the Royal Society. Temple's views were later celebrated by his erstwhile secretary, Jonathan Swift, in *The Battle of the Books* (1704), to which William Wotton was to write a response in 1705, arguing for the Moderns.[3] Joseph Addison's speech in support of the 'New Philosophy', delivered in Oxford in 1693, favoured the Moderns and derided the work of the Ancients, but he was not a natural scientist and his views patently changed in later years. Addison was destined to be a politician and an author and, as such, his growing empathy for the work of the Ancients, in particular poets such as Virgil and Homer, is evident in his writing. Nevertheless, Temple died in 1699 and the argument between Ancients and Moderns dissipated, possibly in acknowledgement that both were important. Temple's second essay is a discourse on the history of 'moral philosophy' and the garden with which it was first associated. The title refers to the Epicurean school and it is not a manual for seventeenth-century garden design; it rather concentrates on the effect of gardens on the senses. He identifies with the philosophical associations of the garden but even here Temple cannot resist another jibe at the Moderns and their pursuit of science: 'I know no Advantage Mankind has gained by the progress of Natural Philosophy . . . excepting always, and very justly, what we owe to Mathematicks'.[4] Although elegant, his writing lacked depth and his understanding of empiricist philosophy and the importance of mathematics was not matched by empathy for empiricist science. According to his biographer, Temple was vain and opinionated, and his refusal to accept the advances of the new science in an age of Enlightenment would appear to support this view, so perhaps his writing does not deserve the attention it has received from garden historians.[5] His pronouncements on *Sharawadgi,* which Temple wrongly interpreted as a Chinese irregular garden style, have diverted modern debate towards Temple's introduction of a winding path into his own garden at Moor Park before 1700, and hence the wider influence of Asia on 'natural' eighteenth-century landscapes.[6] Chinese gardens were divided into rooms that contained references to caves, an association with the Taoist tradition of paradise that had equivalence in empiricist philosophy; but the confusion regarding winding paths arises from a modern interpretation of the words 'irregular' and 'natural'. As we have seen, 'irregular' still had a geometric connotation in the late seventeenth century, and 'natural', that 'proceeds from Nature', had a primary connection to order through the design idea and links to the divine.[7] The Enlightenment understanding of 'natural' was one of underlying order, and had nothing to do with a visual sign such as a winding path. Modern garden historians have lost the understanding that the fundamental form of Nature is repeated symmetry; this is why they struggle with the idea that gardens in the early eighteenth century were called 'natural' and looked to the beauty of Nature, and yet were continuously designed in a systematic geometric pattern. Perhaps Temple's greatest contribution was his *Observations upon the United Provinces of the Netherlands* (1673) in which he first used the term 'pleasures of the imagination', to be famously appropriated by Addison in the title of his philosophical series written at Oxford twenty years later.

Addison finally published his 'Pleasures of the Imagination' articles in *The Spectator* of 1712. His writing owes more than a little to Temple's *Epicurus* and there are several examples of almost direct copy including the paragraph on Chinese garden design; although defined in contemporary dictionaries, plagiarism was common practice at the time and seems not to have attracted the censure that it does now. Addison developed Temple's empiricist ideas with several definitions of beauty including expansive views, the novelties of spring and 'anything which hath such variety or regularity as may seem the effect of design'.[8] Epicurean thinking pervaded Addison's article in *The Tatler* of 1710, which was written in the style of the Younger Pliny's letter to Gallus, and described his fictional garden in which 'the Charms of Nature and Art court all my Faculties, refresh the Fibres of the Brain, and smooth every Avenue of Thought'.[9] However, it was the philosopher John Locke who was the principal exponent of a theory of empiricism that emphasised the role of experience in the formulation of ideas, most notably developed in his *Essay on Human Understanding* (1690). Locke believed that the mind of a newborn baby was a blank canvas and that fundamentally all knowledge came from experience; although he did accept that some understanding of God could be intuitive. Anthony Ashley Cooper, 3rd Earl of Shaftesbury, was tutored by Locke and he was also to become a writer and philosopher, but his views differed from those of his tutor in that Shaftesbury could not deny an element of *a priori* knowledge; his philosophy was therefore a mix of neo-Platonist theory and empiricism.[10] When he started publishing his own work at the end of the 1690s Shaftesbury's writing focused on morality and aesthetics rather than empirical science and, like Temple, he had no time for the Moderns. He argued strongly against natural philosophy in his later *Letters*: 'all those high contemplations of stars and spheres and planets . . . are so far from being necessary improvements of the mind'.[11] Shaftesbury understood the concept of beauty to be imprinted on the mind at birth, but he believed that this innate understanding was later enhanced by the operation of the senses, ultimately resulting in taste. He epitomised, in the matter of aesthetics, the efforts of Enlightenment philosophers to understand how the concept of empiricism could be aligned with an uncomfortable awareness that there was an underlying pattern throughout the universe. Locke was not immune from this battle.

The early English Enlightenment scientists and philosophers, like their Italian forebears, were preoccupied with Nature: from trying to explain what they could see around them and rationalising the role of a deity, to appreciating the importance of peaceful, untrammelled surroundings in the acquisition of knowledge. Shaftesbury writes in *Characteristicks* (1711) that 'if in the way of polite Pleasure, the Study and Love of Beauty be essential; the Study and Love of Symmetry and Order, on which Beauty depends, must also be essential'; an idea that was again to be appropriated by Addison in his observation that beauty is in 'the symmetry and proportion of parts'.[12] The synthesis of Nature with order and beauty was prevalent between 1700 and 1730; it denoted a distinct period of aesthetic development that was unrelated to a smooth transition between formality and Brown's English landscape garden. The references to Nature in contemporary writing together with the absence of obvious signs of what we would define as natural or irregular on garden plans and maps has prompted some writers to try to explain the 'apparent contradictions between theory and practice'.[13] David Leatherbarrow creates a picture of Shaftesbury's own garden at Wimborne St Giles in 1707, in which he highlights the sliding scale of art as yews cut in pyramids and globes near the house gave way to uncut trees in the avenues leading out into the surrounding countryside; although this differs little from the tripartite garden style prevalent in the seventeenth century.[14] Leatherbarrow rightly observes that 'Shaftesbury's praise of uncultivated nature cannot be taken as an anticipation of . . . contrived informality in gardens',[15] but garden history scholarship has yet to acknowledge that in *Characteristicks* Shaftesbury was not writing a prescription for gardening, he was commenting on philosophy. He considers ornament and adornment of person, or indeed gardens, to be irrelevant; it is only what is in the mind that matters: 'But what is there like to this in the minds of those who walk [in the finer sort of gardens or villas], and are the possessors of all this? What peace? What harmony?'[16] It is notable that this quote from *Characteristicks* is only part of a much longer statement from *The Beautiful* that makes it clear that he is referring to philosophy not garden design; its truncation loses the crucial information of Shaftesbury's elucidation that ornaments should be built in the mind, not for vulgar display in gardens.[17] Here, Shaftesbury was elaborating on a theory first expounded in *The Moralists* (1709) that he preferred 'things of a natural kind, where neither Art, nor the Conceit or Caprice of Man has spoil'd that genuine Order' over the 'formal Mockery of Princely Gardens'.[18] 'Genuine Order' is a neo-Platonic reference to the innate form of plants and animals, and his concern with ornate princely gardens was in their inability to promote an appreciation of anything; what was needed for contemplation was a 'bare field or common walk'.[19] Two important elements of philosophy appear in Shaftesbury's writing: the association of Nature with order and underlying pattern (innateness or neo-Platonism), and the connection of natural surroundings with sensory perception and the advancement of knowledge (empiricism); neither would be immediately obvious on a garden plan. Shaftesbury was not able to explain his philosophy in such simple terms, but his contribution is in a discursive style that made his writing on taste and aesthetics accessible; through him a form of early Enlightenment philosophy became commonplace.

During the Exclusion Crisis of 1678 two new terms entered English political discourse: that of 'Whig' was applied to those who opposed the succession of James, the son of

Charles II, on the grounds of his being a Roman Catholic, and that of 'Tory' was originally a nickname given to those who supported him.[20] After his accession in 1685 James
freely promoted Catholics in his standing army and in other civil posts in direct contra-
vention of the Test Act; his subsequent prorogation of Parliament and his progressive
absolutist stance only served to increase public fears. The birth of his son James and the
prospect of a certain Catholic succession was the deciding factor in the decision of seven
Protestant nobles to write to William of Orange, the husband of Charles's Protestant
daughter Mary, promising that he would receive support if he landed in England with an
army. The Glorious Revolution of 1688 achieved the accession of William III and Mary
as joint rulers and the departure of James without a prolonged civil war. John Pocock
argues that James's absolute and often arbitrary decisions regarding the advancement of
Catholics were perceived to be a threat to property and therefore liberty, and that this was
the root cause of the Revolution.[21] But Stephen Pincus asserts that it was fundamentally
a battle between two sets of economic modernisers, the Tories and the Whigs, and that
modernisation was the cause, not the consequence. James deemed the source of wealth
to be land and as this was a finite resource he pursued an agenda of land acquisition;
this attitude influenced his foreign policy leading to an alignment with the absolutist
monarchy of Louis XIV's France rather than the Dutch, whose colonisation aspirations
were seen as a threat.[22] After the Revolution Whig and Tory came to denote two distinct
political parties; James's original supporters, the Tories, wanted to retain the traditional
positions of the monarchy and the church and continued to associate wealth with land;
the Whigs saw wealth in trade and the growth of manufacturing, making it a potentially
infinite resource, and they promoted the role of Parliament as a means of curtailing the
power of both the monarchy and the church.

When William arrived in England in November 1688 he was already at war with
France, a conflict that was to go on for a further nine years. The war led to a financial
revolution in the 1690s and the first national debt financed by the newly created Bank of
England set up specifically to fund the standing army, in what Pincus sees as a victory for
those supporting a manufacturing and increasingly urban culture.[23] At first William had
sought to balance the power of the Tories and the Whigs in government, but the Whig
financial backing for the war, the formation of the Bank of England in 1694 and the failure
of the rival Tory Land Bank consolidated the Whig rise to power. By 1696 the Whig Junto
were dominant, and two of their members, John Somers and Charles Montagu, were
promoted to be Lord Chancellor and First Lord of the Treasury respectively. William's
successor, Queen Anne, favoured mixed ministries, and the early years of her reign from
1702 heralded the demise of the Whig Junto and their replacement by the more moderate
Godolphin–Marlborough alliance, later joined by Robert Harley. The Junto slowly recovered power, with Somers, Thomas Wharton and the 3rd Earl of Sunderland returning to
the cabinet in 1706/7. But in 1710 Sydney Godolphin's dismissal was soon followed by
that of other prominent Whigs and the end of Anne's relationship with the Duchess of
Marlborough prompted the removal of the Duke of Marlborough and the establishment
of a new Tory ministry under Harley. Harley was successful in finally ending in 1713 the
War of the Spanish Succession, which had long been opposed by the Tories, but Anne's
death the following year led to his downfall. The Elector of Hanover, now George I,
saw Harley's Treaty of Utrecht as a betrayal of Britain's allies, and on his accession to the
throne he brought the Whigs back to the ministry.

A legacy of James's rule could be seen in continuing Tory support for land as a means of building wealth, evidenced by the short-lived Land Bank. The association of Tories with land has given rise to a branch of garden history which contends that designed landscapes in the eighteenth century were politically differentiated; that the new extensive gardens were Whig inventions and part of a political project to own the pastoral and morally superior aspects of landscape development that had traditionally been associated with the Tories. Tim Richardson suggests that Tory landscapes had an enduring agricultural focus with decoration as a secondary consideration, whereas the Whigs were creating vast, extravagant showpieces with their new money.[24] In fact, the majority of both political parties were landed gentry and aristocracy, and, although a significant minority of Whigs had made money from trade, the Land Tax that was first raised in 1697 was supported by the Whigs because the substantial tax they paid as established landowners gave them power and influence over other government decisions.[25] The Whig estates at Castle Howard, Claremont and Stowe were financed predominantly from income derived from the ownership of land, whilst the Tory Richard Child, who built Wanstead Park in Essex, inherited the family banking fortune, and James Brydges, who created the wildly extravagant house and gardens at nearby Cannons in Middlesex, was a Tory who made his money out of war contracts. The Whig gardens at Blenheim and Eastbury had their direct equivalents in the Tory gardens of Wimpole in Cambridgeshire and Down Hall in Essex; apart from overt political references such as those at Stowe, there was no obvious differentiation between Tory and Whig landscapes in the first thirty years of the eighteenth century.

The advent of a new patriciate from both political parties followed the Glorious Revolution; Philip Ayres contends that this resulted in a deliberate promotion of the Roman ideal and its association with liberty and virtue, as they tried to detract attention from their increasing power and influence.[26] But the economic revolution produced a multifaceted remodelling of society and there was a fundamental shift in power in the late seventeenth century from those who held arms as individuals to those who financed a standing army, with a concomitant re-evaluation of the meaning of liberty.[27] In giving up the right to bear arms, a mark of the citizen, individuals exchanged money for the service of protection by the state, thereby gaining free time in which to seek 'wealth, leisure [and] enlightenment'.[28] This freedom coincided with advances in science and the associated recovery of ancient texts. The Renaissance humanist approach to education that encompassed not only instructional works but also the revival of classical poetry and prose was not new in England; the nobility had long been taught to read the works of Horace and Virgil in the original. But for those who had not benefitted from a classical education, the lapse of the Licensing Act in 1695 and removal of censorship restrictions led to an explosion in the number of publications of all types in English, from books to the first daily newspaper, the *Daily Courant*, which was launched in 1702. Cheap periodicals and pamphlets became an important means of spreading information; they were read aloud at village gatherings and were indirectly used by the state in support of a political agenda.[29] Copies of news sheets were purchased by the owners of the newly established coffee houses, to inform the aristocracy and the wealthy traders who met there to discuss the events of the day.

The growth in the number of coffee houses was coeval with an increase in gentlemen's clubs; some were devoted only to drinking and licentious behaviour, others had a political focus such as the Whig Kit Cat Club and the Tory Brothers Club; all were places of argument and discussion. Jurgen Habermas has identified a new public sphere in the early Enlightenment composed of the nobility and an upper bourgeois stratum of merchants and professionals, and he refers to a 'certain parity of the educated' in the coffee houses and clubs.[30] In this sphere, those with wealth and influence derived from trade mixed freely with those whose lineage had previously conferred superiority and separateness. There is some dispute over whether this new bourgeoisie, who by virtue of intellect and opportunity had risen above the plebeian tavern, constituted an emerging middle class; certainly this public sphere, which did not involve women, was not wholly inclusive.[31] As Clark asserts, the term 'middle class' was not used in the eighteenth century and no-one recognised the many threads of scientific advancement, latitudinarianism, and commercial and social change as being part of a unified process of modernisation; the Enlightenment is something we see in retrospect.[32] Clark's view is supported by Samuel Johnson's defini-tion of 'enlighten' in his dictionary as 'to instruct' (from Addison); a reference to the instructional properties of ancient texts might be construed from this, but there is no association with the idea of a principiant social democracy that was to protect Britain from the violent revolutions of late eighteenth-century Europe.[33] Yet there is evidence that in the early 1700s the bourgeois stratum sought cultural equality within the public sphere resulting in art, literature and the associative idea of taste becoming commodities.[34] Pocock sees this as a conscious exchange of individual arms for the concepts of manners and politeness, with an attendant expectation that, by investing authority in a civil society and disempowering the clergy, the earlier wars of religion would be curtailed.[35] At the same time the idea of liberty became commercial; the protection of freedom was now the responsibility of the mercantile state.

As the bourgeoisie looked for instruction on matters of taste and politeness Addison's entertaining articles in *The Spectator*, in which he expressed the philosophy of Temple, Locke and Shaftesbury in accessible language, became wildly popular in the coffee houses and clubs. Such instruction would have been thought superfluous by an aristocracy who had hitherto assumed a cultural prerogative: Donald Bond's analysis of letters to the editor of *The Spectator* suggests that the readership was confined to 'ladies of fashion, businessmen, clergymen, players, perplexed parents, footmen, ladies maids, lovers and schoolboys'.[36] The market for translations of classical works into English also grew mark-edly and many of them were published by the secretary of the Kit Cat Club, Jacob Tonson. In the 1680s and 1690s Tonson and the poet John Dryden collaborated on the publication of a number of translations that they purchased from Dryden's Cambridge friends, as well as from Addison, William Congreve and the Kit Cat doctor and poet, Samuel Garth. The nobility supported these works through subscription even though they had little need for English versions of the classics; those written in the style of imitations entertained the educated who compared the originals with the translations in their attempts to identify the inaccuracies and alterations that reflected contemporary cultural mores.[37]

Subscriptions were an important means of patronage; they paid in advance for authori-tative texts that would otherwise not have been published but they also advertised the taste and refinement of the subscribers. Humanists such as Alberti were the most influential scholars of their day and they lent authority to their Medici benefactors in return for finan-cial support. In 1696 Charles Montagu used his new position in the Treasury to award his close friend Isaac Newton the Wardenship of the Mint. Montagu had recently been made President of the Royal Society, even though he had made no direct contribution to the advancement of science; his friendship with Newton was probably a factor but his role as a prominent benefactor and influencer would have been significant. He was a consummate Whig politician, a member of the Junto, who was also a passionate collector of books, art and mathematical instruments. Montagu commissioned Alexander Pope's *Pastorals* and he sponsored Addison's tour of the Continent in 1699 as well as his early diplomatic career. Addison was fortunate; many of his fellow Kit Cat writers applied to Montagu for money with less success. Charles Sackville, 6th Earl of Dorset, was another generous patron of the arts who paid for the author Matthew Prior's education, whilst also supporting the work of poet and fellow member of the Kit Cat Club, William Congreve. Dorset was less forgiving of politics than Montagu, and, after Prior defected to the Tories in 1701, Dorset abandoned him and Prior was forced to turn to Edward Harley for patronage; Harley later commissioned a subscription edition of Prior's poems, the income from which enabled him to buy Down Hall in Essex. Those who had the intellect but no money were reliant on those who had both the money and the wit to realise the importance of sustaining the arts as well as the new science. Although all English monarchs were patrons of the Royal Society, there was no obvious group of intellectuals who gathered around William and Mary or Queen Anne equivalent to the Medici meetings of patrons and scholars, but a similarity may be seen in the more erudite London clubs, particularly the Kit Cat and the Tory Brothers Club.

A nascent neo-classicism was evident in the work of Inigo Jones at the beginning of the seventeenth century but an interest in the lives and work of the Ancients, fostered by the flow of knowledge from the Arabic scientists, could be traced back into the Middle Ages. As the Enlightenment advanced, the recovery of classical literature and natural philosophy intensified the interest in Roman culture, and gave rise to a generation of scientists and gentleman connoisseurs who were keen to prove Britain's Roman heritage. The Society of Antiquaries (founded in 1707) and the Gentleman's Society of Spalding (1710) were both concerned with the study of antiquities. In 1722 William Stukeley set up the *Equites Romani* specifically as a forum for the discussion of Roman archaeology, although he later returned to his long-standing interest in the Druids. The discovery of Roman remains on an estate lent authenticity to the owner's claims of identity with the Ancients; thus, the entrenchments at Castle Howard in Yorkshire and the supposed site of Delgovitia on Lord Burlington's land at Londesbrough, later found to be incorrect, were considered to be of real significance. In a study of the Augustan Age in English literature, Howard Erskine-Hill highlights Dryden's identification of the restored King Charles II as the new Augustus in *Astrea Redux* (1660), although Dryden was later to be disillusioned.[38] In 1686 James II had a statue of himself dressed as a Roman placed in Trafalgar Square, until recently occupying the fourth plinth. The late seventeenth-century identification with Augustus generally ignored the fact that he was not associated with the Republic but held absolute power; only Swift had the courage to observe that 'corruption began to spread at Rome under Augustus'.[39] To bolster and reinforce his power over the Empire, Augustus had cast many portraits of himself in statues and on coins and these had been the subject of interest and collection during the Italian Renaissance. The value of coins and medals was recognised by Addison who, in his 1702 discourse on the subject, noted that coins showing the heads of Roman Emperors and the dates of their reigns were essential tools for the modern historian; they were the equivalent of history painting for an age when canvases did not exist.[40] He went on to observe that 'the plans of many of the most considerable buildings of Old Rome' may be found on medals, where the 'niceti[es] of proportion in the figures of the different orders that compose the buildings' are 'best preserved'.[41] Although it was not published until 1721 his text is indicative of a burgeoning interest in Roman architecture and Roman life, and Addison's reference to medal cabinets clearly recalls the collections of the Renaissance *cognoscenti* 200 years before. In 1727 medals were still considered important; Sir John Clerk of Penicuik recorded a meeting of the Antiquarian Society in his diary where 'all our new discoveries were mentioned here, and such medals, Inscriptions and other remains of Antiquity produced as gave us all mutual satisfaction'.[42]

Pope, like Addison, regularly cited classical authors in his writing. His article in *The Guardian* in 1713 begins with a quote from the Roman poet Martial's *Epigrams,* and proceeds to Homer's *Odyssey*.[43] Both texts are concerned with the virtues of Roman husbandry, a similar premise to that already used by Addison in his commentary for *The Spectator* 477: 'I am more pleased to survey my rows of Coleworts and Cabbages, with a thousand nameless Pot-herbs . . . than to see the tender Plants of foreign Countries kept alive by artificial Heats'. The Roman theme was explicit in *The Spectator* 583 in which Addison discussed the delights of planting 'Prospects of our own making' and reminded readers that 'Virgil in particular has written a whole book on the Art of Planting', although it should be noted that both of Addison's articles were again founded on Temple's *Epicurus*.[44] The promotion of farming in the early eighteenth century was multifaceted: Addison's and Pope's commentaries expressed the desire to identify themselves, and their circle, with the ancient Roman farmer and his villa, whilst the stricture that 'fields of corn make a pleasant prospect' was a response to the prevailing philosophy.[45] But there was also a correlation with the growing movement of 'improvement', whereby landowners sought to enclose agricultural land for reasons of efficiency. Such changes did little to help the workers, who lost their livelihood to landowners who wanted bigger farms and fewer tenants; they were often removed from villages by owners who wanted to reduce their Poor Tax payments, or extend their gardens.[46]

In 1683 Arthur, Earl of Anglesey wrote to Sir Peter Pett Knight from 'my Tusculanum Totteridge', indicating that the connection with the Plinian villa had entered Enlightenment thinking.[47] John Dixon Hunt has found much earlier references to villas in Evelyn's diaries, and in manuscript drawings by John Aubrey of his home at Easton-Piercy in Wiltshire dated 1669.[48] Newbiggin House on the estate of Penicuik in Scotland was not rebuilt in Palladian style until 1761, but its owner Sir John Clerk referred to the old seventeenth-century house as a villa before 1710:

> The villa is seven or eight miles from Edinburgh. This distance is particularly pleasant to me, and would be, as I suppose, to all men immersed in public affairs, more agreeable than a retreat nearer the city. For, as Pliny, the younger, says of his Tuscan home, here is the most profound and undisturbed ease, there is no need to sport fine clothes, no neighbour calls, and all things give rest and quiet.[49]

John Macky's tour of 1712–13 took in the many villas near 'Twittenham', including Orleans House, which even had a vineyard, and at Stoke Park he fancied himself 'in some antient Villa near Rome'.[50] Five years later Stephen Switzer's *Ichnographia Rustica* was replete with references to the Roman way of life:

twas in their Villa's that the Ancient Greeks and Romans pass'd away the happiest Part of their Times. How does Horace exult in his Sabine Villa! and with what wonderful energy did Tully there compose his Orations, and by the way we may observe that there Habitation was surrounded rather than with the general View and Prospect of their extensive Villas than contracted gardens.[51]

Prior, the Whig turned Tory who had been expelled from the Kit Cat Club, sounded surprisingly reminiscent of Switzer when in 1721 he declared that he loved his estate at Down Hall 'more than Tully did his Tusculum, or Horace his Sabine field'.[52] The affiliation with Ancient Rome was characteristic of both political parties, as the refined gentlemen of 'taste' sought to draw attention to the classical foundation of early eighteenth-century knowledge and philosophy.

It was as important for a gentleman to have his name on the list of subscribers to Colen Campbell's *Vitruvius Britannicus* (1715) or Giacomo Leoni's English translations of *I Quattro Libri* (1715–20) and *De re aedificatoria* (1726) as it was to belong to the right club. But such essential additions to country house libraries were not necessarily for instruction; one example being Robert Castell's 1728 English translation of the Younger Pliny's letters, which includes drawings of the gardens.[53] The villa at Laurentum is depicted with an area of woodland composed of informal recesses, pyramids, temples and winding paths, although Radice's translation proves that Pliny's gardens were formal and contained no such ornamentation (Figure 2.1).[54] Castell appears to have deliberately misread Pliny; he suggests that Pliny was describing an *imitatio ruris*, an imitation of Nature in the garden, when in fact Pliny was describing the view outside his garden. Written in the form of an imitation rather than direct translation, Castell was seeking Roman justification for a fashion in gardening that was already being followed by his patron, the 3rd Earl of Burlington, at Chiswick; although there were no winding paths at Chiswick in the 1720s (Figure 2.2). The men who created Castle Howard and Blenheim in the early years of the eighteenth century read the Latin original of Pliny, or Jean-François Félibien des Avaux's 1699 French translation, not Castell who was published nearly thirty years later.[55] They copied Pliny's garden in its formality and architectural plan and they correctly interpreted Pliny's philosophy of landscape; the addition of buildings was a reference to the Roman countryside, not the Roman garden, and the only winding paths were relics of ancient woodlands or they were of geometric form. The impact of Castell as a formative influence on early Enlightenment gardens must therefore be discounted.

The increase in the number of published books, many of which were translations, has led scholars to follow the progress of garden history in the early eighteenth century by using a timeline of English books; from Timothy Nourse's *Campania Fœlix* of 1700 through to Castell's 1728 *Villas of the Ancients Illustrated*.[56] Architectural innovations during this period have also been charted using references to Colen Campbell's *Vitruvius Britannicus* and English translations of Palladio and Alberti from 1715 onwards, even though these works had long been available in French, Latin and Italian. As we have seen, the impact of English works on the nobility may have been largely irrelevant; in researching Enlightenment architecture and gardens, earlier translations of Alberti and Palladio such as Jean Martin's *L'Architecture et Art de Bien Bastir du Seigneur Leon Baptiste Albert* (1553) and Roland Fréart's *Les Quatre Livres de l'Architecture d'Andre Palladio* (1650) become important. There were thirty-one different editions of Euclid's *Elements* published in English and Latin before

FIGURE 2.1 Pliny's gardens at his Laurentum villa: Robert Castell's interpretation (top) and Félibien's (bottom). Robert Castell, *Villas of the Ancients Illustrated*, (London: Robert Castell, 1728). Special Collections, University of Bristol. The Younger Pliny, *Les plans et les descriptions de deux des plus belles maisons de campagne de Pline le Consul*, Vol. 6, translated by Félibien des Avaux, (Paris: Florentin & Pierre Delanine, 1699). The Bodleian Libraries, University of Oxford, Vet E4 f62 p126 Tabula III.

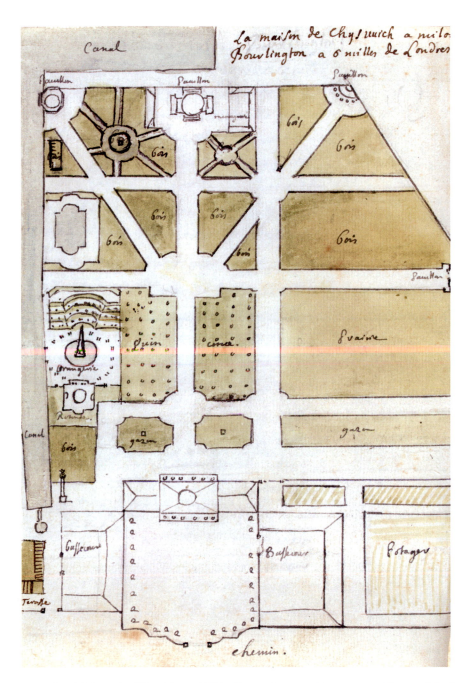

FIGURE 2.2 *La Maison de Chiswick, c.* 1728. Pierre Jacques Fougeroux, *Voyage d'Angleterre d'Hollande et de Flandre*, manuscript. © V&A Images, Victoria & Albert Museum, London, 86.NN.2.

1700; in 1650 Thomas Brush wrote that 'when a man is to make a gardain he must first measure ye ground and take ye plot of it by ye sector and compasses upon paper', and Moses Cook's book of 1676, which is ostensibly to do with the practical management of woodland, invokes Euclidian geometry in large sections of the text, from the method of measuring the height of a tree, to surveying areas of land and planting trees in even rows.[57] Geometry was commonplace as was proportion; Evelyn's comment in 1693 that gardens should be laid out in a 'Beautiful Square . . . especially [where] the Length may be above once and a half or twice as long again as it is broad' comes from Vitruvius.[58] In 1703 Vanbrugh asked his friend Tonson who was travelling on the Continent to buy him a copy of the 'Palladio in French, with the Plans of most of the Houses he built'.[59] In a letter four years later to the Earl of Manchester regarding rebuilding part of his castle at Kimbolton, Vanbrugh expressed the hope that his Lordship:

> won't be discourag'd, if any Italians you may shew it to, shou'd find fault that 'tis not Roman, for to have built a Front with Pillasters, and what the Orders require cou'd never have been born with the Rest of the Castle.[60]

Manchester was ambassador to Venice and he must have asked for a design that incorporated the classical orders, possibly a villa in the style of Palladio. In 1717 Vanbrugh was a subscriber to Leoni's translation but he was familiar with the architectural style and the writing of Palladio long before that.

The value of studying early eighteenth-century English literature is not in its erroneous ability to predict or even engender the arrival of 'natural' landscapes or classical architecture, but rather in its documentation of the prevailing aesthetic. By the time that John James translated Dézallier d'Argenville's *La Théorie et la Pratique du Jardinage* in 1712, the application of Euclid's propositions to the construction of gardens was routine. James acknowledges that to be an 'excellent Geometrician' is 'above the reach of the Gardener', but the basic rules of geometry were fundamental to creating gardens.[61] He gives instruction to gardeners on how to lay out triangles, squares, hexagons and other complex figures on the ground using the semi-circle (Alberti's horizontal astrolabe), the protractor, the theodolite and the 'line' (knotted string). They must also have used an odometer, a marked wheel of known diameter that measured distances; it was described by Vitruvius, although Switzer does not mention it.[62] Switzer copied much of James's *The Theory and Practice of Gardening* word for word in the second volume of his *Ichnographia Rustica*. It is in the first volume that we find specific reference to architecture in the garden: Switzer refers to Sir Henry Wotton as 'the first that had any Thoughts of that *Rule, Proportion and Design* which has *since took place* in Gard'ning'; if he had read Wotton then he would have been familiar with the references to Alberti and Vitruvius.[63] Later in the text he alludes to the architectural garden at Winchendon as though it were a new phenomenon:

> we have . . . [the] *beginnings* of designing and laying down some little spots of Gardening, in the Manner that the Ichnography or Plan of a Building is; and by the means of Eugh and other tonsile Greens, to imitate the Elevation thereof, in Columns, Pilasters, Niches &c.[64]

On this particular point it is interesting to compare the 1712 and 1728 editions of James's

Theory. There are two important additions to the later edition: the first is a section on what he calls 'architecture in green' relating to hedges cut into columns and arches;[65] the second is the inclusion of the sentence: 'the general Proportion of a Garden is to be one third longer than it is wide, or the Length may be once and a half of the Breadth; that the parts, by being longer than they are wide, may be more pleasing to the Eye'.[66] These additions are significant because they indicate that Albertian ideals of the architectural garden had pervaded the English consciousness, and that they were considered not old ideas but new and innovative.

In 1725 Richard Bradley published his book *A Survey of the Ancient Husbandry and Gardening*: 400 pages of instructions on Greek and Roman gardening and design. In it he observes that 'when [the Ancients] laid out their Gardens in any Figures . . . those Figures were either Squares, Circles or Triangles, which they commonly encompass'd with Groves . . . [such designs have been] hardly mended by our extraordinary Regularity'.[67] Johnson's dictionary suggests that Bradley did not like predictability (Regularity) but he was advocating mathematical forms masked from immediate view by trees; he evidently admired Burlington's new geometric grounds at Chiswick. Bradley's writing suggests that he understood the need to mix order with Nature; he argued, like Switzer, against landscapes 'brought to a Level at an immense expense [that] then give us so little Amusement'.[68] There was no sign of a diminution of interest in Ancient methods of gardening and geometry in general during the 1720s. Two years after Bradley, Batty Langley was enthusiastic about the latest fashion for 'serpentine Meanders' as part of an 'artinatural' style that still included 'fine large open Lawns . . . [such as] the Triangle Semicircle, Geometrical Square, Circle or Elipse'.[69] A look at the plates from the book (Figure 2.3) tells us that Langley did not understand 'natural' as we know it. The instructions on how to create his serpentine meanders using mathematics had already been documented in his book *Practical Geometry*; this was a combination of Euclid and the work of the great architects including Palladio, Serlio and Vignola published in 1726. It is easy to misread Langley; he was a strong believer in architectural gardens but he advocated, as Switzer and others had before him, that estate owners should not waste money obliterating Nature (topography), but rather should incorporate it. He despises the 'regular coxcombs' who level their plots and destroy existing trees but then advocates that 'Hills and Dales, of easy Ascents, [should] be made by Art, where Nature has not perform'd that work before'.[70] Admiring the evergreens at Kensington shaped into columns and pedestals, Langley contends that 'the Beauty and very Life of Architecture depends on good Proportions', and he even includes the derivation of the Golden Ratio in his geometric practices.[71] When Willis commented on a plan of Eastbury (*c.* 1718) that 'even the sight of the deer playing sportively in the fields, cannot compensate for the essential rigidity of the layout', he was expressing the commonly held belief that by this time geometry in the garden was outmoded.[72] But the evidence suggests that, far from eschewing geometry, the English gardener of the 1720s was still intent on following Vitruvius's and Alberti's advice that the visual harmony of proportion that could be found in the human body and in architecture should be codified in their gardens and parks. To them, this was the definition of 'natural'.

The two important elements of philosophy that had the power to influence the Enlightenment garden were the association of Nature with order, and the connection of natural surroundings with heightened sensory perception and learning. James and Switzer were not philosophers but they understood the humanist aesthetic, the impact of Nature

FIGURE 2.3 Design for a garden. Batty Langley, *New Principles of Gardening*, (London: A. Bettesworth and J. Batley, 1727) Plate II. Special Collections, University of Bristol.

on the senses. James quotes extensively from Vitruvius in discussing the 'Conveniency of the Place', and from Palladio on the situation of a house.[73] His description of a suitable prospect from a garden, where 'Woods, Rivers, Hills and Meadows . . . make a beautiful Landskip' evokes the writing of Pliny.[74] Switzer's source for his observation on 'the Gardens of Epicurus in Athens, a Person (if Pliny speaks right) that first us'd this extensive way of Gard'ning and of bringing the Pleasures and Produce of the Woods and Fields under the general title of Hortus' is obscure.[75] It was not Pliny or Temple's *Epicurus*, but he appears to be trying to claim a classical source for his theory of 'rural and extensive gardening', in which Nature is brought into the garden by removing visual barriers. Switzer continues with a quotation from Pope's *Essay on Criticism* (1711):

> First follow Nature, and your Judgment frame . . . .
> That Art is best that most resembles her,
> Which still presides, yet never does appear.[76]

It is earlier in Pope's verse that we find a direct reference to the contemporary belief in the divine aspects of proportion and its antique provenance: 'Learn hence for Ancient Rules a just Esteem, To copy Nature is to copy Them'.[77]

Martin Battestin argues that, although harmonic proportions were used in buildings such as Robert Morris's Marble Hill (from 1724), there is little indication beyond Morris's *Essay in Defence of Ancient Architecture* (1728) that 'these ideas influenced contemporary theory'.[78] Yet this contention is not supported by the literary evidence already presented here, which suggests that geometry and the rules of proportion were endemic in garden theory of the early eighteenth century. Like Willis, Battestin struggles with the idea that 'strict geometrical designs [in the garden] forced nature into conformity until well into the . . . century', despite the apparent desire for 'things of a natural kind'.[79] Both authors are looking at it from a modern perspective. Philosophers such as Shaftesbury were not writing about garden design; they were interested in the effects on the senses of all things natural, whilst still believing that there was an element of beauty in the order and regularity of Nature. Although his interest was in aesthetics, Shaftesbury was trying to explain the apparent philosophical dichotomy between innate knowledge and learning from experience. For garden designers, Shaftesbury's philosophy meant that walls should be lowered to incorporate distant views and topography should be used to advantage, not flattened, because the sight of Nature lent a contemplative spirit to the garden. Hence, overt geometry sat comfortably beside the apparent disorder of Nature in the landscape well into the eighteenth century. William Hogarth railed against the influence of harmonic proportions in the assessment of beauty, and derided the universal application of Palladian architecture in 1753, but a new wave of neo-classicism was about to take hold as the archaeological discoveries at Pompeii and Herculaneum sparked a renewed interest in the antique style, particularly in interior decoration.[80] Indeed, John Phibbs has analysed the use of geometry in late eighteenth-century landscapes and found evidence that Brown 'reached first and instinctively for geometry to give himself a solution'.[81]

In 1718 Switzer wrote about Ray Wood at Castle Howard as an example of rural gardening, noting that 'the Romans had doubtless the same extensive kind of Gardens'.[82] By this time Vanbrugh had bestrewn the estate with classical references: Roman walls around the wood and obelisks and pyramids elsewhere in the park were followed in the 1720s by temples and an obelisk parterre on the south front. Classical allusions were not new in the eighteenth century, there was a ramped amphitheatre in the garden at Wilton by 1640, but, as the century advanced and the architectural garden took hold, such references became increasingly common, culminating in thickly templed and ornamented layouts, such as that at Chiswick and the vast grassed amphitheatre at Claremont. The Enlightenment had fostered the revival of the Roman landscape in the garden, reminiscent of the Italian Renaissance. It is worth noting here the difference between the original Roman garden and its later reincarnations. There was a temple to the goddess of agriculture, Ceres, on Pliny's estate but this was a real temple used by the local populace as a place of worship, not a garden ornament. Similarly, the Temple of Venus and the Greek Theatre in the grounds of Hadrian's estate were used for worship and to stage plays respectively; none of these were representations, they were functional buildings. The gardens of Pliny's villas exhibited only references to architecture: a plan of a hippodrome was laid out in box hedges and there were 'small obelisks of box'.[83] As we have already seen, Alberti advised that 'geometric shapes that are favoured in the plans of buildings can be modelled out of laurel citrus and juniper', a clear allusion to Pliny's architecture in box. But during the *Cinquecento,* in an important break with Plinian tradition, these plans were accompanied by scaled-down reproductions of the buildings that had been scattered about the classical countryside. Miniature theatres, loggias and obelisks became commonplace in the garden and *barco*, at the same time as Palladio was putting the temple portico on the front of his villas.[84] The amphitheatre at Claremont and the temples at Castle Howard and Stowe were similar architectural reproductions, but plans of buildings laid out in vegetation were also present – during the 1720s the evergreens at Kensington were shaped into columns and pedestals. Alongside references to classical architecture, allusions to Augustan literature could also be found in the early Enlightenment garden: as Switzer observed, 'From the metamorphoses of Ovid, the Designer may collect Statues and Ornaments for the adorning of his Villa'.[85] Writing in 1718, Switzer was some way behind Lord Carlisle and Vanbrugh who had completed the Ovidian garden in Ray Wood by 1710. Carlisle would have expected his contemporaries to be able to decode an allegorical garden like this with ease, as a classical education was an essential element of the upbringing of an eighteenth-century gentleman. He was fluent in Italian, and would have naturally turned to Cesare Ripa's *Iconologia* (1593) in search of emblems to decorate his house and garden; indeed, Saumarez Smith has demonstrated that Pellegrini's decorations beneath the dome in the Great Hall of the house were consistent with the emblems in this book.[86] Ripa's important work was an iconographic dictionary of representations with its roots in Egyptian hieroglyphics, which is thought to have influenced artists as well as those attempting to appreciate all forms of art.[87] The association of Ripa's book with Carlisle is supported by Colen Campbell's use of emblems in his engraving of Castle Howard in *Vitruvius Britannicus*, Vol. 3 (1725). Consultation of *Iconologia* suggests that these were representations of Perfection, Prudence and Equality, but whether these additions were at Carlisle's prompting or Campbell's instigation is unknown.

It was usual that a part of a young man's education would be effected by travelling abroad and Carlisle was no exception; he spent some time in Italy in the 1680s.[88] Addison wrote of his travel experiences in *Remarks on the Several Parts of Italy &c.* (1705); the tours of others were recorded in letters and diaries.[89] A tour of Britain was, however, an important prerequisite, as Locke observed: 'being acquainted with the laws and fashions, the natural and moral advantages and defects of his own country, [the traveller] has something to exchange with those abroad, from whose conversation he hope[s] to reap any knowledge'.[90] Hadrian's Wall and the Peak District became well-known attractions, and travellers were advised to make 'a reasonable stay at all places where there are Antiquities, or any Rarities to be observ'd', no doubt relying on information that was helpfully offered by guide books.[91] In 1701 a young John Percival set off to explore Britain with his tutor William Byrd and he carefully recorded his experiences in his diaries. This early training was evident in Percival's detailed accounts in letters to his brother during a tour of the great houses and gardens of southern England taken much later in 1724. Other descriptions of journeys were published: John Macky made his *Journey through England* in 1712, when he also visited the country houses and villas of the nobility, and he was followed some years later by Daniel Defoe. Such books were not only travel journals; they were commentaries on the style and taste of the time, often with 'encoded political positions'.[92] The writing of Macky and Defoe was as avidly digested as the classical works of Ovid and Vitruvius, or Shaftesbury's philosophical edicts.

The Grand Tour exposed the wealthy, such as Carlisle, and those whose journeys were subsidised by their patrons, such as Addison, to the palaces and gardens of the Continent. It is reasonable to suppose that, as such tours became increasingly popular during the seventeenth century, travellers would be influenced by the designs they saw in Italian Renaissance gardens or at Versailles and Fontainebleau. In *Garden and Grove* Dixon Hunt argues that foreign travel was the overriding influence in the transfer of the Italian Renaissance garden into an English context during the seventeenth century.[93] In the particulars of garden content – waterworks, grottoes, mounts and amphitheatres – the styles were similar and the argument for cross-fertilisation of such detail, particularly in the more eclectic designs, is strong. But examination of the lunettes of the Medici villas by Gustave Utens highlights an important feature of these Renaissance designs: although differentiated into areas of groomed garden and designed woodland, they were contiguous; there were no fields or wild countryside visible within the boundary walls. Alberti brought geometry into the garden at Fiesole, but Palladio combined references to the order of Nature within the estate with the beauty of the countryside outside it. He did it by using low walls and an underlying geometry to bring together the disparate elements of his designs into one complete composition that included distant mountains and fields as well as the house and its immediate surroundings. It is this aesthetic that was different and made his work stand apart. During the Renaissance Alberti and the Medici had recovered the geometry and the philosophy of Nature from the Ancients and translated it into a new style of building and landscaping that was later to be developed so effectively by the skills of Palladio. Renaissance landscape design therefore emerged from a distinct combination of people, philosophy and socio-economic context and was not the result of copying garden styles from elsewhere. Foreign travel cannot be completely discounted as an influence on the English garden, especially in the seventeenth century, but it was not the instigator of the distinctive style that emerged in the early eighteenth century. There were certain contextual similarities between the Italian Renaissance and the early Enlightenment in England; what was needed was someone who could interpret this unique character in designed landscapes.

When John Vanbrugh returned to England in the 1690s he entered a world where financial and political revolutions were transforming society; it was a place of opportunity.

The new science was generating an atmosphere of enquiry and a desire to further the knowledge of the Ancients, and it resulted in an invigorated demand for classical texts of all kinds. Impoverished authors found employment in translating the classics into English, financed by the patronage of the rich, whilst an emerging merchant and professional class and a burgeoning publishing industry furthered the demand for their work, and made it more easily accessible. Clubs and coffee houses fostered discussion of science and the arts and brought men together who had previously been separate; there were new chances to make money from trade and in a nascent finance industry. The advent of a standing army meant that individuals no longer needed to bear arms; the protection of liberty became a commercial transaction and men had free time to consider matters of taste and politeness. Finally, the Enlightenment humanists questioned the role of the Church, reassessing man's place in the world and his relationship with Nature. Although Pincus suggests that the Ancients had no relevance to an emerging mercantile state, it is evident that classicism was one element in an exceptionally complex group of factors that comprised the early English Enlightenment.[94] It was against this backdrop that Vanbrugh decided to reinvent himself as an architect of buildings and of landscapes. Under his influence, gardens and parks began to convey the deep changes in society: they expressed taste and politeness in their classical associations; they were used by wealthy traders as well as by traditional landowners to symbolise power and control. With the advent of mausoleums in parks they even articulated the re-evaluation of the place of the Church. But most profound was Vanbrugh's demonstration of the philosophy of the age in his laying out of the great estates of the early eighteenth century. Other garden designers understood that proportions and overt geometry in small sections of the garden were an allusion to divine order, and should be mixed with sections of natural woodland or views of distant hills as references to Nature untamed. These were philosophical associations at a simplistic level, but Vanbrugh saw further than that. He understood that a landscape is composed of layers: on the surface it can appear to be wild, free to grow as it wishes, but underneath is a strict system of pattern that is present in all natural things. Like Palladio, he was to devise a system of underlying geometry that symbolised the innate beauty of Nature by using the proportions described by Vitruvius, and pulled together all of the elements of the composition into one complete whole. Thus, Vanbrugh's parkscapes became philosophical statements that expressed the early Enlightenment struggle to resolve neo-platonic theory and empiricism. It seems that, despite the supposed hegemony of Nature over Art that has long been associated with the evolving eighteenth-century garden, this mathematical framework may never have left the landscape. Regardless of the surface decorations, whether they were overt classical references or the eclectic forms of William Kent or Pope, the underlying geometry remained. Vanbrugh was to become the leading interpreter of Enlightenment ideas in English landscape design.

3

JOHN VANBRUGH (1664–1726)

A short biography

John Vanbrugh was born in 1664 in London, the son of a cloth merchant of Dutch descent called Giles Vanbrook (Figure 3.1).[1] He grew up in the Roman town of Chester and initially followed in his father's footsteps as a merchant, becoming a factor for the East India Company in Surat, India in 1683.[2] The job was clearly not to his taste for he had returned home to take a commission as an ensign in Lord Huntingdon's regiment at Hounslow by 1686, before resigning eight months later to accompany distant relations Robert and Peregrine Bertie, travelling on the Continent. The three men were in France at the outbreak of the war with the United Provinces in 1688, when Vanbrugh was arrested and accused of having spoken in support of William of Orange. In conjunction with the Dutch derivation of his name this was enough for him to be detained, although the real reason for his imprisonment appears to have been the desire to hold him hostage to assure the safety of a French spy who was in London. Vanbrugh remained immured for four years, being transferred in 1691 to the Chateau de Vincennes and then to the Bastille in Paris. Bertie tried to support his friend in his absence by conferring on him the income from a position in the Duchy of Lancaster, but the complex diplomacy required to eventually release Vanbrugh in exchange for the Jacobite Thomas Maxwell did not produce results until 1692. He was obliged to remain in Paris on bail before finally sailing for home in 1693. There was a brief spell at sea under Lord Carmarthen's command; Vanbrugh was then back in London looking for new employment.

The writer and dramatist William Congreve staged three comedies in the early 1690s and possibly influenced Vanbrugh's decision to write his first play, *The Relapse*, which was well received in Drury Lane in 1696. This brought him to the attention of the Kit Cat Club and its patron, Charles Montagu, who commissioned the writer's second play *The Provok'd Wife*. Vanbrugh was undoubtedly an intelligent man with wide-ranging artistic talents and an enquiring mind, and his ability to identify and exploit an opportunity is demonstrated by his espousing a career as a writer of marriage comedies, just as they were starting to become popular on the London stage. His character suggests that it would have taken little thought before he proposed himself as an architect, and as a rival to William Talman who was Comptroller of the King's Works. The decade saw a burgeoning

FIGURE 3.1 *John Vanbrugh*, Sir Godfrey Kneller, *c.* 1705. © National Portrait Gallery, London 3231.

appetite for building country houses and Talman submitted proposals to another member of the Kit Cat Club, Lord Carlisle, for his new project at Henderskelfe in Yorkshire in 1699.[3] But Carlisle was not happy with Talman's designs and soon afterwards he took the extraordinary decision to replace him with Vanbrugh. Adolf Loos's nineteenth-century aphorism that an architect is 'a mason who knows Latin' was as valid during the English Enlightenment as it was during the Italian Renaissance. In the early eighteenth century architecture did not have to be a profession, and, just as Italian Renaissance sculptors, stonemasons and painters had been appointed to the position of architect, so Carlisle must have appointed a dramatist in the belief that Vanbrugh's imagination could conceive the modern building he wanted to replace his crumbling castle. His new architect may not have known Latin, but Vanbrugh was fluent in French; he staged six adaptations of French plays in London between 1697 and 1707. He could read the architectural treatises of Alberti and Palladio that had been translated into French but not into English, and, through them, he could access the words of Vitruvius.

At least at the beginning, Vanbrugh did not work alone. Nicholas Hawksmoor had studied under Wren in the 1680s, and by 1698 he was already a prominent architect and the Clerk of Works at Greenwich Hospital. He would have been known to members of the Kit Cat Club and the earliest drawings of Castle Howard suggest that Hawksmoor was there from the instigation of the assignment. It was not unusual at this time for gentlemen architects to be assisted by an experienced team of surveyors and project managers: Henry Joynes and Tilleman Bobart supported Vanbrugh at Blenheim, and William Etty was Clerk of Works at Castle Howard and Seaton Delaval; John Smallwell started as a joiner but rose to be Clerk of Works at Claremont. Vanbrugh's letter to the Duke of Newcastle in 1718 after the death of Smallwell emphasises the importance of these local managers: '[I] am at a Cruell loss for something as a Clerk of Works, to explain this And Other things to, as formerly to Smalwell'.[4] The Castle Howard accounts reference measurements done by 'Mr Hawksmoor and Will Etty', and Hawksmoor's written instructions to the masons and carpenters annotate several drawings.[5] Vanbrugh had the vision, which he must have discussed and agreed with Carlisle, but in the early days it is likely that Hawksmoor decided what was practicable. That a mutual respect grew between the three men over the 26 years of their association is evidenced by their surviving letters. Vanbrugh's design authority was expressed in his letter to Joynes in 1706 regarding the addition of the ornaments and cupola to the drawings of Castle Howard: 'I'll get Mr Hawksmoor to Add them here'. But the partnership between Vanbrugh and Hawksmoor was already evident in 1705 when Vanbrugh wrote to the Duke of Marlborough regarding 'a Project of Mr Hawksmoors' for Blenheim and in 1707 when he wrote about the design of the stud: 'Mr Hawksmoor is of the same opinion with me'.[6] It is clear that as the two men worked together on Castle Howard, Blenheim and Kimbolton between 1700 and 1710 Vanbrugh's innate self-confidence meant that he never felt threatened by Hawksmoor's proficiency and professional training; in return Hawksmoor must have benefitted from a collaboration that brought him to the attention of Vanbrugh's influential associates. Both men suffered at the hands of William Benson when he was appointed to the Surveyorship of the Board of Works in 1717 and promptly sought to destroy the reputations of Hawksmoor, Vanbrugh and Wren.[7] Hawksmoor was most affected, losing his job as Clerk of the Works, and over a period of years Vanbrugh tried to persuade the Earl of Sunderland, and later Lord Carlisle, to reinstate him in the post. In 1725 Hawksmoor repaid his efforts by writing to the Duchess of Marlborough praising Vanbrugh's work and advocating that Vanbrugh be paid the money still owing to him for his work at Blenheim. This was a brave act that was hardly likely to endear Hawksmoor to the Duchess who disliked Vanbrugh, and which could have put his future commissions at risk.[8]

Almost immediately Vanbrugh seems to have been accepted by his peers as an architect: very early in 1700 the 2nd Earl of Burlington diverted him on a trip to Yorkshire to view his house at Londesbrough, possibly with the intention of employing him, and by 1703 Vanbrugh had produced designs for Welbeck Abbey in Nottinghamshire for the Duke of Newcastle, where he was again in competition with Talman. Although Newcastle abandoned the project it provides early evidence that Vanbrugh was also to be a landscape architect. That year Sir Godfrey Copley wrote to his friend Thomas Kirke: 'I am told great Lakes are now the mode; Vanbrook set out one for the D. of Newcastle, to front his new house, of 40 acres'.[9] Many gardens contained canals at this time, but lakes of any size were rare, and such a large one would have been a feat of engineering. Even with a lining of clay eight inches thick there was no guarantee that the water level could be maintained. This is the first indication that Vanbrugh was never going to conform to the prevailing mode; his creativity and his lack of formal training as either an architect or a gardener coalesced with an innate propensity to push the boundaries of the accepted norms; he was going to disregard the existing rules of landscape design.

The first house to be completed to his design was Vanbrugh's own, erected on the site of the burnt-out palace of Whitehall in 1701–2. The rounded-arch loggias on the first and second floors and the rustication of the central front elevation were combined with a number of square and double square rooms; already Vanbrugh was demonstrating a taste for Palladian motifs. Swift satirised Whitehall in his poem 'Vanbrug's House' written in 1703, calling it a 'Thing resembling a Goose Py', possibly because it was so unusual.[10] In the later *The History of Vanbrug's House*, written after Vanbrugh had received his second commission at Blenheim, Swift makes reference to Vanbrugh's inspiration:

> The Plan he much admir'd and took,
> The Model in his Table-Book,
> Thought himself now exactly skilled,
> And so resolved a House to build.[11]

This was possibly an allusion to Vanbrugh's travels during the summer of 1699 when he had 'seen most of the great houses in the North, as Ld Nottings: Duke of Leeds Chattesworth &c'.[12] The poet meant to pour scorn on such amateur methods and so deliberately misunderstood the importance of such a trip. In 1704 John Churchill exhorted travellers to 'always have a Table-Book at hand to set down every thing worth remembering, and then at night more methodically transcribe the Notes they have taken in the day'.[13] Despite Swift's jibe that 'Vanbrug's Genius, without Thought or Lecture, is hugeley turn'd to Architecture',[14] there is evidence that the architect not only researched existing buildings, but also consulted the treatises of Alberti and Palladio, a contention that is inadvertently supported by Swift's later observation that:

> Vanbrug is become by due Degrees,
> For Building fam'd and justly reckon'd,
> At Court, Vitruvius the Second.[15]

At a time when the recovery of classical writing and method was almost an obsession, to be the 'second' Virgil, Homer or Cato was the highest form of approbation, but Swift had no intention to flatter. Vanbrugh had to endure much teasing by the Duchess of Marlborough over Swift's writing and he never forgave the poet for his taunts. When they met at Sir Richard Temple's house for dinner in 1710, Swift recorded in his *Journal to Stella* that 'Vanburg, I believe I told you, had a long quarrel with me about those Verses on his House; but we were very civil and cold'.[16]

Edward Ward wrote in 1709 that the publisher Tonson pursued his own self-interest in setting up the Kit Cat Club where he encouraged 'a Parcel of poetical young Sprigs' who had 'more Wit than Experience' to meet at his friend Christopher Cat's tavern.[17] Here, Tonson plied them with Mr Cat's famous pies and 'finding that Pies to Poets were as agreeable Food, as *Ambrosia* to the Gods, very cunningly propos'd their Weekly Meeting at the same Place', his aim ostensibly being to obtain first refusal on the publication of their work.[18] Although the club may have had a literary bias at its foundation and attracted a number of poets and writers in the 1690s, including Congreve and Addison, the rise of Somers and Montagu to become prominent Whig politicians during this period suggests an underlying political interest. Gradually the Kit Cat evolved into the most influential political club of the early eighteenth century, promoting Whig policies of parliamentary control and religious tolerance and, in particular, the assurance of the Protestant Hanoverian succession. Tonson's loyalties to the Whig cause do not appear to have been in doubt; Vanbrugh accused him of having reasons to be in Amsterdam in 1703, other than working on Caesar's *Commentaries*:

> do you know that the Torys . . . have been very grave upon your going to Holland; they often say that Caezar's CommTs might have been carry'd through without a voyage to Holland; there were meanings in that subscription, and that list of names may serve for farther engagements than paying three guineas apiece for a book.[19]

He is suggesting that Tonson has been sent as an undercover envoy, to provide the future George I with the names of supporters of a Protestant succession hidden in a subscription list.

The Whigs' power fluctuated in the early 1700s but during their time out of government the political manoeuvrings of the Kit Cat Club reached their zenith, when they tried to stage a demonstration against the Tory policy to end the war and generally made life so difficult for the Tories in the Lords that twelve Tory peers had to be quickly created in 1712 to regain control of the House. The organised structure and strong political bonds within the club enabled it to make firm plans to assure the accession of George I after Queen Anne's death: 'Measures were early concerted by the Kit-Cat Club with a Major-General [Cadogan] . . . To seize the Tower upon the first appearance of Danger and to secure in it such persons as were justly suspected to favour the Pretender'.[20] In the event these plans were unnecessary, and the Hanoverian succession was secured without incident in 1714, prompting Horace Walpole to write: 'The Kit-cat-club, generally mentioned as a set of Wits, were in reality the Patriots that saved Britain'.[21]

Alongside its political influence the Kit Cat Club retained its strong literary inclination. In part this was motivated by the desire to impart Whig principles either through poetry and plays such as Addison's *The Campaign* and *Cato*, or through highly influential pamphlets and periodicals. Sir Richard Steele edited *The Tatler*, and in 1711 joined with Addison to edit *The Spectator*, both of which claimed to expound Whig and Tory views equally, although *The Tatler* was certainly associated with Whig propaganda when it closed.[22] The *Whig Examiner* was started in 1710 by another Kit Cat member, Arthur Maynwaring, and was blatantly political. There was a genuine interest in the arts within the Club, quite apart from this political programme, which was cultivated by Tonson in his position as Club Secretary, and the writers and patrons of literature who were members. Subscriptions from the Kit Cats and others financed the building of the Queen's Theatre in the Haymarket on land already owned by Vanbrugh, and in 1709 the club gave 'a subscription for four hundred guineas for the support of good comedies'.[23] Tonson appears to have been a key figure in keeping the Kit Cats together, possibly because it indirectly supported his publishing business. He was certainly shrewd and, early in Dryden's career when they produced *Miscellany Poems* together in 1684, Tonson recognised Dryden's potential and was careful to buy the rights to his work thereafter. The publisher was equally astute in his dealings with John Milton and had all of the rights to *Paradise Lost* by

1690. Tonson is depicted holding a copy of *Paradise Lost* in his 1717 portrait by Sir Godfrey Kneller, one of a set of similarly styled portraits painted by Kneller of members of the Kit Cat Club, now in the National Portrait Gallery in London.

It is reasonable to assume that Vanbrugh became a member of the Kit Cat Club soon after *The Relapse* was staged in 1696. The Kit Cat already comprised a number of distant relations of his mother (the Carleton family), including the Earls of Huntingdon, Stanhope and Carlisle, and the 1st Duke of Devonshire, and Vanbrugh was readily accepted into this mix of aristocracy, gentry, writers and military men. His talents as an architect appear to have won him the respect and a level of friendship from his aristocratic employers, many of whom were also Kit Cats, and his letters to them, although polite, were never subservient; indeed they were often quite forceful, particularly when he wanted to make a point about the 'correct' rules of design. Vanbrugh would spend weeks staying at his patrons' houses, whether working there or not, and he would travel around the country with them during the summer, visiting other estates as was the custom of the time. Over the following years Vanbrugh grew close to Tonson, who frequently travelled to the Continent, especially to Amsterdam, in search of new authors and foreign language publications that he might translate. These trips were later useful to the architect who would ask Tonson to procure books not available in England. Vanbrugh's letters to the secretary whilst he was abroad had a different tenor to those he wrote to his aristocratic friends; sometimes crude, they are full of gossip about Club members and provide evidence of the lighter side of his character. On the possible marriage plans of John Dormer in 1703 he wrote: 'Dunch is overjoy'd to see Dormer buzzing about the Candle', and on what turned out to be the exaggerated death of another Kit Cat, Lord Wharton, he reported that Wharton had 'recommended himself heartily to the Kitcat and Dyed', only to be fully recovered the following morning.[24]

Vanbrugh's surviving letters to Carlisle and the 1st Duke of Newcastle attest to a lifelong concern with politics; whilst writing about progress of building on their estates he would often add a comment about the latest debate in Parliament. His interests were wide ranging, from the new inoculation against smallpox '[there is no fear] that those who go through the Small Pox that way, will have them again', to the operas that 'are Establish'd at the Haymarket, to the generall likeing of the whole Towne'.[25]

Even those with substantial incomes such as Carlisle and Newcastle would spend beyond their means and Vanbrugh seems to have been short of money for most of his life. There is only scant evidence of payments to him in the Carlisle, Newcastle and Ancaster accounts, and some of these may have been associated with gaming, which was a popular pastime.[26] Carlisle substantially supplemented his income through gambling, making a profit of £2,683 (£390,000 today) in 1707 alone; this was essential money as he and Vanbrugh sought to manage the enormous cost of building Castle Howard.[27] Carlisle certainly seems to have economised on his architect; Downes has suggested that Vanbrugh was paid in kind by being given the position of Comptroller of the Queen's Works, replacing Talman in 1702, and an introduction to the College of Heralds, both possibly at Carlisle's instigation.[28] Vanbrugh is depicted in his Kit Cat portrait of around 1705 (Figure 3.1) dressed in the regalia of the Clarenceux King of Arms, and holding the compasses of an architect.[29] Vanbrugh's knighthood in 1714 may also have been due to the influence of the Duke of Marlborough, perhaps as recompense for his not receiving what had been an agreed salary for his position as Surveyor of the Works at Blenheim. By

1719 Vanbrugh had still not been paid by the Duchess of Marlborough and he complained bitterly to Tonson: 'I have a further misfortune in losing . . . £6000 due to me for many years Service, Plague and Trouble, at Blenheim, which that Wicked Woman of Marlb: is so far from paying me'.[30] This would be over £800,000 today and the Blenheim accounts appear to support his contention, as the architect received nothing between 1707 and a final settlement that was awarded in 1725 of £1700.[31] He was not alone in not being paid by the Duchess, but the delay of such an amount must have been difficult. In such circumstances the regular income that came from official posts was important, so the loss of his position as Comptroller of the Board of Works in 1713 in a political move by Harley would have been a blow. However, the accession of George I brought a change of fortune for the Whigs, who had been out of power since 1710. The King immediately showed his gratitude to his supporters, particularly the members of the Kit Cat Club, by granting promotions and elevations to the peerage; Vanbrugh was the first man to be knighted by the new monarch. He was subsequently reinstated in his position at the Board of Works in 1715 and given the post of Surveyor of Gardens and Waters in the same year, which Hawksmoor thought was 'made for Sr John V'.[32]

But Vanbrugh's trials were not over. He had 'a very hard Disappointment of not being made Surveyour of the Works', as he told Tonson in 1719, and his financial difficulties continued with losses from the Queen's Theatre and the South Sea Company.[33] In 1720, again writing to Tonson, Vanbrugh reported that 'Our South Sea, is become a sort of a Young Messissipy, by the stocks rising so vastly', and that like many of his contemporaries his brother 'had about £5000 there, which is now near doubled'.[34] He could not foresee the collapse of the Mississippi, which came only three months later, triggering a stock market crash in France and the bursting of the South Sea Bubble in England the following year. His comments on the South Sea crash evidence the depth of the impact across polite society, and his own losses:

> the South Sea is so hatefull a Subject one do's not Love to name it; And yet it do's so interfere with almost everybodys Affairs more or less, that all they have to do, is in some degree govern'd by it. Even I, who have not gain'd at all, Shall probably be a Loser near £2000.[35]

Vanbrugh achieved some financial stability towards the end of his life. In 1719 he sold the Queen's Theatre to his brother Charles, and with the final Blenheim payment and the sale of his position in the College of Heralds he had a substantial sum to invest in stocks, the annuity from which would support his unmarried sisters, and his new wife.

In 1718 there is the first hint to his friends that at the age of fifty-four Vanbrugh might finally be 'buzzing about the Candle' himself, when he wrote to the Duke of Newcastle that is was 'so bloody Cold' at Castle Howard that he had 'almost a mind to Marry to keep myself warm'.[36] Within a month he was married to Henrietta Maria Yarburgh, a second cousin to the Duchess of Newcastle. This would appear to have been an advantageous marriage, drawing him closer to one of his patrons (Vanbrugh was working at that time on Newcastle's house at Claremont); he made a point of the relationship when he wrote to the Duke that his new wife was 'pretty nearly related to the Dutchess [which] gives me the more hopes I may not be mistaken. If I am, 'tis better however to make a Blunder towards the end of ones Life, than at the beginning of it'.[37] At fifty-four Vanbrugh would expect to be towards the end of his life, and this must have prompted his marriage, for until this point he appears to have been happy with his freedom to follow a 'sinfull life' and was somewhat scathing about his friends who had been ensnared.[38] He alludes to his previous views on marriage in his comment to Tonson in 1722 that:

> I am now two Boys Strong in the Nursery but am forbid getting any more this Season for fear of killing my Wife. A Reason; that in Kit Cat days, wou'd have been stronger for it than against it: But let her live'.[39]

Having signed a lease for Sir William Saunderson's house at Greenwich in March 1718, Vanbrugh had built his own castle on the hill, with magnificent views across the Thames and the city to the north. On its completion in 1720 it became a home for the architect, his new wife and later his sons Charles and John. In 1722 Vanbrugh proudly wrote to Lord Carlisle of his two-year-old son Charles:

> I fancy your Lordships Godson will be a Professor that way [in architecture], for he know Pillars, & Arches and Round Windows & Square Windows already . . . and is much pleas'd with a House I am building him in the field at Greenh: it being a Tower of White Bricks only one Room and a Closet on a floor'.[40]

John died an infant and only Charles survived into adulthood; to become a soldier and not an architect. Vanbrugh continued with his many projects but his health deteriorated with increasingly common attacks of asthma. He wrote his last letter to Carlisle regarding the design of the Temple at Castle Howard just days before his demise from a throat abscess in March 1726. By then the Kit Cat Club meetings no longer took place but the friendships had endured; a few months earlier Vanbrugh had written to Tonson: 'both Lord Carlisle and Cobham exprest a great desire of having one meeting next Winter, if you come to Towne, Not as a Club, but old Friends that have been of a Club, and the best Club, that ever met'.[41]

4

INFLUENCES ON VANBRUGH'S LANDSCAPE STYLE

Vitruvius, Alberti and Palladio

In 1703 Vanbrugh wrote to Tonson asking him to purchase a copy of the 'Palladio in French' whilst he was in Amsterdam, and he was still reliant on the work in 1711 when he enquired of Joynes at Blenheim: 'Pray ask Kitt Cash if the French book of Paladio be not in Mr Strongs Shedd; I thought we had had it in Towne but don't find it'.[1] His first design for Castle Howard clearly displayed the triadic composition around a central axis with a hierarchic system of rooms arranged symmetrically on either side; all fundamentally Palladian elements.[2] Indeed, an early elevation of the south front that the Duke of Devonshire thought to be a 'plain low building like an orange house' was reminiscent of the Villa Emo at Fanzolo with its long wings and terminating dovecots (see Figure 1.4).[3] Vanbrugh knew Palladio's *Quattro Libri* long before he subscribed to Leoni's English translation in 1717 and he was specific that he wanted the version with the woodcuts of Palladio's building designs when he wrote to Tonson. The set of Palladio drawings originally owned by Jones were the property of John Oliver when he was working with Wren and Hawksmoor, and it is possible that Vanbrugh saw the drawings before they were sold to his rival Talman in 1701. From the start Vanbrugh used standard room sizes in the same way as Palladio: the Great Hall at Castle Howard and the salon at Blenheim both exhibit proportional ratios of 9:7, and other ratios of 7:5 and 3:2 occur frequently.[4] In 1707 the architect wrote to Manchester about his new salon at Kimbolton: 'I wish it cou'd have been made a reall Salon, by carrying it up into the Next Story . . . 'Twill however be eighteen foot high, which is no contemptible thing, tho' *not what in Strictness One wou'd wish*'.[5] Following Palladio's stricture that 'the closer [halls] are to being square the more praiseworthy', Vanbrugh built a number of square rooms at his own house at Chargate, and in later projects he went on to use the double square in the Great Hall and in the salon at Eastbury, with a triple square appearing in the salon at Seaton Delaval in 1719.[6]

Palladio was a stonemason and had no formal training as either a painter or a sculptor, but became an architect under the patronage of Giangiorgio Trissino and was an early member of the Accademia Olimpica (founded in Vicenza in 1555), which had evolved from Trissino's informal meetings of literate friends. The membership of the Accademia was a mixture of scholars, mathematicians and wealthy patrons who were keen to advance developments in science and the arts, in what Ackerman has described as a 'new social conformation', an association of gentlemen and technicians.[7] The Accademia has associations with the Medici Academia Platonica of the *Quattrocento*, and the parallels with the late seventeenth-century Kit Cat Club are striking. The Kit Cat Club included politicians and military men amongst its members and was also an association of gentlemen patrons and technicians, most notably writers, interested in the advancement of science and the arts. The club was in part the result of the political, social and economic changes affiliated with the Enlightenment, and its *Cinquecento* and *Quatrocento* counterparts had similar foundations. The political affiliation to the Whig cause and the assurance of the accession of the House of Hanover distinguished the Kit Cat from the apolitical academies, but both Vanbrugh and Palladio turned to architecture after following other careers. The Kit Cat Club paid by subscription for Vanbrugh to build the Queen's Theatre in the Haymarket, which opened in 1705 with the opera *The Loves of Ergasto*, whilst 120 years previously the Accademia had commissioned Palladio to build the Teatro Olimpico in Vicenza, also funding it by subscription. Vanbrugh founded his theatre design on a sphere of twenty feet radius, which explains the enormous proscenium arch. The theatre was a 'unified architectural structure' that was proportional in three dimensions, constructed according to Vitruvian rules.[8] It is possible that, by using circles, Vanbrugh reproduced Palladio's mistaken understanding of Vitruvian theatres, which resulted in the audience being too far from the stage.[9] In 1740 Colley Cibber described the problems with the barrelled ceiling of the theatre, which 'occasion'd such an Undulation from the Voice of every Actor, that generally what they said sounded like the Gabbling of so many People in the lofty Isles in a Cathedral'; the ceiling was subsequently levelled in an effort to improve the dreadful acoustics.[10] The set within Vanbrugh's arch was painted with retreating columns, and, although Palladio's original drawings for the *frons scaenae* at the Teatro did not include receding streets, he had included them on other projects and probably intended to use them here.[11] Palladio's Teatro was also based on the semi-circular outline, but it was constrained by a pre-existing building and may have been acoustically more successful than Vanbrugh's because of this; although opera as an art form was not officially recognised until later, the opening production in Vicenza in 1585 was Sophocles's *Oedipus* set to the music of Andrea Gabrieli.

Other similarities exist between the two architects: Palladio made several studies of military formations, and in 1574 he applied for permission to print Julius Caesar's *Commentaries* with his own illustrations. Vanbrugh sponsored one of the plates in Samuel Clarke's version of the *Commentaries*; the book mentioned by him in the subscription list letter of 1703 that was published by Tonson in 1712. His illustration is very similar to one of Palladio's drawings and Vanbrugh's own skills as an artist are supported by his letter to Godolphin regarding 'a picture I have made [of the landscape at Blenheim]'.[12] He could also see the advantage of publishing a book of the plans and elevations of his houses in the same style as the *Quattro Libri*, for he wrote to the Duke of Marlborough in 1710: 'I propose to adjust all the prints [elevations] to a scale that they may form a book as is usually practised abroad in such cases'.[13] Here, Vanbrugh anticipated Colen Campbell's *Vitruvius Britannicus* by five years, and it could be argued that he was the original source of Campbell's idea, given that many of Vanbrugh's earliest plans for Blenheim and Castle Howard appear in Volume I.[14] Neither man had been trained in painting, but both Palladio and Vanbrugh appear to have used innate painterly skills and both men were influenced by Alberti and, through him, by Vitruvius. As Palladio had for the members of the Accademia Olimpica, Vanbrugh designed and built houses or made alterations for several members of the Kit Cat Club, and there is a possibility that he was somehow considered to be the Kit Cat's 'Palladio'.

Susan Lang has suggested that Alberti directed Vanbrugh's *Proposals for Building ye New Churches* (1711), and she equates several passages in the manuscript directly to *De re aedificatoria*.[15] In the first book of the *Quattro Libri* Palladio referred to buildings he had 'read about in Vitruvius and Leon Battista Alberti'.[16] It is likely that Vanbrugh also read Alberti's book and, although he makes no direct reference to him in his letters, the evidence is in his use of language. When Vanbrugh wrote to the Earl of Manchester in 1707, ''tis certainly the Figure and Proportions that make the most pleasing Fabrick, And not the delicacy of the Ornaments', he was expressing Alberti's conviction that 'beauty is that reasoned harmony of all the parts within the body . . . ornament may be defined as a form of auxillary light and complement to beauty'.[17] Vanbrugh employed a version of the Vitruvian Triad in a letter to Lord Poulet in 1710 when he said of Blenheim 'that it might have ye Qualitys proper to such a Monument, Vizt Beauty, Magnificence, and Duration', and he used it again in 1721 with regard to Lumley Castle, where he was 'altering the House both for State, Beauty and Convenience'.[18] Alberti's views on the appropriateness of design, particularly in terms of correct ornamentation and control of expense, pervaded Vanbrugh's work and are again manifest in his letters.[19] As an untrained architect looking for inspiration, Vanbrugh understood Alberti's statement that beauty could be equated with the correct proportions in buildings, and he created harmonised layouts by applying the rules of Vitruvian proportion to all of the elements of his designs.[20]

Much of this equivalence between the words of Vanbrugh and those of Alberti could also be construed from the writing of Palladio or indeed from their original source, Vitruvius; but sometimes the precise phrasing suggests Alberti rather than any other, and Palladio did not write about planting. In 1708 Alberti's edict that 'rows of trees should be laid out in the form of quincunx' was recalled by Vanbrugh when he wrote to Joynes at Blenheim:

> Pray tell [Mr Bobart] I am glad there's so good a Progress made in things without doors; but I should be glad to know what he do's About the Forrest Trees in the Quarters of the Woodwork I mean as to bringing Lines of 'em every where behind the Hedges, for I take that to be the grand point of all.[21]

Vanbrugh was the landscape architect; he was not particularly interested in the choice of plants but he was concerned with how the planting contributed to the overall form of the layout of the gardens. In 1721 he wrote of Castle Howard that it:

> will be (beyond all contest) the Top Seat and Garden of England. Of the House I say nothing. The others I may commend, because Nature made them. I pretend to no more Merrit in them than a Midwife, who helps to bring a fine Child into the World out of Bushes Boggs, and Bryars'.[22]

Alberti had observed that the Ancients 'drew [the art of building] out from, the very bosom of Nature' and Vanbrugh's letter hints at the two key components of his theory of landscape design: that he associated Nature equally with beauty and with an underlying order.[23]

Each of Vanbrugh's landscape projects will be examined in detail in succeeding chapters, but his first project at Castle Howard is briefly considered here as an illustration of how he used Vitruvian principles in gardens and parks, as well as in his buildings. Lord Carlisle's new house in Yorkshire was to be situated in a rolling landscape with an ancient hunting park to the west and a mature woodland, called Ray Wood, to the east. London's first design before the arrival of Vanbrugh (Figure 4.1) shows Talman's proposed building with its east front facing into Ray Wood and the main west front with an enclosed courtyard and long approach avenue. A formal parterre lies to the south of the house and the villagers of Henderskelfe, whose houses would be demolished by the construction of the new estate, have been relocated to a model village. This was the design that was rejected by Lord Carlisle, who then turned to Vanbrugh for inspiration. London's slightly later plan (see Figure 0.2) shows Vanbrugh's redesigned house situated in a landscape similar to the original, but Ray Wood has been obliterated by an elaborate star.

All of the research on Vanbrugh's landscapes presented in this book has been carried out using the traditional methods of research in libraries and archives and site visits, but this has been combined with computer-aided analysis. The most useful computer tool is digital overlaying – in which photographs of historic maps and plans as well as aerial photographs are overlaid on modern and first edition Ordnance Survey maps using photographic software. Each map is stored as a layer and moving through the layers exposes

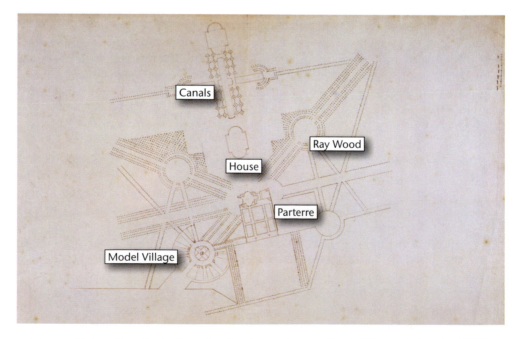

FIGURE 4.1 George London's first plan for the gardens at Castle Howard showing William Talman's house, *c.* 1699. © V&A Images, Victoria & Albert Museum, London E434.1951.

the evolution of the landscape over time. Photographic software is the preferred methodology for overlaying because it allows historic maps to be rescaled to fit as closely as possible to the base Ordnance Survey map without stretching or warping. This study is about the proportions of the original designs, so preserving the intended proportions of the early eighteenth-century maps was essential. Geo-referencing was used afterwards to check results and three-dimensional modelling also informed the study of many of the landscapes in this book. The methodology of the computer analysis is explained in detail in Appendix C.

The landscape at Castle Howard as it was a year after Vanbrugh's death is illustrated by an estate plan of 1727 (Figure 4.2). In searching for clues as to why Vanbrugh's design was so different from London's we must return to the estate plan of 1694, which shows the original landscape with the old castle and church before building began. In Figure 4.3 the plan is overlaid on the first edition Ordnance Survey map of 1891. It appears that several elements of the 1694 estate influenced the new layout: the orientation of the old castle is the same as that of the new house; the position of the south wall around Ray Wood defined the Temple Terrace; and the alignment of other walls to the east of the church dictated the line of the access road into the wood. Significantly, the boundaries

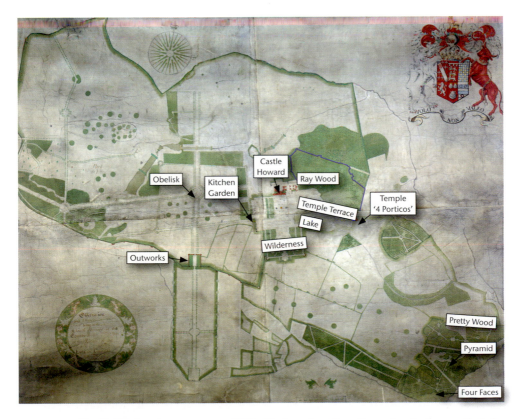

FIGURE 4.2 Castle Howard estate map, 1727. Vanbrugh referred to what is now called the Temple of the Four Winds as the Temple with the four Porticos. Castle Howard Archives P1/4. Annotations: author.

Ordnance Survey 1891.
© and database right "Crown Copyright and Landmark Information Group Ltd." (All Rights Reserved 2011).

FIGURE 4.3 *Observations and Demensions of Land Lying in the Manour of Castle Howard in the County of York*, Ralph Fowler, 1694. Castle Howard Archives P1/2. Overlaid on Ordnance Survey 1st edn 1891.

of the fields to the south of the castle appear to map the north extent of the wilderness and the highlighted field boundary was to form the main axis of the design; these features become clearer in Figure 4.4 in which this main axis is shown in pink. This initial examination begins to explain Vanbrugh's unusual decision to cut Ray Wood in half with a wall, as further analysis of the 1727 map shows how the design became a master class in Vitruvian proportion (Figure 4.5). There is no evidence that Vanbrugh actually drew the outline of a man over his landscape plans as shown here; this would have been unnecessary although there is Renaissance precedent for it.[24] Da Vinci's study of a man 'in the manner of Vitruvius' has been used as a research tool to simplify the proportional analysis of Vanbrugh's landscapes.

Castle Howard was Vanbrugh's first project as a landscape architect and, although the influence of Lord Carlisle cannot be discounted in the details such as the interior of Ray Wood, it appears that the overall design was Vanbrugh's, particularly as the principles seen here reappear in so many other of his projects. It is significant that the arrangement shown in the 1694 plan in some part directed the new layout; Vanbrugh was sympathetic to the topography and the original form of the landscape and he had no intention of flattening the hill on which Ray Wood stood or of obliterating it with a star of avenues. He also used

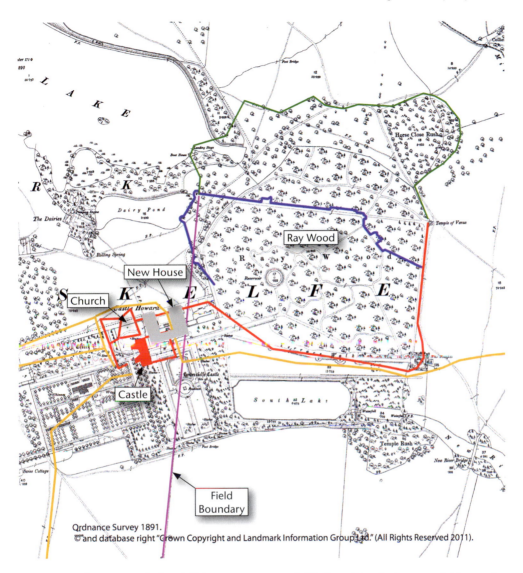

FIGURE 4.4 Elements of the 1694 estate map and Vanbrugh's design overlaid on the Ordnance Survey map of 1891. Original walls in red and roads in yellow. The walls that Vanbrugh built to divide Ray Wood are in blue; the north-east corner was revised when the Temple of Venus was built (1731–5). The green line marks the extent of the northern section of the wood separated by the new wall. All Ordnance Survey maps are oriented N–S. Annotation: author, 2009.

the lines of existing walls that followed the natural rise and fall of the land to demarcate new approach avenues with dramatic effect. Vanbrugh drew attention to both the beauty and the order of Nature in his design; he not only copied Palladio's architectural style but also composed his building sympathetically within the landscape. There is no evidence that he ever went to Italy so he could not have seen Palladio's villas in their settings, although his father Giles was in the Veneto in 1655 and he may have talked about the

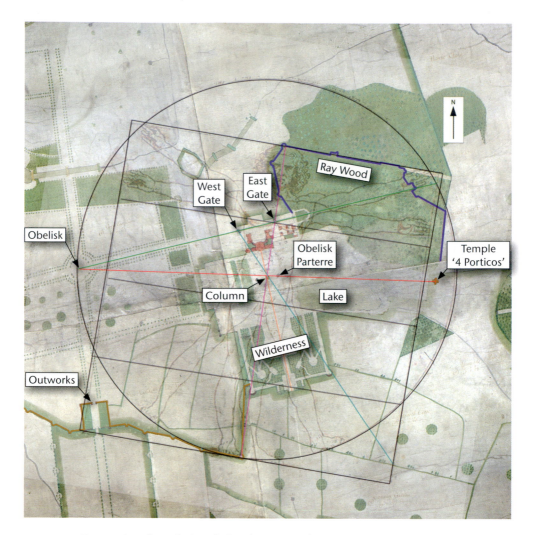

FIGURE 4.5 Proportional analysis of the design in the 1727 estate plan. The main axis (pink line) measures 55 chains using the scale on the map; the distance to the Column on the Obelisk Parterre (position of navel) is 22.1 chains; the Column therefore divides the main axis into two sections in the ratio 2:3. The red line from the Temple to the Obelisk also runs through the Column. The East Gate is positioned on the first quarter line (in black); the angle of the green line that runs along the approach road from the Obelisk to the north front and into Ray Wood is 20° to this quarter line (i.e. the same as the uplifted arm). The orange line measures 25.1 chains; the distance from the south front of the house to the Wilderness is 12.52 chains ~ 1/2. The angle between the light blue line that runs from the West Gate to the east edge of the Wilderness and the pink line of the main axis is bisected by the orange line through the Wilderness. Castle Howard Archives P1/4. Annotation: author.

architect or even, as Lang suggests, have brought home books or manuscripts.[25] Vanbrugh was a natural innovator but both he and Palladio had empathy for landscape, and both men used geometry as a means of setting houses in their backgrounds.

Vanbrugh's task of overlaying a Vitruvian grid on the land would have been so much easier if the land had been flat. In fact, the majority of his sites were composed of interesting and, in some cases, spectacular topography. Had he simply imposed the grid the result might have been temples in valleys or houses with their main front facing into a hill; this would not have achieved the objective, which was to represent both the order and the beauty of Nature. Vanbrugh must have decided on the position of the house and the access roads first, utilising the flat area to the east of the castle and recognising the dramatic possibilities of the existing roads and walls. A line from the wall at the south-east corner of Ray Wood to the crossroads of the avenues (red on Figure 4.5) would naturally have come next. The old field boundary seems to have inspired the angle of the main axis (pink) but its length would be derived from the point at which it crossed the red line, which divided this axis in the ratio 2:3. This then defined the cut-off point for the blue wall across Ray Wood. All other elements would be placed according to Vitruvian rules; this was easily achieved with compasses and a ruler and by folding the paper. Many of Vanbrugh's designs exhibit the ratio 2:3 in the definition of a focal point; at Castle Howard Vanbrugh placed a column at this point on the Obelisk Parterre. The angle between the two positions of the arms (20°) and other human proportions are often discernible in his compositions. 'Vitruvian Man' appears to be the source of the unique layouts, which were different from the symmetrical stars favoured by other designers of the time. These designs were subsequently realised on the ground using surveying instruments and triangulation. Proportion was already fashionable in some aspects of the garden, such as the parterre; Vanbrugh covertly applied geometry to the entire landscape design and he did it without flattening the topography. It has not been possible to find this sort of geometry aligned with topography by any other designer, until Bridgeman started using the technique in the 1720s, in a style that must have been based on Vanbrugh's principles (see Chapter 15).

Later additions to the landscape at Castle Howard that are not shown on the 1727 estate plan also appear to fit into the Vitruvian design (Figure 4.6). The mausoleum was mentioned by Vanbrugh in a letter dated 1722 although it was not started until the 1730s; the Temple of Venus (1731–5) and the Carlisle Pyramid (1728) were also built after Vanbrugh's death. The positions of the Temple of Venus and the 'Temple with the four Porticos' suggests that they might have been planned early in the design process, but it is difficult to imagine that Vanbrugh had placed the mausoleum and the Pyramid in his mind in 1700.[26] What is important is that the later additions fitted with the scheme, which indicates that it was known and understood by those working on the project as well as by Lord Carlisle. The offset of the Carlisle Pyramid from the axis that dissects the house and wilderness is now explained by its presence on one of a pair of lines that run from the walls of the north entrance courtyard and define features on the apse of the wilderness. The light blue triangle defined by the column on the Obelisk Parterre, the Pyramid and the Temple with the four Porticos is equilateral with a tolerance of 3 per cent.

All measurements were checked using the first edition of the Ordnance Survey map (Figure 4.7) and a modern Ordnance Survey map; on these maps the Pyramid triangle was equilateral with a tolerance of 2.8 per cent. Comparison of distances on the Ordnance

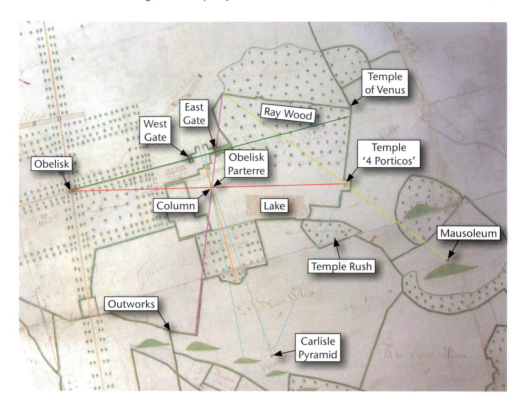

FIGURE 4.6 Proportional analysis of the landscape at Castle Howard in 1744. The light blue triangle defined by the Column on the Obelisk Parterre, the Pyramid and the Temple with the four Porticos is equilateral with a 3 per cent margin of error. The yellow line connects the Mausoleum to the Temple and the north-west bastion of Ray Wood. Castle Howard archives P1/11. Annotation: author.

Survey maps and those on the eighteenth-century maps showed a margin of error for the historic maps ranging from 0.2 per cent to 1 per cent, indicating that measurements using the astrolabe, theodolite and odometer were reasonably accurate. Some of the historic maps had distorted as a result of age and the two pages of the 1727 map had been badly joined such that the column and the Temple with the four Porticos were positioned about fifteen feet south of where they actually were. It is significant, however, that the proportional analysis remains valid on modern maps where positioning is precise and accurate measurements are obtained using geo-referencing. Although it has been thought that no master plan existed at Castle Howard and that the landscape simply evolved, this exercise shows that this was not the case.[27] Vanbrugh created a grid that lay *underneath* the topography; actual measurements across the ground would not have been proportional because of the rise and fall of the land. Vitruvian proportion applied in this way must therefore have had symbolic significance on the plan. For those walking around the estate the upper layer comprising the topography, the fields, woodlands and parterres was the most obvious. These drew attention to the beauty of Nature and the philosophical associations of the garden.

The form of the Medici Villa at Fiesole outside Florence is a perfect cube and it has long been acknowledged that the square plan of the house is reproduced in the design

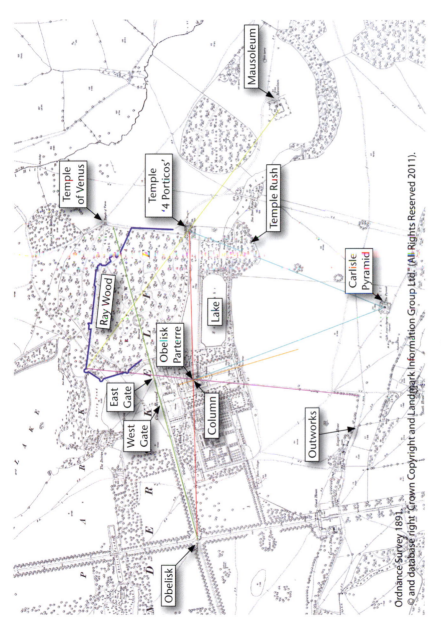

Temple of Venus

Temple '4 Porticos'

Temple Rush

Mausoleum

Ray Wood

Carlisle Pyramid

Obelisk Parterre

Lake

East Gate

West Gate

Column

Outworks

Obelisk

Ordnance Survey 1891.
© and database right "Crown Copyright and Landmark Information Group Ltd." (All Rights Reserved 2011).

FIGURE 4.7 Proportional analysis of the landscape at Castle Howard on the 1st edition Ordnance Survey map of 1891. The analysis has been verified by overlaying it on a modern Ordnance Survey map. The dark blue line shows the position of the wall around the north and west of Ray Wood built by Vanbrugh, which was positioned by overlaying the 1727 plan. This was demolished at some time in the late eighteenth century. Annotation: author.

of the gardens.[28] Mazzini's firm attribution of the villa to Alberti is relatively recent and is based on modern geometric analysis, but Alberti wrote about the cube in *De re aedificatoria*: 'the primary cube whose root is one, is consecrated to the Godhead, because the cube of one remains one'.[29] Mazzini's work is founded on the reconstructions by Clemens Steenbergen and Wouter Reh, who have traced the use of geometry from the Renaissance into the gardens of seventeenth-century Europe at Versailles and Vaux-le-Vicomte, and then into England.[30] At Vaux the authors draw attention to the situation of the garden in a valley, which effectively shuts out the surrounding landscape; the philosophy of Roman design, the opening of the garden to the countryside beyond, was evidently not reproduced in France.[31] In 1700 Nourse remarked of Versailles: 'there lying nothing but dead Plains beyond it, in which the sight, I say, is soon lost, receiving in but little Variety'.[32] In Britain, Steenbergen and Reh perceive an Arcadian landscape at Castle Howard, with garden buildings that were designed to be viewed as elements of a picturesque composition, thus taking a similar stance to that of Giles Worsley and Whistler, who describes it as an example of the 'new landscape gardening'.[33] The inference is that the Picturesque, often associated with the pictures of Claude Lorrain and Nicolas Poussin, signified 'the end of the classical landscape ideal of the Enlightenment'; in other words, Castle Howard had already advanced along an inevitable path towards the unsystematic landscape gardens of Lancelot Brown, away from strong geometrical form.[34] For this reason they propose picturesque sight lines from the centre of the south front of the house to the Carlisle Pyramid and the Temple with the Four Porticos, forgetting both the topography and the height of the trees. Analysis using three-dimensional modelling indicates that in the eighteenth century it would have been impossible to see the Temple or the Pyramid from the south front, or the Pyramid from the Temple, which were separated by a belt of ancient woodland known as Temple Rush (Figure 4.8). The work of Steenbergen and Reh is important in supporting the argument for geometry in eighteenth-century landscapes, but their assumptions regarding overt display and sight lines render the geometrical analysis flawed. It is possible to be deceived by two-dimensional maps and plans into conjecture about what could or could not be seen 300 years ago; three-dimensional modelling goes some way towards helping us get closer to the original design and what it was like to be in the landscape, but the essential tool is an understanding of the context. Here, philosophy and the atmosphere of the Enlightenment were the overriding controllers of the layout.

Vanbrugh undoubtedly had an eye for the picturesque; his letter to the Duchess of Marlborough advocating the preservation of the old manor at Blenheim is often quoted as proof of this.[35] Although he alludes to the historical associations of Henry II's old palace and its importance as an attraction on the summer tour circuit, Vanbrugh seems to have been most interested in composing the view from the north front of Blenheim Castle, so that 'all the Building left . . . might Appear in Two Risings amongst [the trees], it wou'd make One of the Most Agreable Objects that the best of Landskip Painters can invent' (Figure 4.9).[36] This was indeed an attempt to pioneer the use of the artistic concept of scene extension in landscape design, but it should not be confused with the *subject* of Claude's or Poussin's paintings and we should not assume that the romantic scattering of ruined buildings in the Italian countryside influenced the gardens of the early eighteenth century. Vanbrugh did not aspire to this sort of romanticism; indeed, he never placed a house, garden building or piece of designed landscape randomly. All of the elements in his

FIGURE 4.8 Three-dimensional reconstruction of the gardens on the south front of Castle Howard, *c.* 1727. The Doric column and Obelisk Parterre face the wilderness. The lake and statues are centre right. Ray Wood with its bastions can be seen behind the house and one of the two sets of entrance gates stands to the left of the house. The predominant colour is green. Digital elevation model by permission of Ordnance Survey on behalf of HMSO. © Crown copyright (2011). All rights reserved. Ordnance Survey Licence number 100050286. Layout taken from map P1/4 Castle Howard archives. 3D model: author, 2010.

FIGURE 4.9 View from the north front of Blenheim palace with a reconstruction of the old palace of Woodstock on the north bank of the Glyme river. Photo and reconstruction: author.

schemes were obviously different – in size, colour or form – but Vanbrugh grouped them together in a systematic pattern so that they were all connected on the plan. This was a reference to the symmetry and order of Nature; Vanbrugh's designs were linked by philosophy, not by lines of sight. Hart asserts that 'in its associational intentions [Vanbrugh's] work should be viewed as the forerunner of the picturesque idea of Richard Payne Knight and Capability Brown', yet Brown enclosed his gardens with shelter belts, he did not open them to the world outside.[37] The two components of the picturesque composition – the method and the subject – need to be separated when discussing Vanbrugh's work. Vanbrugh used the method of landscape painting, the means of creating depth and space, the opening of views; he could see the picture, and in this aspect his oeuvre was indeed picturesque. But it had none of the romantic mood, the unconstrained subject; it was founded on a strict geometrical design. In this respect Vanbrugh's projects exhibited the fusion of beauty and order found in Nature and epitomised the treatment of landscape already seen in the work of Palladio; as Vanbrugh said: 'Nature made them'.[38]

The overall outline of the 1727 plan of Castle Howard is pleasing to the eye yet the underlying geometry that makes it so does not stand out. There are overt references to geometric forms in some parts of the garden – in the wilderness, the approach avenues and the Obelisk Parterre – but at first the individual elements appear to be randomly positioned. The effect on a person walking around the grounds would be the same: some parts were obviously strictly ordered, others appeared suddenly at some distance as the visitor walked around a corner or emerged from woodland; everywhere there were hills and valleys. The effect was completely different from the seventeenth-century formal arrangement of contiguous garden rooms. Vanbrugh was still using geometry but in an innovative way – he brought to life the philosophy of the Enlightenment, the fusion of 'natural' with mathematics, and applied it to the estate, not just the garden near the house. He understood that topography should be part of the composition and not flattened, that views outside the garden of grazing animals or distant hills were important references to Nature and that the site of the house was fundamental to the design. The evidence is in his letters: in his references to Nature; his knowledge of Vitruvius that came from Alberti and Palladio; and his obsession with using the correct proportion in buildings. Analysis of maps and plans of the landscapes with which he is associated has revealed the underlying Vitruvian framework of all of his compositions. The lines on Vanbrugh's designs were not sight lines; all of the elements were connected in an iconographic Enlightenment parkscape that would have been understood by his patrons and visitors alike. Modern scholars have assumed that there was no overall preconception at Castle Howard: Neil Levine refers to the unexplained axial misalignment of the Carlisle Pyramid with the centre of the south front of the house; and Lance Neckar maintains that Castle Howard 'resisted preconceived geometries'.[39] The geometry was there, it is just not obvious to us.

Fortification

We know from the Castle Howard accounts that the garden in Ray Wood was surrounded by high walls and bastions, and the coeval Woodwork at Blenheim was built in the same style.[40] The military theme of Vanbrugh's bastion gardens could have been inspired by the walls of Chester where he lived as a boy, but Alberti described Roman fortifications and how they were made and so the method and the idea may have come from *De re aedificatoria*.[41] The fortresses designed by the prominent French military engineer Sébastien Le Prestre, maréchal de Vauban, in the late seventeenth century followed the design of the early Romans, and Vauban was working at Calais in the 1690s when Vanbrugh was released from prison. In 1694 Nicholas de Fer published in French an illustrated description of the fortified towns of Europe that included Vauban's masterpiece, the star-shaped citadel at Lille.[42] The trace of Vauban's first method would appear to be the pattern for the distinctive diamond-shaped bastions that Vanbrugh built at Castle Howard, Claremont and Grimsthorpe. Alberti observed of Roman walls that 'the earth excavated with the ditches can be used for the rampart'; Vauban's bastions had high walls sunk into the ground, the interior being built up into a terrace to give the soldiers a clear view of approaching attackers.[43] Early eighteenth-century copies of Vauban's drawings are held in the Ancaster (Grimsthorpe) and Manchester (Kimbolton) family archives, both sites where Vanbrugh was employed (Figure 4.10).[44]

Although the presence of these drawings is not proof of a connection with Vanbrugh, they do provide evidence of an underlying interest in Vauban and fortification design amongst Vanbrugh's contemporaries. A map of the new fortifications at Plymouth dated 1718, again associated with Vanbrugh, is also in the Ancaster archives.[45] Vauban, Alberti or a combination of the two inspired Vanbrugh to sink the wall of his woodland garden into a ditch, and to use the excavated earth to build up the ground on the inside. The effect at Ray Wood (and at Blenheim) was that the wall appeared only a foot high to those inside the garden but was seven feet high from the base of the ditch making a strong military statement with its bastions on the outside, as well as forming an effective barrier against

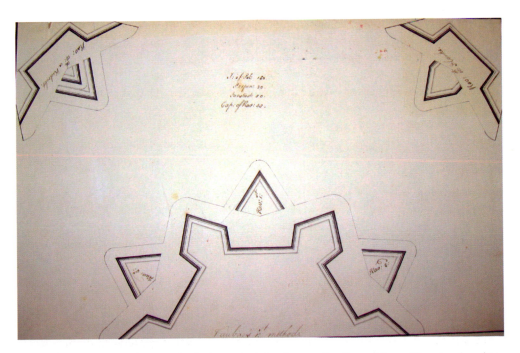

FIGURE 4.10 Vauban's first method. From the Manchester family archive at Huntingdonshire Archives M1B/3-1.

animals. The ditch and terrace idea was ascribed to Vanbrugh by Switzer in 1718 when he wrote:

> The Ditch of Graff, on the outside being what supplies the Inside, and raises up the Terrace, was certainly a very good Thought, tho' I presume it has not been much practis'd by us in England, and was first deliver'd to us by a Gentleman that is deservedly honour'd with some considerable Posts belonging to the Architectural Province, &c in his Majesty's Works.[46]

This innovation allowed those walking in the garden to see over the low barrier into the countryside beyond (Figure 4.11), and effectively joined garden and landscape into one composite picture, reminiscent of the painting in the garden room at the Villa ad Gallinas. By removing the barriers between Ray Wood and the fields and distant hills at Castle Howard, Vanbrugh had invoked the philosophy of the Roman garden by bringing in 'the Liberty of all the Beauty that Nature affords without'.[47] Interestingly, Palladio also surrounded his early villas with walls that were two feet high looking from the inside but eight feet high looking from the outside. Like Vanbrugh's bastions they were symbolic forms of protection that did not obscure the view. The effect can still be seen at the Villa Godi (Figure 4.12), and at the Villa Almerico-Capra (La Rotonda), both in the Veneto in Italy.

It appears that the early eighteenth-century ha-ha may have derived from this style of fortification. James is credited with the first reference (in an English text) to the ha-ha in 1712, when he describes it as providing 'Thorough-Views, call'd Ah, Ah, which are Openings in the Walls, without Grills, to the very level of the Walks, with a large and deep Ditch at the Foot of them'.[48] Earlier in the text he mentions a 'low Terrass-Wall' at the end

FIGURE 4.11 *The Dutchess's Bastion at Grimsthorpe*, William Stukeley, 1736. The Bodleian Libraries, University of Oxford MS. Top. Gen. D14 f38v.

FIGURE 4.12 The low wall and the view from the Villa Godi near Vicenza, Italy. Palladio's
first villa. Photo: author, 2008.

of a great walk 'from whence you have a View of the Country round about'.[49] It is evident
that both the 'Ah, Ah' and the 'Terrass-Wall', as James understood them, were sporadic
features that did not completely enclose the garden. Vanbrugh's inspiration was that he
encircled the garden with the sunk wall and terrace walk; as Switzer observed: 'The first
[fortification] was the *Ambit* of the Gardens at Blenheim; but that is after the ancient
Roman Manner'.[50] Willis observes that, 'although it seems unlikely that they did so prior
to about 1720, both [Vanbrugh and Bridgeman] used ha-has when working together at
such houses as Blenheim, Eastbury and Stowe'.[51] However, the ha-ha was a direct result
of Vanbrugh's fortification style dating from the early 1700s, thus preceding d'Argenville's
book and any real association with Bridgeman by some years. Writing to his brother after
a visit to Stowe in 1724, Viscount Percival declared that: 'What adds to the beauty of
this garden is that it is not bounded by walls but a Ha-hah which leaves you the sight
of the bewtifull woody country'.[52] Jacques Rigaud's series of paintings of Stowe in the
1730s indicates that the gardens were in fact encompassed by low walls and hedges, and a
stockade (Figure 4.13).[53] It appears that Vanbrugh's innovation was termed a 'ha-ha' at this
time. Only about a foot high and put there simply to prevent the visitor from falling into
the deep ditch beyond, the low wall or hedge did not obstruct the view in any direction. It

FIGURE 4.13 The ha-ha at Stowe. *View of the Queen's Theatre*, Jacques Rigaud, 1739 (detail).
© The British Library Board Maps 7.TAB10, view 8.

may not have been until later that the wall disappeared completely, resulting in the ha-ha as we now understand it.

Vauban's second method of fortification was the use of covered bastion towers that could be defended even when attacked from above, and such towers appeared in the curtain walls of the outworks that Vanbrugh built at Castle Howard (Figure 4.14).[54] In 1724 Vanbrugh wrote to Carlisle about the caps for the towers: 'I have seen one upon a round Tower on the Walls of Chester that I thought did extreamly well'.[55] The association with Vauban and with Chester points to a Roman precedent for Vanbrugh's outworks, and not a mediaeval one. Hart argues that both mediaeval and Roman influences pervade Vanbrugh's work, resulting in a mix of Gothic and classical styles, but as Mowl asserts Vanbrugh never used the ogee window, and the castellated detail in Vanbrugh's buildings did not represent an intention to mediaevalise.[56] The Mount (now the Belvedere) at Claremont has been labelled 'neo-Norman' by Downes, and Hart contends that its mediaeval character served to differentiate it from the classicism of the house.[57] However,

FIGURE 4.14 The outworks at Castle Howard. Photo: author, 2007.

the Mount was originally plastered and painted white, a device used to hide the use of bricks that were cheaper than stone, also seen in Roman buildings and, incidentally, in Palladio's villas (Figure 4.15).[58] Vanbrugh's crenellations owe their origin to the Romans who first built them in Britain on city walls and watch towers. There is no evidence of the mediaeval in Vanbrugh's landscape architecture, and the argument that the Mount is a copy of one of the miletowers on Hadrian's wall or modelled on the gate of a Roman fort must, therefore, be worthy of consideration.

Vanbrugh's outworks actually appeared at more sites than has previously been thought; the tower in the south wall of the garden at Eastbury shown in a late eighteenth-century painting is evidently part of another set of Roman outworks (Figure 4.16). They also appeared at Claremont: the Newcastle accounts include an entry for a 'Necessary House in the wood by the Mount and outworks'; there were outworks at Seaton Delaval; and an unrealised drawing of a defensive structure around the Great Court at Kings Weston shows a wall flanked by a ditch, and a gate very similar to the Pyramid Gate in the outworks at Castle Howard.[59] Vanbrugh's fortifications were bold statements that were much admired; he enthusiastically reported to Lord Carlisle only days before he died that the Duke of Grafton and the Lords Bathurst and Binny were 'all vastly Surprised and taken with the Walls and their Towers [at Castle Howard]'.[60]

In 1606 Sir Henry Fanshawe was building 'a fort, in perfect proportion, with his rampars, bulwarkes, counterscarpes' in his garden at Ware Park in Hertfordshire,[61] and a manuscript in the British Library written by a gardener called Thomas Brush (*c.* 1650) includes transcripts of Edmund Gunter's instructions on how to build garden fortifications.[62] But Vanbrugh's liberal use of the style in the grounds of the most important

FIGURE 4.15 The Mount at Claremont at the end of Vanbrugh's approach ramp, reconstructed in its original colour. Photo and reconstruction: author, 2008.

buildings of the new century must have set the trend for the early 1700s. Batty Langley included an illustration of 'An Arbor in a Fortified Island' in his *New Principles of Gardening* (1727), a design similar to Viscount Castlemain's fortification at Wanstead Park, which was built before 1725 (Figure 4.17). Vanbrugh appears to have felt some ownership of the style and observed in a letter to Newcastle that the Duke of Rutland's new curtain walls at Belvoir Castle were 'like a pasteboard work . . . for want of being rightly understood, the whole grace of them is lost'.[63] He was always prompt to criticise projects where he had not been employed. After visiting Cannons in 1720 he remarked to Newcastle that the Duke of Chandos:

> has done great things since I was there both in Building and Gardening, in which I do Assure you, he has sav'd nothing by not letting me be his Architect; For I had Cutt him out less Expence, And you may be Sure, (I think) a Better house.[64]

FIGURE 4.16 A painting of the west front of Eastbury, attributed to A. Grant, *c.* 1795. Note the tower with a pyramid roof on the far right sitting atop a substantial wall. The outworks stood to the south of the house, which is mostly demolished. Source unknown.

The classical landscape

There is no mention of ornamentation other than seats and fountains in Pliny's gardens, and, although there are reconstructed statues at the end of the canal at Hadrian's Villa Adriana, their placement is only conjecture. Real temples to Isis, Vesta and Mercury abounded in Roman cities, whilst those to Ceres, the goddess of agriculture, could be found scattered around the *campagna*. The Pyramid of Cestius in Rome was built as a tomb around 12 BC and the city was crowded with obelisks taken from the ancient temples on the Nile by the emperors of the first century; all would have been important sights on the Grand Tour. Miniature theatres, obelisks and loggias started to appear in the garden and *barco* during the Italian Renaissance: Lazzaro refers to the temples and loggias seen by a visitor to Reggio Parco in Turin in 1605, and to the sixteenth-century Tempietto in the Sacred Grove of Bomarzo.[65] Michel de Montaigne saw 'a high pyramid [*guglio sudante*] which spouts water in many different ways' at the Villa Lante in 1581, and there were eight pyramids surrounding the central fountain.[66] These gardens were a mix of utilitarian planting (fruit trees), iconographic representations (temples and statues) and pure entertainment (water music and fountains).

By 1706 there were antique piers with pyramidal tops and pyramids decorating one of the bridges at Castle Howard, and a 'four square summerhouse' made of wood but again

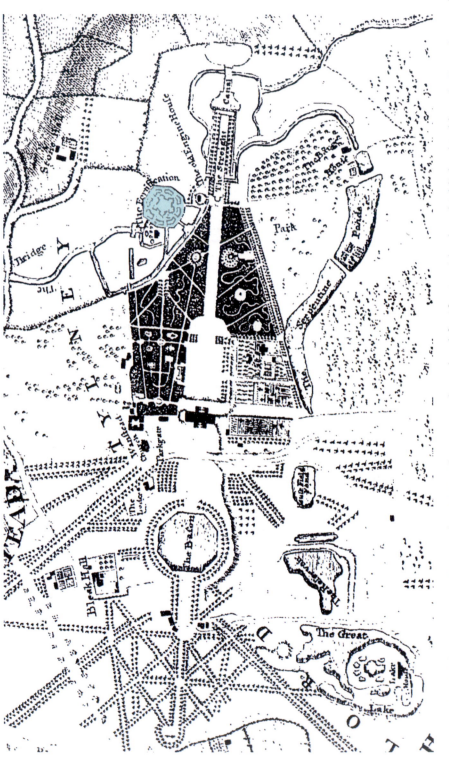

FIGURE 4.17 Lord Tylney's estate at Wanstead in 1746. The octagonal pond and fortification island are highlighted in blue. *An Exact Survey of the City's of London Westminster, ye Borough of Southwark and the Country near Ten Miles Round*, John Rocque, 1746. © The British Library Board CRACE PORT XIX 18.

painted to look like stone stood at the north-east boundary of Ray Wood (Appendix B).[67] The shape of the summerhouse is interesting, and Thomas Player's description of 1710 of a 'little regular front adorned with images of shepherds' with another shepherd on the roof does suggest a classical style, particularly as the building faced a 'rectangular circled' (octagonal) pond.[68] Although there is no direct evidence, it is reasonable to assume that the summerhouse and the bowling green house, mentioned in the accounts of 1710–15, were both designed by Vanbrugh.[69] The classical bowling green house with a temple portico can be seen next in Kip and Knyff's engraving of Chatsworth in the 1690s, and Celia Fiennes described the grounds in 1697 as having 'two piramidies full of pipes spouting water'.[70] Palladio paid scant attention to gardens in the *Quattro Libri*, even though Alberti had been specific about what should be 'within the gates' of a villa when he wrote that 'there should be no shortage of semiprivate spaces, walkways, promenades, swimming pools, areas grassed and paved over, porticoes and semicircular loggias'.[71] Vanbrugh was working with patrons who had been on the Grand Tour and who had seen obelisks and pyramids in the cities of Italy, as well as the decorations in Renaissance gardens; they would not have questioned the placement of buildings and ornaments in the landscape, which would be understood as references to the classical provenance of the design. Hart suggests that the pyramids were an allusion to archetypal tomb architecture, possibly inspired by the English Cemetery in Surat, but Vanbrugh would have considered them to be consonant with his theme of Roman gardens and outworks, and he may have sought advice from Alberti on their construction and elevation.[72]

The bowling green house at Castle Howard was soon followed by the Mount at Claremont; Vanbrugh augmented an existing hill in order to exploit the extensive views of Surrey from the roof of this building. The proximity of the Mount to the house would have enabled it to be used as a summer dining parlour, and a billiard table was constructed there in 1716.[73] The Mount was coeval with the Round Seat or Temple at Claremont, the exact location of which is uncertain, but it may have been the building later fronted with a temple portico, which can be seen in an engraving of the 1720s (Figure 4.18). This seat with a domed roof is mentioned in Lawrence Eusden's poem on Claremont of 1717: 'Where Domes, and distant Turrets fill the Sight'.[74] If it is the building shown in the engraving, it would be an early example of Vanbrugh siting a garden building in a prominent position on the edge of a landscaped park, specifically to take in the view. Later examples would be the Rotundo at Stowe, the Ionic Temple at Duncombe (attributed to Vanbrugh by Whistler), the Temple with the four Porticos at Castle Howard and the Temple Pavilion at Claremont (Figure 4.19). When Vanbrugh wrote to Carlisle in 1724 about the Temple at Castle Howard he was clear that it was not a belvedere but a temple:

> I have some doubts about the Name of Belvedere, which is generally given to some high Tower; and such a thing will certainly be right to have some time and in Some Place, tho' I can't say I do at present think of one about the Seat, where the View is better than this, But this Building I fancy wou'd more naturally take the Name of Temple *which the Situation likewise is very proper for.*[75]

Alberti observes that 'every place was not suitable for [temples to] every god' and that those to gods of pleasure or strife such as Venus and Mars should be built *on the very edge of the city*; Vanbrugh seems to have followed this advice.[76] Although Palladio is keen to

FIGURE 4.18 Domed temple above the round pond at Claremont. The Bodleian Libraries, University of Oxford Gough Maps 30, fol. 58.

point out that 'by God's special grace, [we] are free of that darkness and have deserted [the Ancients] foolish and false superstitions', he stipulates that modern temples (i.e. churches) should still be carefully placed, and those on the edge of the city must 'look out over public streets or rivers';[77] his churches in Venice are evidence of this. All of Vanbrugh's temples were on the edge of parks or gardens, visible from outside but rarely visible from the house; they made a bold statement about the possession of the land, and their Roman provenance underlined the classical standing of their owners.[78]

Vanbrugh's temples were all raised on earth or stone podiums following Alberti's dictate that 'the whole temple should be raised above the level of the city', and in the Temple with the four Porticos he built a perfect cube, copying on a smaller scale Alberti's '*cubo pitagorico*' at the Medici Villa in Fiesole.[79] The height of the podium of the Temple measured exactly one-sixth of the width, thus invoking the method of 'almost all the best architects' in antiquity.[80] Vanbrugh used the Ionic order for his temples, and the Doric for his pavilions (or 'seats'), apparently eschewing at the Stowe Rotundo the Vitruvian principle of using the feminine Corinthian order for temples to Venus. The evidence from all of Vanbrugh's garden buildings suggests that, although he followed Alberti's guidance on placement and form, neither he nor Hawksmoor followed Vitruvius in the orders of capitals suitable to a particular god; one possible explanation for this is that Alberti omitted from *De re aedificatoria* Vitruvius's explicit directions on the capitals to be used.[81]

FIGURE 4.19 Vanbrugh's temples. Clockwise from top left: Rotundo, Stowe; Ionic Temple at the end of the Terrace at Duncombe; Temple with the four Porticos, Castle Howard; Temple Pavilion, Claremont. Photos: author, 2008. Bottom left: *Plan of Claremont*, John Rocque, 1738 (detail). © The British Library Board Maps K.Top 40 19a. The roof of the Rotundo was lowered by Giovanni Battista Borra in 1752. All four temples were features on the edge of Vanbrugh's designed landscapes.

Nevertheless, Hawksmoor's 1724 letter regarding his alternative design for a building on the eastern edge of Ray Wood exposes the social significance of classical tradition at this time:

This turret must stand upon a square Basement *after ye manner antique*; and if I dare answer for ye Beauty Conveniency and Duration of this fabrick, and them 3 things are ye chief in all Buildings. I would not mention Authors and Antiquity but that we have so many conceited Gentlemen full of this science, ready to knock you down, unless you have some old father to stand by you. I dont mean to Coppy them but to be upon ye same principals.[82]

Hawksmoor associates the Vitruvian Triad with his 'turret', but then reveals a frustration with those who sought to impose strict classical rules upon architectural design. His letters were usually deferential and far less forceful than Vanbrugh's, but there are other examples in which Hawksmoor was careful to draw attention to the Vitruvian authority for his work. Regarding the later Octagon Temple (Temple of Venus), also on the eastern boundary of Ray Wood, he wrote that 'the proposition is according to what Vitruvius mentions & directs in this Sort of Temple which he calls monopter'.[83] Saumarez Smith makes reference to the argument about the mausoleum at Castle Howard (1729–45), where Hawksmoor was criticised by Sir Thomas Robinson and the 3rd Earl of Burlington for using an incorrect intercolumniation, and Hawksmoor's subsequent wounded and defensive response.[84] Hawksmoor was a veteran neo-classicist who had been using Palladian motifs in his buildings when Burlington was still in the school room; however, he does seem to have attracted more criticism than Vanbrugh from these amateur arbiters of taste in all things architectural.[85] Vanbrugh was probably saved from such attacks only by his death, although he had his detractors during his lifetime: Blenheim was famously described by the Duke of Shrewsbury as a 'great pile of stones above ground', and Vanbrugh wrote of Castle Howard in 1721: 'I think no Place I ever Saw, will dispute with it, for a Delightfull Dwelling in generall, *let the Criticks fish out what particular faults they please in the Architecture'*.[86] In the event, Vanbrugh's design for the Temple with the four Porticos for Ray Wood was preferred over Hawksmoor's turret, and Hawksmoor later wrote to Carlisle, without rancour, that 'What Sr John proposes is very well, and founded upon the Rules of the Ancients I mean upon Strong Reason and good Fancy, Joyn'd with experience and tryalls, so that we are assured of the good effect of it'.[87] The location of this Temple, and of the later Octagon Temple, seems never to have been in dispute, and, although Downes claims that the significance of the garden buildings at Castle Howard 'is neither geometrical nor symbolic', the buildings do fit exactly with the proportional landscape design revealed earlier in this chapter.[88] Vanbrugh had never seen Palladio's Villa Almerico-Capra outside Vicenza, although he would have been familiar with Palladio's description of 'the most beautiful vistas on every side, some of which are restricted, others more extensive'.[89] Yet he situated his Temple with the four Porticos with open views in three directions and a restricted view to the west, thus precisely emulating Palladio's placement of the building. His first temple was at Chargate; a pencil addition, 'Temple Pavilion', to an early garden plan probably dates to around 1717 when Newcastle began to enlarge the gardens after his marriage. Lord Burlington's first building in his gardens at Chiswick, the Casina, was designed in the same year and his Ionic Pagan Temple was finished in 1719; they prompted the Duchess of Marlborough to comment to Lady Cairns: 'at Rosamonds Bower [at Blenheim] I will have something like those temples which they talk of that are at my Lord Burlingtons country house'.[90]

Alongside his references to the classical landscape there are also examples of Vanbrugh's use of James's 'architecture in green' at Blenheim, Grimsthorpe and Stowe. Between 1706 and 1710 the Blenheim accounts have many references to pyramid yews, 'shapt pyramid Hollys' and 'square pyramid true Phyllareas'.[91] Stukeley's view of the parterre at Grimsthorpe (Figure 4.20), which may have been of Vanbrugh's invention, shows that it was an architectural construction of shaped pyramid yews, and the parterre at Stowe was surrounded by a high hedge cut with alcoves: 'an Amphitheatre of Ewe Niches with the Muses etc between them'[92] (Figure 4.21). Vanbrugh placed statues in each of the niches, an

FIGURE 4.20 *The Parterre at Grimsthorpe*, William Stukeley, 1736. The Bodleian Libraries, University of Oxford MS. Top. Gen. D14 f37v.

FIGURE 4.21 Statues in yew niches at Stowe, Jacques Rigaud, 1739. © The British Library Board Maps 7.TAB10, view 14.

effect he later reproduced in stone at the temple at Eastbury and which he may have copied from Palladio, whose statues in niches decorate the facades of his Venetian churches.

After the death of Marlborough in 1722 Vanbrugh wrote to Carlisle that 'I have taken the liberty to mention to my Lord [Godolphin] what your Ldship designs at Castle Howard [for a Mausoleum], and has been practic'd by the most polite peoples before

Priestcraft got poor Carcasses in their keeping, to make little money of'.[93] This short statement not only dates the mausoleum at Castle Howard, or its inception at least, to 1722, but also hints at Vanbrugh's sceptical view of the Church. The architect had proposed a plain and durable monument for Marlborough to be erected in Blenheim Park, but he was overruled by the Duchess who insisted that the Duke was buried in the chapel. There is further evidence from analysis of the landscape at Seaton Delaval that Vanbrugh may have proposed the mausoleum there, although it was not built until 1776. Williams suggests that the mausoleum in the English park may have had its origin in the graves in the cemetery in Surat, where Vanbrugh was employed as a factor in the 1680s.[94] However, Howard Colvin highlights the association of Vanbrugh's mausoleums with Palladio's church for the Barbaro family on their estate at Maser in the Veneto, which had the form of an antique mausoleum.[95] Analysis of the site using Google Earth suggests that the alignment of the church at Maser on the Roman Via Appia and its geometrical relationship to the house and the garden are equivalent to Vanbrugh's careful placement of buildings. The Roman associations of the mausoleum were further strengthened by Gaius Cestius Epulo's pyramidal tomb in Rome and Hadrian's circular mausoleum, now the Castelo di Angelo. The idea of the mausoleum was not unknown in Britain in the seventeenth century, although there were only a few burials outside the grounds of the church, and these had no 'architectural consequences' before Vanbrugh.[96] In the event, the Carlisle mausoleum was not started until three years after Vanbrugh's death, and Hawksmoor's design for it was founded on Bramante's Tempietto, illustrated by Palladio in the *Quattro Libri*.[97] Whether Vanbrugh had given an opinion on its form in 1722 is unknown, but the choice of style was in keeping with the classical theme and the building was accurately positioned according to Vanbrugh's geometrical plan for the estate.

Heraldry and the theatre

The post of Clarenceux Herald was conferred on Vanbrugh in 1703/4 by Lord Carlisle, when he was temporarily Earl Marshal during the Duke of Norfolk's minority.[98] Hart makes a case for Vanbrugh's use of iconography in his house architecture in *Storyteller in Stone*, where he focuses on the heraldic theme, seeing it as major force in the formation of Vanbrugh's architectural style: 'his frequent use of medieval ornament and architectural forms . . . should instead be seen as a kind of heraldic celebration of the nation's chivalrous history'.[99] His views follow Downes's assertion that 'maybe not at first, but at some time Vanbrugh came to understand the seriousness of the job [of Herald]'.[100] It is difficult to be precise about Vanbrugh's opinion of heraldry, as he seemed to be making fun of it in his play *Aesop*. But it is worth reviewing the few comments that the architect made in his letters about the role of Clarenceux, in an effort to understand its significance. In July 1703 he wrote to Tonson:

> There was a great deal of Saucy Opposition, but my Lord Treasurer [Godolphin] set the Queen right, and I have accordingly been Souc'd a Herald Extraordinary, in order to be a King at Winter. Ld Essex was left Deputy to do the feat which he did with a whole Bowle of wine about my ears instead of half a Spoonful.[101]

As we have seen, Vanbrugh's true feelings are most readily revealed in his letters to Tonson rather than to his patrons, and the impression from this account is that Lord Essex, a close Kit Cat friend, had made the ceremony into a huge joke. Vanbrugh seemed to remember this after finally giving up the post of Clarenceux in 1725, as he told Tonson: 'I got leave to dispose in earnest, of a Place I got in jest, Clarx King of Arms, and I sold it well'.[102] Such a long-lasting appointment would have been financially important to Vanbrugh, who was always short of money, and he may well have seen it as pecuniary rather than anything else. As was usual, his tone changed completely when telling Carlisle the news:

> I don't remember whether I acquainted yr Lordp in my Last, that I had made an end of my affairs at the College and rec'd my money £2,400 . . . My Parting with that office while I am Living, has made your Ldps Gift of it to me Still the more Valuable.[103]

A sum of £2,400 would be worth over £330,000 today. Although the association of medi-aevalism with Vanbrugh's garden designs is disputed here, he did make frequent use of emblems in the ornament of his buildings. Given the strong contemporary interest in such matters, they could have been sourced either from heraldry or from Ripa's *Iconologia*, or other emblem books of the period.

Finally, there has been some discussion of the impact of the theatre on Vanbrugh's building and landscape style.[104] Despite his having told Tonson that he had 'drawn a design for the whole disposition of the inside' of the Queen's Theatre, there is no evidence that Vanbrugh designed the scenery himself, and it appears that James Thornhill's contemporary set designs were commissioned for the theatre in the Haymarket.[105] McCormick draws attention to the spatial complexity and depth in Vanbrugh's buildings and postulates that elements of Vanbrugh's architecture 'owe less to the Continental Baroque than they do to the trappings of the contemporary English stage – in particular to wing and shutter scenes'.[106] Vanbrugh utilised the method of landscape painting in his designs for parks, gardens and houses; perspective is obvious in his projects but its origins appear to be in classical and Renaissance writing, rather than in the theatre. Vanbrugh's landscape ethos was original in England and, assuming that he had never experienced Palladio's framing of the mountains at Fanzolo, his inspiration should be sought in the atmosphere of the Enlightenment and in his innate artistic talents.

Contemporary writers and gardeners

George London (died 1714) and Henry Wise (1653–1738)

London and Wise first started working together at Brompton Park Nursery, west of London, in 1681. London had trained in France where he was influenced by the garden designs of André le Nôtre at Vaux-le-Vicomte and Versailles. He set up the nursery with Moses Cook (the author of *Forrest-Trees*), and Wise worked there as an apprentice during the early years, rising to the position of partner by 1687. The two men started at Longleat in 1682, they were at Chatsworth in the 1690s, and were responsible for many of the great geometric gardens of the late seventeenth century that were illustrated in Kip and Kynff's

Britannia Illustrata. Vanbrugh appears to have quickly supplanted London as landscape designer after his arrival at Castle Howard in 1699; as Switzer put it: 'That beautiful Wood belonging to the Earl of Carlisle at Castle-Howard, where Mr. London design'd a Star, which would have spoil'd the Wood; but that his Lordship's superlative Genius prevented it'.[107] Although Switzer ascribes the demise of the star to Carlisle, it was Vanbrugh's bastion garden that replaced London's circular scheme of avenues in Ray Wood. London continued to regularly supply seeds and trees for the estate from Brompton until 1712, but after the accession of Queen Anne in 1702 Wise was promoted to Superintendent of the Royal Gardens, and London's career started to wane; he worked alone at Wanstead and Cannons until his death in 1714.

Wise translated two gardening books from the original French with London: Jean de la Quintinie's *The Compleat Gard'ner* (1699) and Francois Gentil's *The Solitary Gard'ner* (1706), reinforcing his position as an accomplished garden practitioner. But as Vanbrugh instigated his own style the role of the gardener was to change. Landscapes were transformed from contiguous garden areas that were levelled and groomed and, most of all, predictable to new parkscapes. When Vanbrugh was promoted to the newly created post of Surveyor of Gardens and Waters in the Office of Works in 1715, Wise was no longer in sole control of the royal gardens. 'Surveyor of Gardens' was the eighteenth-century terminology for a landscape architect; Vanbrugh's post was a tacit acknowledgement that the new style required an architect to be involved in the management of the King's gardens, working alongside the gardener.

London and Wise's formal gardens could not have been more different from Vanbrugh's landscapes and it is clear that they had little influence on his work. As the 1710s progressed, their obviously symmetrical garden rooms, star avenues and enclosed broderied parterres were displaced by Vanbrugh's encompassing vistas, his low walls, lakes, bridges, garden buildings and underlying geometry. And yet both London and Wise were essential to the projects at Castle Howard and at Blenheim; between 1704 and 1712 London supplied trees and seeds totalling nearly £100 from his nursery to Castle Howard.[108] There is no evidence from the accounts that London visited Henderskelfe during that time, and a letter from Lord Carlisle to his agent reveals that it was he who was responsible for the selection and ordering of plants, not London.[109] However, it was Wise who took this role at Blenheim, supplying (again from Brompton) the trees and flowers that would fill Vanbrugh's Woodwork and park, as well as managing the labourers. As time went on, Vanbrugh exasperated both of the Marlboroughs with his forceful ideas on all aspects of the design of the house and garden at Blenheim, but Wise was a trusted servant: 'for the gardening and plantations I am at ease, being very sure that Mr Wise will bee diligent', the Duke wrote to his wife in 1706.[110] The classical parterre at Castle Howard was designed by Vanbrugh but it is most likely that Wise was responsible for the fussy *parterre à l'anglaise* at Blenheim, as Vanbrugh would have had no interest in such detail. Indeed, it is clear that the architect concerned himself only with the form of plants and the impression they would make as part of the overall 'construction', the exception being those in kitchen gardens; he often commented on the progress of fruit trees, reporting to Manchester of his gardens at Kimbolton: 'a Mighty prospect of Grapes, which have fail'd almost every where [else]'.[111]

Assuming that Vanbrugh was no more than an architect of bridges and garden buildings, scholars have sought the 'garden designer' in Vanbrugh's projects: Neckar and Dixon Hunt look for Switzer at Castle Howard;[112] Whistler suggests London and Wise;[113] Downes attributes the Blenheim design to Wise, and Eastbury and Stowe to Bridgeman.[114] Whistler ponders Vanbrugh's contribution to landscape gardening, but eventually decides on a collaboration of architect, patrons and gardeners.[115] To a degree he is right; to look for the landscape architect who was responsible for the underlying form and the message of the design, and the gardener who oversaw the detail of the planting, brings us closer to the truth.

Joseph Addison (1672–1719)

Addison was a politician and a writer who was responsible for a series of highly influential articles in *The Spectator*, in which he expressed the philosophy of Temple, Locke and Shaftesbury for the education and betterment of the emerging bourgeoisie. Vanbrugh and the aristocratic members of the Kit Cat Club, who owned the estates on which he was working, frequented the coffee houses of London and mixed with the writers, merchants and professionals who congregated there. Consequently, it has been argued by Mavis Batey and others that Addison's essays would have influenced all members of the coffee-house society, and were thus significant in the 'evolution' of the natural garden during the early eighteenth century.[116] However, Addison's articles may not have had such a strong impact on Vanbrugh and his contemporaries. *The Spectator* was satirical and was designed to appeal to the merchant and professional classes who wanted advice on matters of culture and good taste. Addison gently mocked the landed gentry in the guise of the ineffectual and unintelligent Sir Roger de Cloverley and placed more positive emphasis on the businessman Sir Andrew Freeport; he waged 'war on false values, foppery and folly'.[117] Vanbrugh, Carlisle and their social group were all enthusiastic gamblers, yet Addison railed against gambling as a vice, and against the 'tastelessness of aesthetes and the eccentricities of the learned', both character traits that Vanbrugh's patrons, if not Vanbrugh himself, would have identified with.[118] It is difficult to see how Addison could have been the profound influencer of taste in the world of the *cognoscenti* that has been assumed when his articles were unlikely to have been of interest to them and may even have alienated them. His strictures on the importance of the Roman virtues of husbandry and his advocacy of the 'wild fields of nature' over the 'stately garden' were philosophical rather than garden advice.[119] They may have prompted country squires to tend to their vegetables and expand their plantations, but Addison's authority over Vanbrugh and his style of landscape architecture is highly questionable. Classically educated patrons such as Carlisle and Newcastle would have been more inclined to turn to Shaftesbury and Locke than to Addison's satire for their philosophy. A subscription edition of any learned book in the early eighteenth century was automatically supported by a selection of the aristocracy; the list of subscribers to the collected edition of *The Spectator* (1712–13), which was published by Tonson and included a number of Kit Cats, is therefore not a reliable source when evaluating the real impact of literature at this time. There is no evidence that Addison was particularly close to Vanbrugh; although they were members of the same club, the Kit Cat seems to have divided into factions. Apart from Tonson, Vanbrugh's friends were his aristocratic relations Carlisle, Cobham and Newcastle, as well as Essex, Dormer and Garth; Addison was closest to his Kit Cat patrons Montagu and Wharton, and to the soldier John Tidcomb.[120] Vanbrugh opened his gardens and parks to the surrounding countryside and included fields in his schemes long before Addison first published an article in *The Tatler* or *The Spectator*. Enlightenment philosophy pervaded English culture and Vanbrugh would not have been immune; we do not know whether he read Locke or Shaftesbury, but he read Palladio's descriptions of the sites of his villas, and the evidence supports the theory that he also read Alberti's account of those essential elements of the country estate: 'meadows full of flowers, sunny lawns, cool and shady groves, limpid springs, streams, [and] pools'.[121] The effect of the meadows and fields of cattle around Ray Wood at Castle Howard seen over Vanbrugh's low walls would have been of an early *ferme ornée*; this combination of profit with pleasure was possibly the source of the idea attributed to Viscount Bolingbroke at Dawley Farm, much later in 1724.

Addison's actual knowledge of gardening appears to have been limited. He purchased an estate at Bilton in Warwickshire in 1713, and set about planting with great enthusiasm.[122] The gardens were described *circa* 1800 as predominantly unchanged:

> The gardens attached to Bilton Hall are rather extensive: they continue as they were long since laid out, in *straight lines with long and thick hedges of yew*. On the north side of the grounds is a long walk, still called 'Addison's Walk', once the promenade of that great writer. Its seclusion was deepened by rows of trees, some of which were Spanish Oaks, raised by Addison himself from acorns given him by Secretary Craggs.[123]

The impression is of a geometric garden with a broad avenue to the rear and to the front of the house, and open views over fields of crops and cattle to the south; it seems that Addison had indeed made 'a pretty Landskip of his own Possessions'.[124] Addison's purchase of Bilton may have been prompted by the Tory Act of Parliament which stipulated that an MP must have an income from land, and his years in the political wilderness before the death of Queen Anne could also have influenced the decision.[125] However, Addison left Bilton soon after the end of November 1713, and, although he continued to spend money on it, he appointed a distant relative to manage the estate. His steward wrote in the following year that 'what you planted last year are all dead, a few Cherries and Apples excepted', the game was 'mostly destroyed', and the neighbours were taking advantage: hunting, shooting and fishing on the estate without hindrance.[126] As his political career recovered following the accession of George I, Addison was less and less at Bilton. He had spent a summer and a great deal of money creating his own *ferme ornée*, only to abandon it soon afterwards. Addison was not as interested in pursuing the life of a country squire as his writing suggests; it seems that the Warwickshire estate was a political expedient, and his articles in *The Spectator*, which closed in 1714, may only have been a diversion during a downturn in his career.

As Smithers observes, Addison's 'interest in planting was aesthetic rather than practical', and this may explain his attitude to topiary, which was not consistent with the developing fashion for 'architecture in green'.[127] At the same time that Lord Burlington was buying twenty-eight pyramid yews for his estate at Londesbrough and the Woodwork at Blenheim was sinking under vast numbers of them, Addison was admonishing his readers:

> our trees rise in cones, globes and pyramids. We see the marks of the scissors on every plant and bush . . . for my own part I would rather look upon a tree in all its luxuriancy and diffusion of boughs and branches, than when it is thus cut into a mathematical figure'.[128]

Pope enthusiastically embraced the cause, although he was less concerned with globes than with the intricate designs that had, in fact, been favoured by Pliny: 'we run into Sculpture, and are yet better pleas'd to have our Trees in the most awkward Figures of Men and Animals'.[129] Such aberrations he ascribed to those of 'the common Level of Understanding . . . [who] constantly think that finest which is least Natural'.[130] This was before Pope started to develop his own garden (where straight lines and quincunx were prominent), and it was left to Switzer, the only practical gardener amongst them, to make the more reasoned point that 'we don't by this absolutely reject in some few proper Places something of that kind [i.e. pyramids], yet why should that be thought such a Beauty and to exclude things that are more Natural?'[131] Pope and Addison had no hand in the banishment of topiary; it went unhindered into the 1720s, with Vanbrugh's yew niches at Stowe and Burlington's Orange Tree Garden at Chiswick, driven by the obsession for green architecture in the garden.

Stephen Switzer (1685–1745)

Switzer was a writer and a gardener; his *Ichnographia Rustica* in three volumes (1718) was a combination of theory, practical advice and descriptions of contemporary gardens. Switzer's books were common on the shelves of country gentlemen, but how often his work was purchased by the aristocracy, to whom he dedicated his work, is unclear. Never prone to modesty, Switzer informed his readers of his 'great command of water' in *Ichnographia*, and in 1729 he published a book on 'hydrostaticks and hydraulicks'.[132] His association with hydrodynamics has led some authors to link Switzer with early eighteenth-century landscapes where there is water, and no other name presents itself, but William Brogden's unpublished thesis proves how little real evidence of his work as a garden designer really exists.[133] He links Switzer with some gardens based solely upon his book dedications, but, as Pope described them in 1713, these 'prostitutions of Praise' were more likely to be attempts to gain commissions.[134] Brogden admits that there was no stylistic consistency in Switzer's recognised designs that might be used as a guide to his work.

Switzer was apprenticed to Wise at Brompton Nursery in the 1690s, which explains his employment at Blenheim in 1705, when he was paid £3 for working for six weeks looking after the quarries.[135] By his own account he planted about 10,000 hedge-yews in the Woodwork in 1706 and was responsible for the 'Carriage that plays the Engine at Blenheim', possibly a reference to digging the canal for Mr Aldersea's water engine.[136] However, a letter from Samuel Travers dated 1707 indicates that Wise did not think Switzer capable of supervising the already planted gardens at Blenheim; he was to be employed 'about the business of the Bridge'.[137] Wise gave the job to Tilleman Bobart instead, a botanist of some distinction who went on to work as garden designer to the Duke of Chandos at Cannons in the 1720s. In 1718 Switzer was dismissed from an important project at Caversham in Berkshire after an argument with Lord Cadogan over money, and in 1720, when both Vanbrugh and Bridgeman were weighed down with work, Switzer was actively seeking employment at Hursley in Hampshire, but was unsuccessful.[138] Even in 1724, Switzer's tentative letter to William Stukeley, when he was working at Spye Park in Wiltshire, does not suggest the confident hydrological engineer who wrote *Hydrostaticks* just four years later: 'My chief aim is to know how much fall in a mile is Requisite at the least to convey water by. We are prodigious Busied here on acct of waterworks and should have been glad of your assistance and advice'.[139] It is possible that this request to Stukeley was meant to flatter, but Switzer's sense of urgency and strict instructions on where Stukeley was to send his reply indicate that it was not. It is another letter to Stukeley dated 1711 that has formed the basis for Brogden's attribution of the bastion garden at Grimsthorpe to Switzer.[140]

Switzer realised that geometry could be combined with Nature in the early eighteenth-century garden. This insight was expressed in *Ichnographia*, and was conveyed to writers in the 1720s such as Langley, arguably making Switzer as influential as Addison amongst the squirearchy and their gardeners. Yet Switzer's known designs before 1730, such as those for Caversham, Marston in Somerset and the fruit garden at Spye Park, were unremarkable and demonstrated none of the inventiveness of Vanbrugh's work. At Broadley in Hampshire Switzer insisted that the road next to the house was moved to enable him to complete a viable design, a costly solution that did not win him praise, or a contract, from his client. As Brogden affirms, Switzer's 'attitude to the site seems rather cavalier and he is very far from consulting the genius of the place'.[141] His later design for Beaumanor, Leicestershire (1737) does exhibit the prevailing fashion for asymmetry, with detached groves and an irregular lake, although it is not known whether this design was ever realised. The gardens at Leeswood in Flintshire, the estate of George Wynne, have been attributed to Switzer and may support an argument for a change in his style after 1730.[142] The evidence for Switzer's presence on the estate is in a payment to him from Wynne in March 1733, and the observation in *Archaeologia* of 1786: 'The gardens [at Leeswood] laid out by Switzer (author of *Ichnographia Rustica*) in Bridgeman's first style'.[143] The payment of £53.05 is not substantial enough to denote a major project, being the sum that might be expected for a plan or for provision of plants or seeds. It seems more likely to have been a plan, as Switzer drew up a design for another garden on the instructions of Wynne in 1739.[144] What is interesting here is the report in *Archaeologia* that the gardens were in 'Bridgeman's first style'. Although attributions at this distance of time are often unreliable, analysis of a late eighteenth-century plan of the site suggests that the designer had indeed tried to emulate what was originally Vanbrugh's landscape architecture, later copied by Bridgeman (Figure 4.22). A geometrical framework is obvious, with one centre on the Mount, and some proportional rules have been used, although a modern site report indicates that 'a great deal of earth-moving' was required to create the slope between the house and the White Gates to the north, and it is consequently unclear how much sympathy Switzer really had with the natural topography.[145] Lack of proven Switzer gardens makes it difficult to ascertain his contribution to landscape architecture, and certainly in the 1720s there is no evidence that he physically promoted the style that he wrote about in his books. Nevertheless, Vanbrughian elements can be seen in the garden designs of the 1730s for Beaumanor and Leeswood, and it is reasonable, therefore, to draw the conclusion that Vanbrugh influenced Switzer, rather than the other way around.

Alexander Pope (1688–1744) and Lord Burlington (1694–1753)

Pope was eleven when Vanbrugh started work at Castle Howard and Burlington was only five. Pope was a Catholic although he suppressed his religious views until the Tories took power in 1710, when he was persuaded to write the political poem 'Windsor-Forest'

FIGURE 4.22 The underlying geometry of the landscape at Leeswood, Clwyd. The coloured layer refers to elements taken from a late eighteenth-century plan that are overlaid on the Ordnance Survey map of 1872: green = original extent of woodland, red = buildings, brown = outline of the kitchen garden. Plan: 'Rough Draft of the Estate at Leeswood' from David Jacques and Jane Furze, *Report of the Historical Interest of the Gardens and Grounds at Leeswood Hall, Clwyd*, Garden History Society (1981). Annotation: author.

in support of the peace negotiations with France. Addison disliked Pope but he tried to court him fearing that he would write for the Tory opposition, and his fears were now realised. Tonson always had an eye for talent regardless of politics or friendship, and had written to Pope in 1706 offering to print his *Pastorals*, a work that was eventually published as part of Tonson's sixth *Miscellany Poems* in 1709. This was followed by the poet's *Essay on Criticism* (1711), a work of 'an intellectual brilliance and eloquence'.[146] Not surprisingly, Pope was soon established as one of the first financially independent essayists of the eighteenth century.[147] Pope was close to the Tories Robert Harley, Lord Lansdowne and Viscount Bolingbroke and he was at risk when the accession of George I led to the return of the Whigs, and the trials of his friends for treason. There is evidence that the Pope family was protected by Burlington when they moved to a rented property in Chiswick in

1715, and thereafter Pope was less inclined to advertise his politics or his religion.[148] The close ties to Burlington continued throughout the 1720s and resulted in Pope's *Epistle to Lord Burlington* (1731), in which he famously advised consulting 'the genius of the place', although this was hardly an original phrase, having been used by Dryden in 1701 and by Addison in 1713, in relation to the gardens at Fontainbleau.[149] Pope's *Epistle* added little to the understanding of Art and Nature in the garden over and above that previously defined by Switzer, and yet both Pope and Burlington were considered by their contemporaries to be arbiters of taste, and are thought by modern writers to have been influential in the development of eighteenth-century garden style.[150]

In 1719 Pope acquired the lease on a piece of land next to the Thames at Twickenham, and he constructed a villa with a garden that was necessarily separated from the house by the route of the road to London; he connected the two by a tunnel that ran under the road. There are some features reminiscent of Vanbrugh in Pope's bastion and mount, but the closest that Vanbrugh came to a villa was Seaton Delaval, and Pope's garden design owed nothing to Vanbrugh's careful placing of house, garden and classical garden architecture, or his passion for topography. In its apparent eclecticism, Pope's work at Twickenham was further differentiated: by 1725 he had made the underground tunnel into a *camera obscura*, such that when the doors were shut 'all the objects of the river, hills, woods, and boats, are forming [on the walls] a moving picture in their visible radiations'.[151] The *camera obscura* had been known to the Ancients and this is an interesting use of it in a garden context that could be interpreted as a reference to the scientific foundation of the Enlightenment. Pope's garden temple composed of shells really was eccentric and was hardly in keeping with Burlington's strict classicism at Chiswick, although Vanbrugh did build grottoes at Claremont and at Blenheim. The geometry at Twickenham remained strong into the 1740s: a great avenue replacing an original diagonal crosswalk was flanked by quincunx and symmetrically arranged statues, and terminated by an obelisk to the west. Morris Brownell argues for a garden laid out in accordance with Pope's 'theory of picturesque design', but it is difficult to see it here: the garden seems to have been enclosed and the only views were from the top of the mount.[152]

Burlington did not reach his majority until 1715 when he was already into the second year of his first Grand Tour. In Italy he became interested in architecture and on his return to his Jacobean house at Chiswick he began construction of the Casina, under the mentorship of the architect Colen Campbell, which presaged a complete redesign of his garden. Campbell was at the peak of his career; he was about to publish the second volume of *Vitruvius Britannicus,* and had been given a place as clerk in the Board of Works by his friend William Benson.[153] Benson had been made Surveyor of the Board of Works in 1717 and quickly placed his friends and family in prominent positions, removing Wren and Hawksmoor. He was soon proved to be incompetent and was summarily removed from his post by Lord Sunderland after he advised that Wise and Carpenter should be replaced as Royal Gardeners by Thomas Ackres. Vanbrugh survived the upheaval, probably because of his connection with Newcastle who was related to Sunderland, but he disliked Benson and must have been wary of Campbell as a result.

Burlington went back to Italy in 1719 to study the work of Palladio in the Veneto, where he purchased a large number of his drawings. The only illustration of the finished garden at Chiswick in the 1720s was made by the French traveller Pierre Jacques Fougeroux who made a tour of England in the late 1720s (see Figure 2.2). His descriptions and drawings of the estates that he visited are valuable records of the important gardens of the time, although they are stylised and sometimes curiously inaccurate, reversing elements of a garden from right to left, and even missing out the Woodwork at Blenheim altogether.[154] Fougeroux's plan of Chiswick demonstrates a strict geometrical garden with temples at the end of a *patte d'oie*, another in the Orange Tree Garden (Figure 4.23), and a straight canal with a mount at its eastern end, which, like Pope's, afforded views of the Thames. Burlington was again restricted by the London road between his villa and the river, but the garden seems to have eschewed Nature; the impression is that it was inward-looking and lacked Vanbrugh's distant eye-catchers. This was not a 'Palladian garden'; Palladio had little interest in gardens, and the essential element of assimilation of the house with the landscape that was an identifying factor in his compositions, and in Vanbrugh's designs, was patently missing at Chiswick. In its overt geometry and green architecture Burlington's design had classical authority; he even planted his cedars in the 1:3:9:27 proportional sequence recommended by Alberti.[155] But his strict interpretation of Palladianism appears to have blinded him to both Pliny's and Palladio's landscape aesthetics; his design did not 'call in the Country'.[156] In 1724 Burlington started building a new villa at Chiswick, a derivative of Vincenzo Scamozzi's Rocca Pisani and Palladio's Villa Almerico-Capra, yet he set his 'belvedere' flat on the flood plain of the Thames without any reference to its surroundings; he completely missed Palladio's sense of place. In recognising the overt geometry but failing to comprehend the philosophy, Burlington eradicated 'the very qualities that differentiated the real works [of Palladio] from the graphic records of them'.[157] It is notable that Vanbrugh's sites were rarely flat, the one example being Seaton Delaval; yet even here he managed to bring the surroundings of the garden and park into the composition, to emphasise the beauty of Nature.

FIGURE 4.23 *The Orange Tree Garden at Chiswick*, Johannes Michel Rysbrack, 1748. The Bodleian Libraries, University of Oxford Gough Maps 17, fol. 41b.

Burlington was a late member of the Kit Cat Club, possibly through an association with Tonson; as Vanbrugh wrote to Tonson in 1719: 'I hear my Ld Burlington is arriv'd, and design (on what you say to his advantage) to go and wait upon him'.[158] Evidently Vanbrugh did not know Burlington before this date, but as a celebrated publisher Tonson would have been well known to the British *cognoscenti*; he had been offered, but had turned down, a place in Burlington's coach between Paris and London when Burlington returned from his second Italian tour. Although Burlington and Campbell are credited with the adoption and spread of neo-Palladianism in England, Vanbrugh was already an established architect by the time that he met Burlington in 1719, and his buildings had exhibited Palladian elements since his first projects at Whitehall and Castle Howard. Pope and Burlington are also believed to have been strong influencers in the development of the landscape garden, but neither could have had any impact on Vanbrugh's style, which was fully developed whilst they were still minors. Vanbrugh's Mount at Claremont pre-dated Burlington's Casina, and, although their construction of temples appears to have been coeval, the octagon pond and the square summerhouse in Ray Wood preceded the first work at Chiswick by ten years.[159] The introduction of overt green architectural features, such as the amphitheatre at Sacombe in Hertfordshire (1715–20), again anticipated Burlington's designs for an exedra and amphitheatre at his villa by the river in the 1720s.[160] Ironically, the one thing that Burlington did not do at Chiswick was consult 'the genius of the place', and his more imaginative landscaping of his country estate at Londesbrough in Yorkshire did not commence until after 1728. However, Pope's eclectic garden decorations at Twickenham cannot be ignored; they were a distinct deviation from the prevailing classical taste, and a precursor to William Kent's memorial to Congreve at Stowe and his remarkable Merlin's Cave at Richmond.

Charles Bridgeman (died 1738)

Bridgeman's early career is obscure; the first mention of him is at Blenheim in 1709 and it is possible that, like Switzer, he was apprenticed to Wise at Brompton Nursery. Although a landscape plan dated 1709, which now hangs in the Great Hall of Blenheim Palace, was drawn by Bridgeman, there are no payments to him in the Blenheim accounts for this period and no mention of him in letters. This was an early stage in his career and it is likely that he was working as a draughtsman for Wise; he hints at his role by signing the cartouche on his plan '1709 Bridgeman discrip.', meaning copy or transcript, rather than the more usual 'delin.', meaning drawing. There is evidence that he was at Stowe in 1716, but in 1714 London had died, and Wise went into partnership with Joseph Carpenter at Brompton, overlooking Bridgeman in the same way that he had dismissed Switzer as a gardener in 1707.[161] It is difficult to see any reason for this decision other than that Bridgeman was still considered a relative 'unknown' in the gardening fraternity. In the early years he worked at Stowe as a gardener rather than as a garden designer. Possibly he was introduced to Lord Cobham (another member of the Kit Cat Club) by Vanbrugh, who was advising on alterations to the house. Yet in 1715 Bridgeman was employed at Sacombe, where he was to receive over £650 in payments during the following three years.[162] There can be no doubt that Vanbrugh was with him at Sacombe; the kitchen garden was typically Vanbrughian with huge diamond and round bastions, and was described by Nathaniel

Salmon in 1728 as 'finished with walling equal to that of Blenheim'.[163] Willis observes that Sacombe demonstrates 'Bridgeman's typical axiality, and his use of dense woodland, rectilinear canals, a rectangular kitchen garden, an amphitheatre and an octagonal basin'; in this statement Vanbrugh's role in the development of landscape architecture is overlooked.[164] It was Vanbrugh who introduced the octagon pond, the terrace walk and the ha-ha much earlier at Castle Howard, where he also built the rectangular kitchen garden and was instrumental in saving the trees in Ray Wood. Vanbrugh's sympathy for topography combined with his hidden geometry was well established before Bridgeman copied the plan of Blenheim, and there is no reason to suppose Bridgeman's influence in any of these aspects of his style. Bridgeman could not have impacted the evolution of Vanbrugh's landscape architecture; he was the essential 'gardener' to Vanbrugh's landscape architect until the late 1710s, yet he was to become a popular designer in his own right during the 1720s. There is evidence that he absorbed Vanbrugh's ideas and adopted them in his own designs, but Bridgeman was no architect, and it is significant that he went on to work with other architects, such as James Gibbs, to achieve the distinctive landscape style that was not his invention, but Vanbrugh's legacy. This legacy, and its impact on Bridgeman's career, is further examined in Chapter 15.

This chapter has evaluated Vanbrugh's landscape style and considered the many possible influences on its development. It has uncovered little evidence to support the contention that his work was founded only on the theatre, had mediaeval roots or was guided unduly by the rules of the College of Heralds. In a replication of the *Quattrocento*, the move of the architect into the garden in early eighteenth-century England resulted in the rules used to build houses being adopted in the design of landscapes; Vanbrugh was to apply Vitruvius's strictures, informed by Alberti and Palladio, to the plans for all of his estates, from Castle Howard to Seaton Delaval. His character and innate self-confidence suggest that he would have eschewed guidance from established garden designers, but Vanbrugh appears not to have been a plantsman, and he could not have achieved the realisation of his projects without the participation of gardeners such as Wise and Bridgeman, Clerks of Works such as Etty and Smallwell, patrons who had been on the Grand Tour or, indeed, Nicholas Hawksmoor. When he started his contract at Henderskelfe in 1699, fortification gardening was not unknown, but the other elements of his style – the application of Vitruvian proportions to create integrated parkscapes, his sensitivity to topography and the allusions to Roman roads, Roman buildings and Roman walls – all point to him being an innovator who was influenced by the atmosphere of the early Enlightenment.

5

CASTLE HOWARD, YORKSHIRE

Charles Howard was born at Naworth in 1669 and was a descendant of Lord William Howard, a younger son of the 4th Duke of Norfolk, who had made the family's fortune. In 1688 Howard married Lady Anne Capel, the daughter of the 1st Earl of Essex and sister of Kit Cat Club member Algernon Capel, who was to become the second Earl. As Lady Anne was only thirteen, Howard spent the next three years on a Grand Tour of the Netherlands, Germany and Italy before returning in 1691 to settle at Naworth and to enter local politics. After four years Howard, now the 3rd Earl of Carlisle, moved the family to Carlisle House in London, where he was an enthusiastic supporter of the Whig party, and became a member of the Kit Cat Club, probably through the influence of Essex. By 1698 he was established in London society and, although he was to wait another two years before being appointed Gentleman of the Bedchamber to William III, Carlisle's political career was in the ascendancy. The old house at Naworth did not match his newfound power and ambition, and in 1698 he leased an estate at Henderskelfe in Yorkshire from his grandmother, with the intention of building a new home. Carlisle asked the eminent architect William Talman and the garden designer George London to draw plans for a house and gardens to replace the old castle, which had been largely destroyed by fire in 1693; he thereby unwittingly set the scene for Vanbrugh to adopt his fourth career, as an architect.

Downes has highlighted the simplicity of Vanbrugh's initial designs for Castle Howard, Blenheim and Welbeck, suspecting that later embellishments to these houses were at the insistence of their owners (Figure 5.1).[1] Both Levine and Dixon Hunt see the house as Palladian, Levine ascribing the design to Palladio's Villa Trissino at Meledo, although the influence appears to be a combination of Trissino for the north front and the Villa Emo for the south front.[2] The Renaissance villas of the Veneto had to express the status of their wealthy owners as well as provide practical housing for farm animals and equipment; hence, the low wings of the Villa Emo housed the dairy and stables and were terminated by dovecots. Palladio could have built the Villa Emo on an east–west axis but instead he turned it to face south-east, creating an avenue three kilometres in length that ran perpendicular to the ancient Via Postumia in the south, cutting through the centre of the

FIGURE 5.1 The south or garden front of Castle Howard. The termination of the west wing, which originally had a bow window, was altered by Sir Thomas Robinson in the 1750s. Photo: author, 2008.

house and continuing towards Monte Grappa in the foothills of the Alps. The line of sight from the *piano nobile* across the square garden on the north front and out into the *campagna* was directed by Palladio's avenue as far as the mountains in the distance (see Figure 1.5). Although the rooms at Castle Howard were all grand apartments, their symmetrical layout around a central hallway, the later addition of the *piano nobile* set above a basement floor and the vista through the house to the north and south were all features mirrored in the design of the Villa Emo.[3] Like Palladio, Vanbrugh had re-oriented the house towards the south-east, and, although there was no avenue through the house, he was later to build geometrical approach roads leading from the Roman road between York and Malton.

Vanbrugh spent the summer of 1699 visiting 'the great houses of the North', but his initial simple designs for the south front of Castle Howard, with low wings, which the Duke of Devonshire thought to be 'like an orange house', bore little relation to anything that he had seen.[4] By December the design was greatly embellished 'with those Ornaments of Pillasters and Urns', as Vanbrugh wrote to Manchester, and in the final design a cupola was added to the roof.[5] The Doric pilasters were plain on the north front but the walls were rusticated with antique statues in niches, whereas on the south the Corinthian pilasters were fluted and the walls undecorated – a deliberate use of the masculine Doric order for the entrance front, and the feminine Corinthian order for the garden front.[6] By the end of 1701 the Earl was at the peak of his political career; he had just been appointed First Lord of the Treasury and he intended to make a clear statement on his authority and wealth in the extent and ornamentation of his house.

As Vanbrugh took over the hard landscaping from London, the star in Ray Wood, the proposed canals and avenues to the north of the house, and the model village were all abandoned. A large-scale plan of the new house and Ray Wood (*c.* 1706) indicates that work was concentrated on the house and its immediate environs (Figure 5.2). The building appears to be unchanged from London's plan (see Figure 0.2), although the separate office blocks have gone and the kitchen and stable courts are attached to the house. The bow window at the west end of the south front, which was designed in 1707, is missing, indicating that it was not part of the original scheme; the east end of this front was already built and never had a bow window.[7] An enclosing courtyard to the north of the entrance drive has been roughly sketched in; this appears to be completed in the 1727 plan. The accompanying notes to Figure 5.2 refer to a new wall around the north of Ray Wood 'which is built', and the accounts of October 1706 include an entry for work on 'ye wall of Ray Wood being seven foote high'.[8] A pre-existing wall on the south side of Ray Wood had bastions added to it in 1705, and the new wall to the north and west, also with bastions, enclosed the woodland garden.[9] In June 1706 the labourers were 'making ye Ditch Round Wraywood', and there is surviving evidence that the garden was surrounded by a high wall sunk into the ditch with the ground built up on the inside to form Vanbrugh's terrace walk.[10] It is clear that an 'air of Defence' was always intended, for here are the first drawings of the diamond and rounded bastions of a fortress garden, a theme that was to be reproduced much later in curtain walls to the south of the house.[11] The military leitmotiv evident in Ray Wood was coeval with that at Vanbrugh's second project at Blenheim; differing shaped bastions in a military garden was a recurring theme in Vanbrugh's work, and they appeared in so many of his landscape designs over the following twenty years that they must be ascribed to him.

The notes attached to Figure 5.2, probably in Clerk of Works Will Etty's hand, indicate that it is a topographical plan for the new gardens.[12] The annotations to the plan carefully plot the rise and the fall of the land around the house, and the incline into Ray Wood, indicating that there was never any intention to level the ground. The notes refer to 'ye Partar' and the 'Kitching Gardin' as well as the entrance to the wood. The kitchen garden was completed in 1705, although probably functional long before then, but a mystery lies in the parterre.[13] London continued to regularly supply seeds and trees for the estate from his nursery at Brompton until 1712, but there is no evidence that a *broderie anglaise* or *gazon coupe* was ever created on the parterre. The old castle of Henderskelfe was still in situ on the west front, and the parts not destroyed by fire remained as a lodging place for the Earl until he could move into the new house in 1712. The accounts for 1706–8 include entries for work 'at ye old castle' to set 'a grate in my lords great dining room', and to re-floor the kitchen.[14] Apart from the kitchen garden and Ray Wood, the only landscaping before 1714 was the planting of the avenues, work that clearly had to be undertaken immediately to ensure that the park was established by the time that the house was built. The abrupt cut-off of the plan to the south of the house suggests that at least one more sheet of paper has been lost, but it is important to note that the straight line of the avenue into Ray Wood, the geometry of the approach roads marked by trees and the striking decision to cut the wood in half are clearly visible on this plan, thus supporting the theory that there was an overall scheme early in the project.

In 1714 there is a reference to building the 'long parterr wall' in the accounts, followed in 1715 by work on the door of the 'bowling green house' and 'stairs down to the bowling green'.[15] There is no obvious place for the bowling green except the south front, so the parterre must have been laid to grass for this fashionable game, probably soon after

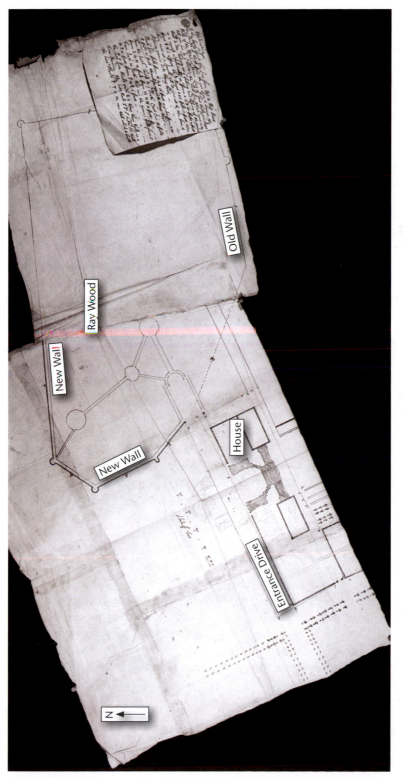

FIGURE 5.2 *The Plan of Henderskelfe Castle and Wray Wood, c. 1706.* © V&A Images, Victoria & Albert Museum, London, E433.1951.

Carlisle took up residence in 1712. Although Vanbrugh had designed the whole estate, for a period of twenty years the principal garden at Castle Howard was Ray Wood. Gardens were meant not only for the recreational use of the family, but to delight, surprise and impress visitors to the estate; it is therefore interesting to consider the reasoning behind Lord Carlisle's initial decision to create what must have been relatively modest gardens for such an imposing house. Carlisle's total annual expenditure already exceeded his income by 1704, although he augmented it by gambling: Vanbrugh reported to Manchester in 1707 that Carlisle had 'won Two thousand pounds of the Sharpers, and is gone downe again to lay it Out in his Building'.[16] Carlisle's financial situation was exacerbated by losing his position as First Lord of the Treasury on the accession of Queen Anne in 1702, after less than a year in the post. Thereafter, the costs of building were carefully managed both by Carlisle and by Vanbrugh, and this must have contributed to the slow development of the landscape. Castle Howard was to be the first of many of projects in which Vanbrugh had to employ strict controls on expenditure, and throughout his career his letters attest to his sensibility to cost, and to his efforts to reduce it.

Figure 5.2 suggests that in 1706 the design of the interior of Ray Wood was still tentative and certainly not complete, although pedestals for the statues were already being carved in 1705.[17] The three circles connected by straight lines suggest a formality at the entrance that is still partly visible today, but the lack of detail on the east side of the wood is frustrating. Figure 5.3 is a reconstruction of the environs of the house and of Ray Wood and draws on information from the archives, together with a contemporary description written by Thomas Player, who rode out from York one Monday morning in 1710 to see 'my Ld Carlisle's house'.[18] In an undated letter, possibly 1706, written by Carlisle to his agent Nevil Ridley in London he asks him to find at the Brompton Nursery '600 Limes 300 Chestnuts and 60 English Elms . . . they must be about 8 feet high'.[19] These trees were planted in avenues on the south front, which were decorated with statuary. As Player described it: 'tis addorn'd with abundance of Images on the south and west side of the house with many very fine walks of trees newley planted of sicamore limes and horse chestnuts'.[20] But it is Player's early account of the interior layout of Ray Wood that is most valuable. Saumarez Smith has discussed the painting in the dome of the Great Hall of Castle Howard as a depiction of the Fall of Phaeton from Ovid's *Metamorphoses* Book 2, and Player's manuscript reveals that in 1710 Ray Wood was also a theatre of Ovidian legend.[21] He entered

> on the north side of the house, [where] one of the largest walks in the park answers the most regular part of the wood. The Wood is upon every side of a little hill covered with large beech trees and oak, the walks which are innumerable are cover'd with the ruins of the building (stamp'd and lifted) first of all in a very broad walk you ascend to the top of the hill where stands a very fine statue of Apollo on one of the pleasantest prospects [crossed out and replaced by 'rocks'] in the world; the whole work seems naturall, but is very curiously work'd, it represents many different prospects as sheep horses goats swans deer dogs and men.[22]

In *Metamorphoses* Book 8, Apollo rests his lyre on a rock and thereafter the stones ring with music. The statue has been moved but Apollo can still be seen at the end of an avenue on the south front carved as though rising out of the rock on which he stands.

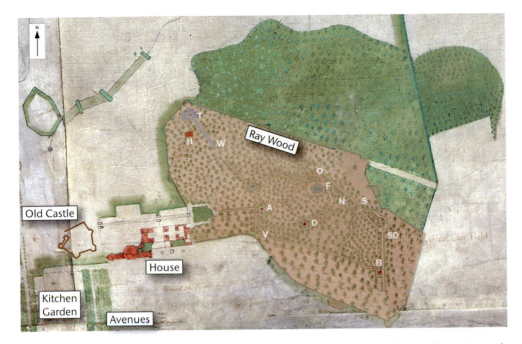

FIGURE 5.3 Reconstruction of the gardens at Castle Howard in 1710. Correctly positioned:
A – Apollo, T – Triton Fountain and Octagon Pond, H – Summerhouse, W –
Cascade. The positions of the following are tentative using Thomas Player's
description: V – Venus, D – Diana, B – Bacchus, S – Satyr, N – Nymph, F –
Swan Fountain, SD – Shepherd with Dog, O – Fruit Garden. Drawing: author,
2007, based on Castle Howard Archives P1/4 and P1/16.

The pedestal is intricately decorated with scenes from the *Metamorphoses* and its position
at the entrance to the wood was clearly meant to announce the theme of the garden. As
he moved around a woodland garden reminiscent of the *barco* at the Villa Lante, Player
saw statues of Venus, Bacchus, Diana with a stag, a satyr and a shepherd with his dog,
each depicting one of Ovid's stories.[23] The statues were in openings in the woods that he
called 'green plats'. Player also noted two fountains, one in the middle of a fruit garden
with a rock in the centre topped by 'a swan seated in a nest of rushes the water gushing
out'. On the west side of the garden he saw a stepped cascade over rocks and 'a very
pretty fountain rectangular circled, where a Triton throughs the water [blank] foot high
amongst the trees'. This octagonal fountain was next to a 'four square' summerhouse 'all
of wood, but the work and paint is so much like stone, that you would guess it to be such
till you touched it'.[24] Beside the summerhouse was a carved figure of a shepherd, representing Daphnis, the Idaean shepherd-boy turned to stone by a nymph in *Metamorphoses*
Book 4.[25] The many copies of *Metamorphoses* in his library and his choice of decoration
for the house testify to Carlisle's interest in Ovid's stories, and suggest that he was the
instigator of the original theme for Ray Wood.[26] In conjunction with the grandeur of his
house, Lord Carlisle wanted to draw attention to his classical education and his taste for
the art and architecture of modern and ancient Italy and Greece. Vanbrugh would have
been familiar with Ovid from Alberti, if not from Tonson and his contemporaries, but

his focus as architect would have been on the bastion walls and terrace walk and the geometric forms of the summerhouse and the octagon pond, all of which defined the landscape as classical.

The accounts attest to a 'new gardin' in Ray Wood in 1718 and further additions in the 1720s that attenuated the Ovidian theme.[27] Lady Irwin's poem of 1732 suggests a more generalised composition of Roman, Greek and Egyptian references in the landscape, and a focus on Diana the huntress in the wood.[28] The Diana and the name 'Ray Wood', which was a corruption of 'roe' the female deer, were references to hunting and possibly an allusion to the mediaeval hunting park that lay to the west. The symbolism of love was combined with an aura of classicism in the statues of Venus, Apollo and Bacchus, but the iconography was not the only defining feature of the wood; the similarity between the situation and plan of Ray Wood and the *barco* at the Villa Lante in Italy has been high-lighted by Dixon Hunt.[29] At the Villa Lante there were fruit trees in circles and squares around fountains that shot water high into the air, an octagon pond with a fountain 'which shoots water through the mouths of 4 eagles', stepped cascades, shaded seats, obelisks and pyramids.[30] All of these were present in the Castle Howard landscape by 1714. Finally, the 'four square' wooden summerhouse adorned with images of shepherds in Ray Wood bore similarities to the garden house of wood painted to look like stone that Ippolito d'Este had built in his garden on the Quirinal Hill in Rome in 1561, although there was little hope that it would last as long in the Yorkshire climate. Although it has been argued in this text that the influence of foreign travel on garden design of the early eighteenth century was very much a secondary factor, it is in the decoration of the interior of Ray Wood that we can perhaps see the effect of Lord Carlisle's Grand Tour.

The ornaments of the Wood were not in formal geometric walled garden enclosures or in a planted fir wilderness; they were in 'little Cabinets and Gardens' of a wood, at the junctions of paths that met at odd angles.[31] The visitor could get lost in a diffusion of differ-ent routes but would often catch glimpses of the 'Padducks and Cornfields . . . Brooks and Streams' outside, over Vanbrugh's ha-ha.[32] In 1715 Switzer wrote of Castle Howard: 'Tis there that nature is Truly imitated if not excell'd, and from which the Ingenious may draw the best of their Schemes in Natural and Rural Gardening'.[33] It is notable that in 1732 Ray Wood was still considered to be at the height of fashion, with 'several openings . . . that as Mr Pope expresses it, Calls in the country catches opening glades'.[34] This is what Switzer meant by 'natural and rural gardening', that the surrounding countryside was part of the ordered garden; the owned landscape and the borrowed landscape were of one composi-tion, brought together by the low wall and terrace walk that surrounded Ray Wood. He was later to observe that 'the Romans had doubtless the same extensive kind of Gardens'.[35]

Brogden, Neckar and Dixon Hunt attribute the cascades and fountains in Ray Wood to Switzer, whereas Whistler suggests London and Wise as designers.[36] The Castle Howard accounts make no reference to the technology required to pump water from the river north of the house to supply the fountains in the wood, although in 1705 five shillings were paid for 'an engine to water the garden with', followed by payments to Mr Norris the gardener, who must have been overseeing the kitchen garden.[37] Switzer was perform-ing only simple supervisory tasks at Blenheim when Ray Wood was being constructed; there is no evidence for his being responsible for any major scheme before 1718, and the first form of the wood was already completed by 1710.[38] The octagonal pond and Triton Fountain on the north-west boundary of the garden were close to the seventeenth-century fish ponds at the bottom of the hill, and it would not have been a difficult task to pump water from the river to the reservoir that fed the fountains and the cascade.[39] The Triton Fountain, with its water jet that was thirty feet high, was low enough to have been operated by gravity from this reservoir.[40] A local hydraulics engineer may have been hired to realise the plans already drawn up by Carlisle and Vanbrugh; it could even have been Robert Aldersea, who had constructed a water engine at Blenheim that was functional by 1706.[41] The names of eminent craftsmen such as Jan Nost appear in the accounts of many of the prominent estates of the period, and competent and reliable workers were re-employed from project to project.[42] The carpenter John Smallwell spent twenty years at Castle Howard, Blenheim and Claremont alongside other commissions.

Only minor changes were made to Ray Wood during the 1710s, as the house was completed, without the west wing, and the sunken bowling green on the south front was laid out. By 1713 Lord Carlisle had spent just over £35,000 (over £4m today) on his house, park and gardens and he had been living there for a year.[43] The 'south terrass' in front of the house was decorated with pedestals next to the stairs, which gave access to the bowling green and the bowling green house.[44] The terrace must have been extended east at this time towards Ray Wood, with the addition of 'the circular seats on the tarrass wall 4 in number'.[45] In 1718 the accounts refer to a new garden in Ray Wood and in 1719 to the building of two greenhouses; this presaged a second period of intense construction, which was to last throughout the 1720s.[46]

As the area to the south of the house was developed, a new entrance to Ray Wood was opened on the south front by removing part of the old wall. In 1720 the South Terrace running in front of the house was extended into the wood and a pedestal was built at this entrance, possibly to support the vase that is still there today.[47] The first mention of 'ruff walling in ye wilderness' appears in the accounts of 1720, followed in 1721 by 'Towers in the wilderness wall', and at the same time the Pyramid Gate was built on the York Road.[48] Evidently the landscaping was now moving south of the bowling green, and the walls of the area that was to become the wilderness were being constructed. The bowling green was to be redesigned into a parterre, decorated with obelisks and a Doric column, but in 1721 the dispute over how it was to look was only just beginning. Etty had had the temerity to submit a design for 'Rock work' on the parterre, but Vanbrugh advised 'a fluted Pillar only', with eight lower obelisks and four vases to be arranged symmetrically around it; rock work, he thought, was more suited to 'some other parts of the Garden more retir'd and solemn where there is Water'.[49] The obelisk and column appeared in several of Vanbrugh's designs, including Stowe and Eastbury. The parterre was a bold statement of architectural geometry, laid out directly in front of the house in a design of strict proportion as Alberti had advocated. Yet the 1727 plan shows that the field boundaries just outside the gardens remained as they had been in the 1690s; sheep and cattle would have been grazing right up to the walls of the wilderness.

Carlisle was concerned that the sloping ground of the new parterre would make the obelisks appear of different height to each other when viewed from the end of the garden, but Vanbrugh thought 'their rising one above another [as in] the view of Townes which ly on the Side of Hills' had a much better effect.[50] He was to debate the height of the obelisks with Carlisle for the next three years, before finally agreeing to make them taller. In March 1724 Hawksmoor was tentatively trying to resolve the situation, when he wrote to Lord Carlisle:

I dont know what to say about ye obelisks may be I may bring Sr John upon my back. but if they were mine I woud not let them stand upon ye cold ground but lift em up ye same sort of pedestal in ye Piazza Navonna don by Dominico Fontana, they are also upon pedestals.[51]

He included a drawing to support his point but it was obviously rejected, as the obelisks were finally constructed without pedestals, according to Vanbrugh's original design (Figure 5.4). The Doric column can just be seen in William Marlow's painting of the 1770s, although the obelisks and vases had by then been removed. Hawksmoor's letter suggests that it was generally unwise to disagree with Vanbrugh; he no doubt found, as did Etty, that his opinions would be summarily overruled. Throughout Vanbrugh's correspondence there are examples of meticulousness verging on the pedantic, but always associated with the design of his houses and gardens. He was evidently confident in his ability and did not hesitate to firmly express his point of view to his colleagues and to his patrons when he was sure that he was right, which appears to have been most of the time.

In November 1722 the masons were 'making the batlements upon the square bastions

FIGURE 5.4 The west front of Castle Howard and the Obelisk Parterre, Anon, before 1756. Mortham Estates (Trustees) Ltd. Reproduced by kind permission of Sir Andrew Morritt.

in the batlement walls', but Colonel Tyrrell had already given people 'a mighty good Acct: of Castle Howd: especially the out Works' after a visit in April that year, so Vanbrugh's Roman city walls to the south-west of the wilderness must have been nearing completion.[52] Tyrrell was later to create his own bastion on his estate at Shotover in Oxfordshire. No doubt impressed by the 'Magnificent Effect' of the walls at Castle Howard, the Duke of Newcastle had been persuaded to build outworks at Claremont, which were under construction in 1723.[53] Just before he died Vanbrugh wrote to Carlisle with regard to the outworks that he 'always thought we were Sure of that Card'.[54] The obelisks on the parterre were less well received: Edward Harley, 2nd Earl of Oxford, recorded in his diary in 1725 that 'It must be easy to guess what a figure this must make except to those who are in love with Obelisks'.[55] In fact, Oxford saw little that pleased him, with the exception of Ray Wood. He believed the house to be cold and damp because of its exposed situation and noted that the Pelegrini paintings in the hall had 'almost gone' because of it. His views do appear to be exaggerated and Neckar has attributed this negative description of Castle Howard to politics, arguing that the Tory, Oxford, was suspicious of Carlisle's affiliation with the ruling Whigs.[56] However, Edward did not follow his father Robert into politics and his principal interests were in the arts and the collection of books. It was Oxford who had helped Prior with the publication of his poems and Swift also benefitted from his patronage. Had he been interested, Oxford would have known that Carlisle was not a supporter of the Walpole–Townshend ministry. In the 1720s he was creating his own expensive design at Wimpole using the architect James Gibbs and the gardener Charles Bridgeman; it seems more likely that his comments had their roots in competition.

In the summer of 1723 workmen began to dig the new lake to the south of Ray Wood. In keeping with the tone of the Castle Howard landscape, the lake was an unusual shape and size for the period; not a rectangular canal but a curious rhomboid that appears to have been designed to follow the line of the original south wall of the wood. Twenty years earlier Sir Godfrey Copley had written to Thomas Kirke: 'I am told great Lakes are now the mode; Vanbrook set out one for the D. of Newcastle, to front his new house, of 40 acres',[57] but the lake at Newcastle's estate at Welbeck was never built. Large ornamental lakes were not common until much later, probably because it was very difficult to keep them full. It is not known whether Switzer's advice that ponds 'should be Clay'd six or eight inches thick at least all over' was followed, but as usual Vanbrugh was at the cutting edge of design, although even he was a little unsure, as he wrote to Carlisle: 'I have the new piece of Water much at Heart; I hope t'will do well but I doubt there's no certain proof till the dry comes'.[58] A visitor to Castle Howard in 1741 described the lake as unfinished, so it is possible that it suffered the same fate as the Chatsworth canal, which was constantly leaking.[59]

As the lake started to fill with water, the architects turned their thoughts to a new building to stand on the existing bastion at the south-east corner of Ray Wood. In January 1724 Hawksmoor sent a letter to Lord Carlisle with 'Sr Johns and Mr Hawksmoors designs for ye Tower at ye east end of Raywood'. Carlisle, as ever concerned with the cost, had asked for modest designs and Hawksmoor's Belvidira was a 'little turret . . . in a square form built with rough stone'.[60] Another battle of wills ensued, but Vanbrugh enlisted the help of Carlisle's son, Lord Morpeth, who 'declar'd his thoughts utterly against anything but an Italian Building in that Place', and his design for the Temple with the four Porticos was eventually chosen for the site.[61] The similarities to Palladio's Villa Almerico-Capra

(La Rotonda) outside Vicenza are obvious; and the square outline, the porticos on each side and the cupola are all equivalences between the two buildings. Only Downes and Whistler mention the fact that the principal section of Vanbrugh's building is a cube, and, although Whistler believes this was a deliberate attempt to contrast the austere shape of the building with the delicacy of its porticos, neither author takes this further.[62] Palladio never used a cube as the form of a whole building, although it frequently appears in rooms within his villas and palaces. Alberti employed the cube for the Villa Medici at Fiesole outside Florence; according to Mazzini:

> from the geometrical point of view it is known how Alberti used the 'root' cube of 2 per side, proceeding to construct with a length of 2, an area of 4 and a cube of 8. It is curious how our villa [at Fiesole] reflects these rules.[63]

Alberti employed the cubic form because such pure proportions were associated with the divine; Vanbrugh used twenty (feet) per side in his Temple with the four Porticos, again mirroring Alberti's construction exactly. Vanbrugh's knowledge of Alberti's writing, and his interest in Vitruvian rules, may have prompted him to build a cubic temple with the intention of drawing attention to his classical sources and to the proportions in his land-scape design. It is worth considering here whether the summerhouse in Ray Wood, which was complete by 1706, and described by Player as 'four square', may also have been a cube.

Whistler is the only author who notes the importance of the approach to Vanbrugh's Temple although he believes that the bend in the terrace, which obscured the Temple from view in the house, simply followed the old line of the Malton Road, and would have been 'twenty years ahead of its time' if it had been deliberately designed.[64] Overlay mapping suggests that the Temple Terrace followed the line of the old Ray Wood wall rather than the road that ran beneath it. The wall was removed when the Temple was being built, exposing Vanbrugh's terrace walk behind it; the statues along the Terrace stand on the original bastions in the wall (see Figure 4.4). The Temple was hidden around the corner of a bend in the wall and the approach is another example of Vanbrugh's innovative treatment of landscape. It is probable that he deliberately augmented the Terrace to create the mound that hid and then slowly exposed the building as the visitor rounded the corner and approached it (Figure 5.5). This would not be the first time that he incremented the natural rise and fall of the ground to create an explicit visual effect: the Mount at Claremont was built on a man-made hill.

The wilderness was planted when the new walls on the south front were finished in 1723/24. It had a broad central avenue, angular crosswalks, two curved paths and openings between the trees covered in gravel or grass. Carlisle had been lucky in the close proximity of natural woodland to his house, which enabled him to create a semi-natural garden in Ray Wood without the expense of planting. Other landowners were not as fortunate and, as the taste for woodlands decorated with classical ornaments became increasingly popular, artificial forests close to country houses proliferated. We know from Lady Irwin's poem of 1732 that the wilderness was evergreen and that this was a deliberate planting decision:

> Perpetual Verdure all the Trees disclose
> Which like true Love no Change of Season knows.

Not crouded with Trifles brought from far:
No Borders, Alleys, Edgings spoil the Scene,
'Tis one unvary'd Piece of pleasing Green.[65]

There is a suggestion here of a conscious simplicity with no ornamentation that was supported by the architectural minimalism of the Obelisk Parterre. Vanbrugh had made a deliberate move away from Wise's intricate broderied parterres. In a poem redolent with references to classical literature Lady Irwin attributed the landscape to her father, Lord Carlisle. Vanbrugh is not mentioned, even though his influence is evident from his letters. Writing to Carlisle in 1725 Vanbrugh was unaware that the new planting was called a wilderness: 'for I don't know anything by those Names; What I incline to fancy [Etty] must mean is the New Plantation of Firs to the Southward'.[66] His visits were infrequent at this time; he was working on Eastbury and Grimsthorpe and was suffering from ill health so he may have had little to do with the internal form of the wilderness.

Comparison of the 1727 estate plan with Campbell's bird's-eye view of the house and gardens at Castle Howard in *Vitruvius Britannicus*, Vol. 3 (1725) highlights several inconsistencies (Figure 5.6). The west wing of the house, the gate in the north courtyard wall and the temple at the south end of the wilderness, all depicted by Campbell, are not on the estate map, and yet the Obelisk Parterre and the lake were nearing completion in 1724 but are not in Campbell's drawing. Further inspection shows Campbell's interior plan of

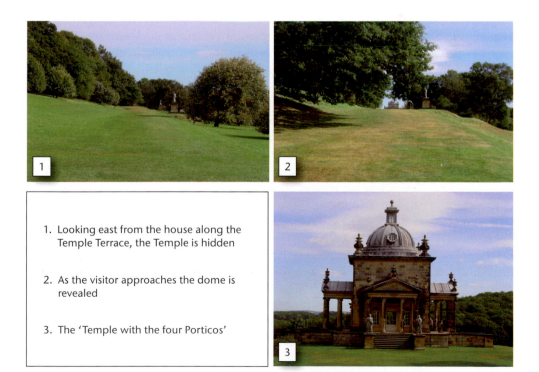

1. Looking east from the house along the Temple Terrace, the Temple is hidden

2. As the visitor approaches the dome is revealed

3. The 'Temple with the four Porticos'

FIGURE 5.5 Vanbrugh's use of topography on the approach to the Temple with the four Porticos. Photos: author, 2007.

the wilderness to be wrong; indeed, the only accuracy in the depiction of the landscape is in the gateways over the north approach road, and the avenues of trees on the south front. Campbell's classical summerhouses on the south wall of the wilderness are clearly fictitious, as Vanbrugh describes the 'Round Bastions at the Southernmost Angles [of the wilderness] . . . as Considerable ornaments and distinguish'd terminations of the Garden'; the bastions can be seen on the estate map.[67] Ray Wood and the outworks are missing altogether; indeed, the whole of Campbell's plan is in the seventeenth-century compact garden style and gives no indication of the innovative parkscape that Vanbrugh had designed. Such deviations call into question Campbell's sources. Vanbrugh must have viewed Campbell with suspicion given his association with Benson, and may not have cooperated with him after Benson's coup at the Board of Works in 1717, but it raises the question of why Carlisle and Vanbrugh would have agreed to such an inaccurate portrayal of Castle Howard being published in 1725. Several of Campbell's engravings are incorrect, which is perhaps not surprising given the inevitable alterations during major building projects that took place over many years. Campbell's drawings came from a variety of sources of different dates; as such they are useful only as indications of how parts of gardens may have looked or were planned, and not as accurate depictions of a point in time.

Lord Carlisle's third area of designed woodland, Pretty Wood, was to the south-east of the house and, like Ray Wood, it was originally an area of natural woodland. Pretty Wood was completed by 1727 when it was depicted in detail on the 1727 estate map and it included the two important ornaments, the Four Faces and the pyramid. The Four Faces could have been a copy of the statue of the Roman God of four faces, Lanus, that was built in Rome in 261 BC, and the pyramid was possibly a small-scale reproduction of the tomb of Gaius Cestius, also in Rome. Panini's *Roman Ruins with Figures* (*c.* 1730) depicts the Gaius Cestius Pyramid in a mythical setting, and gives an idea of the brooding atmosphere that Carlisle and Vanbrugh successfully created in Pretty Wood. This area had Roman entrenchments (extant in the late nineteenth century) that must have influenced the design of this part of the estate.

The three woodlands at Castle Howard that coexisted in the late 1720s were all of a different design and theme. The Ovidian stories of Ray Wood contrasted with the darker subject of Ancient Rome, accentuated by the heaviness of the ornamentation, in Pretty Wood. Both were created from a natural forest and were visibly detached from the house; the fashionable wilderness on the south front displayed overt geometry to match the Obelisk Parterre and was the only wood that was deliberately planted. Close to the house, with gravel walks and evergreens, it would have been a practical addition to the gardens when Ray Wood and Pretty Wood were devoid of foliage, and muddy with winter rain.

The smiths were making 'large plates and nails to ye Octagon windows in the temple' in 1727, so work had progressed as far as the cupola on the Temple with the four Porticos, although the interior was not decorated until 1737.[68] The exterior must have been finished and decorated by 1729 when there is an entry in the accounts for 'mending a vase that was blown down of ye Temple'.[69] Hawksmoor was working on the Carlisle Pyramid, a monument to Carlisle's ancestor William Howard; he 'sent the Drawing of the Pyramid to Mr Etty at York' in June 1728.[70] The close planting and height of the trees in the wilderness meant that it could not have been visible from the house, although it is obviously displayed to the east of the road as the visitor approaches the Pyramid Gate. The alignment of the

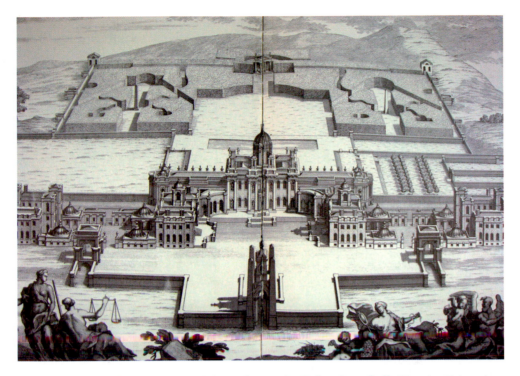

FIGURE 5.6 View of Castle Howard from the north. Colen Campbell, *Vitruvius Britannicus*, Vol. 3, (London: C. Campbell and J. Smith, 1725). Special Collections, University of Bristol.

Pyramid within Vanbrugh's Vitruvian plan suggests that it was intended, although it was not completed until after his death.

In 1731 Hawksmoor was drawing plans for the Octagon Temple (later the Temple of Venus) on the north-east boundary of Ray Wood.[71] At this time the bastions on this boundary were demolished, and the wall was extended towards the new temple, as depicted in the original plan of 1706 (see Figure 5.2). The existing gravel path leading from the bastions to the edge of the wood suggests that an ornament was always intended to be placed at this point. Hawksmoor designed a Vitruvian monopteral temple in which he proposed a 'Greek Venus Gilt'.[72] The Temple of Venus was demolished in the 1930s but the Venus remains in the kitchen garden. The final building to be completed to Vanbrugh's scheme was the mausoleum. Vanbrugh's letter of 1722 regarding the proposed mausoleum for the Duke of Marlborough is evidence that the building was already being discussed. A draft of Carlisle's will written before Vanbrugh's death stipulated that his son should consult Vanbrugh and Hawksmoor on the design, which should be in the form of a 'little chapple . . . with a Cupola'.[73] Only six months after Vanbrugh died in 1726, Hawksmoor was drawing the first plans for the mausoleum, and construction started three years later. Hawksmoor's building attracted much criticism from Burlington and Robinson but he was also to die before it was completed. Burlington seized the opportunity to make alterations, instructing his protégé Daniel Garrett to design the steps at the entrance. Although Carlisle had stated vaguely that his mausoleum should be placed on Lody Hill, this garden building was in fact precisely positioned; it was invisibly connected to the Temple with the four Porticos and the north-west corner of Ray Wood by Vanbrugh's Vitruvian grid. The estate map of 1744 (see Figure 4.6) shows the final version of the landscape, a product of the partnership between Vanbrugh, Carlisle and Hawksmoor. This map only hints at the geometry that underlies the design, that links the dispersed woodlands and garden architecture with the house. The fields of Cow Close, St Ann's Close and Car Fields were an intrinsic part of a scheme that used the rolling topography to maximum visual effect.

FIGURE 5.7 Vertical aerial photograph of Castle Howard, 1993. The trees in Ray Wood were felled in the 1950s, and the new planting reveals the outline of some of the paths laid out before 1710. The boundary of the Wilderness and the north extension of the Outworks are visible in parch marks to the south of the parterre. OS-93066-007 reproduced by permission of Ordnance Survey on behalf of HMSO. © Crown copyright (2011). All rights reserved. Ordnance Survey Licence number 100050286.

Vanbrugh's ha-ha opened the gardens to the views of East Moor Banks in the distance, and the crops and the animals grazing beneath the walls of Ray Wood and the wilderness.

In the following thirty years a number of changes were made: the 1773 estate map shows that the wilderness on the south front was already rooted up and the land returned to pasture. The north wall of Ray Wood was demolished and rebuilt to incorporate more of Low Ray Wood. The reasoning for this is obscure, as the designed area of the wood does not appear to have expanded into the new area. Only four obelisks, the central column and the two buildings remain on the parterre; the other obelisks and the vases have been removed, and Carlisle has finally finished the north-west wing of the house, which was designed by Sir Thomas Robinson in the 1750s. The outline of some of the paths set out 300 years ago in Ray Wood can still be discerned in a modern aerial photograph (Figure 5.7). The overall form of Vanbrugh's landscape remains, although the Great Lake to the north of the house and the New River and cascades leading from the south lake are late eighteenth-century additions. In the mid-nineteenth century William Andrews Nesfield used the gravity flow from the hill in Ray Wood to feed the Atlas Fountain and a second fountain in Vanbrugh's lake (1853), in the same way that it had been used to feed the Triton Fountain 150 years earlier.

By 1721 Castle Howard was an essential part of the summer itinerary of all gentlemen of taste who were interested in architecture and gardening. As Vanbrugh wrote to the Duke of Newcastle in August that year, he believed that he had formed the landscape 'out of Bushes Boggs and Bryars'.[74] Although claiming the overall design as his invention, he acknowledged the truth of Alberti's assertion of the innate beauty of Nature and the order found within it. Carlisle's aim must have been to create a landscape that impressed his visitors, with an iconography that would be understood in the context of the Enlightenment. In its dramatic setting behind fortress walls Castle Howard drew attention to the family's position in society, and Carlisle's own education, power and wealth. Carlisle's gamble on his architect had paid off; for this project, Vanbrugh had proved to be the perfect partner.

6

BLENHEIM, OXFORDSHIRE

In 1704 John Churchill, 1st Duke of Marlborough, was granted the mediaeval park of Woodstock in recognition of his success as joint commander of the Allied forces in the War of the Spanish Succession. Marlborough had seen the wooden model of Castle Howard that had been sent to Kensington in 1700 for the King's approval, and he commissioned Vanbrugh to build both a home and a suitable monument to his achievements in similar style.[1] The use of wooden architectural models dated back to the Italian Renaissance when Alberti observed that 'it is advisable . . . to construct models of this kind, and to inspect and re-examine them time and time again, both on your own and with others'.[2] Like Alberti, Vanbrugh found himself surrounded by a 'great many Criticks', from gentleman amateurs to experts such as Wren and Hawksmoor, and it was important to seek advice from a wide range of people, including the monarch, before a final decision on the design of any major building project was made.[3] Vanbrugh's new assignment at Woodstock was to be named Blenheim, to commemorate the Allied victory near the village of Blindheim in Bavaria in August 1704, and, although there would later be a bitter dispute over funding, the initial intention was that Blenheim would be paid for by the Crown. A wooden model of the new project was sent to Kensington in 1705/6 where Queen Anne 'Expressd her Self extreamly Pleas'd with it', and she gave instructions that the building was to be 'dispatch'd with all Aplication'.[4]

Woodstock Park had been favoured as a royal hunting park since mediaeval times, particularly by Henry II who built a palace there in the thirteenth century on the north bank of the River Glyme; the park had been slowly extended by enclosure of common land since that time. To the south and west of the river lay the dense forests of Hensgrove and Bladon (Figure 6.1); more open country lay to the north in High Park, where the previous tenant Lord Lovelace had held race meetings around the 'four mile course' since 1676.[5] Henry II's palace stood to the east of the remains of Rosamund's Bower, named for Henry's mistress Rosamund de Clifford, which had once had rooms arranged around three ponds and a herb garden.[6] But when John Aubrey sketched it in 1669 the Bower, like the palace, had fallen into disrepair, although he noted the meadows and the 'clowds

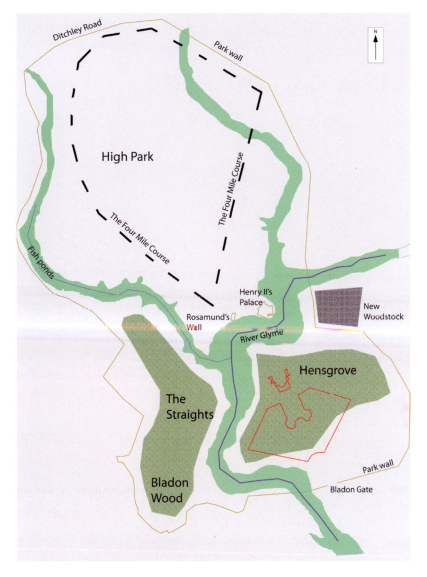

FIGURE 6.1 Woodstock Park before the building of Blenheim Castle. The position of the first design of the house and hexagonal garden is outlined in red in Hensgrove Wood. Plan: author, based on the Bodleian Libraries, University of Oxford MS. Top. Oxon. A.37★ first plan.

of woodes wch yield a very lovely melancholy' to the south of the river.[7] Thirty-five years later these woods were to become the site of Marlborough's Blenheim Castle.

The earliest surviving plan of Blenheim shows Vanbrugh's building with two office wings to the north flanked by courtyards, and a large hexagonal walled garden to the south that Vanbrugh called the 'Woodwork' (Figure 6.2). This would appear to be the first use of the term 'woodwork' to describe an ornamental garden made from established

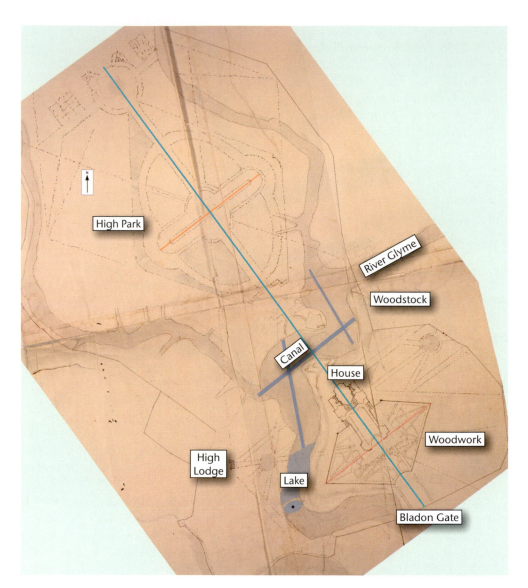

FIGURE 6.2 The first design for the landscape at Blenheim, early 1705. An oval of rides is planned in High Park, which is disconnected from the area to the south of the river – there is no bridge. To the south of the house is the hexagonal garden called the Woodwork. It is laid out with an intricate design of paths in squares and circles. Three canals and a lake in the Glyme valley have been added subsequently in pencil. The whole layout is geometric: the light blue centre line is divided into three equal parts by the canal and the orange line that crosses the oval in High Park. Both of these features are parallel to the red line that runs across the Woodwork. All three are roughly the same length: 3,000 feet according to the scale on the plan. Several other geometries are present but have been omitted here for clarity. The Bodleian Libraries, University of Oxford MS. Top. Oxon. A.37★ first plan. Annotation: author.

woodland (as opposed to a deliberately planted wilderness). The word was not in common use until after the publication of James's *Theory*, and it may have been of Vanbrugh's invention. At this initial stage there is no bridge over the river and no gate onto the Ditchley Road on the north boundary of the estate. The geometry in the design is obvious; it unites the oval of rides in High Park with the house and the Woodwork on the south front. Sight lines along avenues of trees have been constructed towards High Lodge, which was to be the temporary residence of the Duke and Duchess during the building. Three canals and a lake in the Glyme valley have been added in pencil at a later date, but analysis of the measurements on this plan indicate that the canal system must have been intended as an integral part of the original design.

Ratios of 3:1, 2:1, 5:2 and 5:1 can be seen in the divisions of the landscape along the light blue line that runs through the centre of the plan. The allusion to the square and circle in da Vinci's drawing is so obvious in the interior design of the Woodwork that it appears to be a deliberate reference to Vanbrugh's source (Figure 6.3). At Blenheim Vanbrugh was faced with another topographically challenging site of undulating hills dissected by the deep valley of the River Glyme. A geometrical solution would not have been an obvious choice to anyone else, but he applied a proportional framework with a central line running from the north-west of the estate to the Bladon Gate in the park wall to the south-east. The interior of the military garden at Ray Wood was never symmetrical because some of the existing walls and many of the original woodland paths were reused. The first design for the Woodwork at Blenheim is distinctive; the strongly geometrical form of the hexagon is bordered by a terrace walk that would have afforded views of the surrounding woodlands, meadows, lake and canals outside the ordered interior of the garden. Wise was at Blenheim from the instigation of the project, but he had never created anything as unusual as this hexagon, and his use of geometry was limited to the contiguous squares and rectangles of seventeenth-century formality. Scholars have concluded that Blenheim was 'Picturesque', but underneath the rolling countryside was another geometrical framework with carefully positioned elements that was distinctly Vanbrughian.[8]

A second plan must be a little later in 1705 as it shows the final form of the Woodwork with eight round bastions, similar to those in Ray Wood (Figure 6.4). Later, Vanbrugh was to persuade Newcastle to have curtain walls and bastions at Claremont, and he appears to have met no resistance from Marlborough when he proposed a military-style garden at Blenheim, to equal that at Castle Howard. The absence of the office courts on this plan makes it earlier than the winter of 1707, and the canal scheme, which is ink and therefore an original element of the drawing, appears to be the focus of the design.[9] Overlaying this plan on the earlier one has shown how the house was moved north and the whole scheme was rotated in a clockwise direction away from the Bladon Gate. This was a strange decision that may have been forced by the need to accommodate the bridge across the Glyme valley that was not in the earlier plan. The bastion garden is narrower (2,000 feet) and the length of the canal has been altered to match it. The angle of the boundary of the lake to the west has been moved to reflect the revised orientation of the garden, and the pond below it has been replaced by a cascade. These changes are evidence that each of the elements in the design was linked; they must have been part of Vanbrugh's original geometry and not devised by Colonel Armstrong in the 1720s, as has previously been thought.[10]

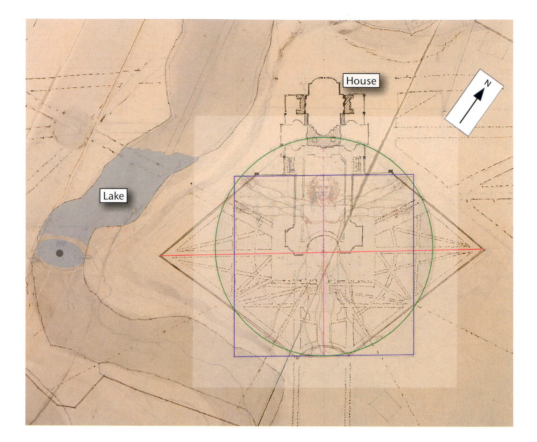

FIGURE 6.3 The Vitruvian proportions revealed in Vanbrugh's first design for the hexagonal Woodwork at Blenheim. The red line divides the height of the hexagon (pink line) in the ratio 2:3 and measures approximately 3,000 feet. In this position the green circle marks the north front of the house. The feature in the centre of the pond to the south of the Lake is positioned on the extension of the red line. The Bodleian Libraries, University of Oxford MS. Top. Oxon. A.37★ first plan (detail). Annotation: author.

Wren submitted a proposal for the bridge in 1706, although his design was soon superseded by Vanbrugh's interpretation of Palladio's unrealised scheme for the bridge over the Rialto in Venice (Figure 6.5); Wise's men started digging the foundations of the bridge in 1708.[11] The depth of the Glyme valley meant that the road running across Vanbrugh's bridge had to be some fifty feet above the water; if the bridge had been any lower the drop into the valley would have been too steep for carriages. The advantage, however, was that the resulting massive structure was able to house Mr Aldersea's water engine, which was to pump water up to the house and was already operational.[12] Downes maintains that the 'necessity for a larger body of water [under the bridge] seems never to have occurred to Vanbrugh', but contemporary descriptions demonstrate that the bridge was designed with a central arch of 100 feet to accommodate exactly the sixty-foot wide canal that the architect had already planned.[13]

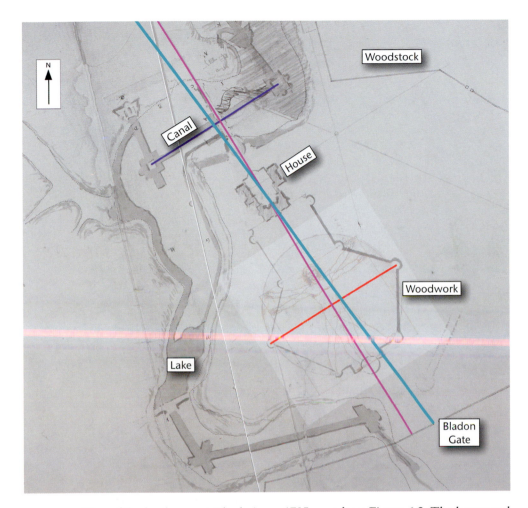

FIGURE 6.4 Plan of the landscape at Blenheim, *c.* 1705; postdates Figure 6.2. The hexagonal garden has moved south of the parterre and eight rounded and two square bastions have been added. The absence of enclosed office courts dates this revised plan to before the winter of 1707. The light blue line marks the orientation of the first plan in Figure 6.2. The main axis of this plan (pink line) has been rotated clockwise. The length of the Canal (blue line) has been altered to match the reduced width of the Woodwork (red line). It is evident that, despite these changes, the Vitruvian proportions have been retained in this design. The star to the east of the house, the Woodstock Gate and the shading of the Glyme valley (top centre) are pencil additions that relate to construction in the 1720s. The Bodleian Libraries, University of Oxford MS. Top. Oxon. A.37★ second plan (detail). Annotation: author.

The accounts in the British Library provide fascinating detail of every step of the development of the landscape at Woodstock from 1705 to 1710, and they are carefully documented by Green in his book on the building of Blenheim Palace.[14] It is not intended to reproduce the complete story of the gardens here, but to reconsider evidence in the

FIGURE 6.5 Vanbrugh's bridge across the River Glyme was a version of Palladio's unrealised design for a bridge over the Rialto in Venice. The valley was flooded by 'Capability' Brown in the 1760s, which raised the water level and flooded the lower sections of the bridge. The wide arch in the centre was designed for a canal and the two side arches were for the stream that fed the water engine (right) and the overflow for the river (left). The proposed superstructure was never built although the bridge had iron railings in the 1720s. Photo: author, 2007.

accounts and in correspondence that particularly relates to Vanbrugh's work as a landscape architect. On 9 June 1705 Vanbrugh was appointed Surveyor of all the Works and Buildings at Blenheim by decree of Lord Sidney Godolphin, Lord High Treasurer. He was to be assisted by Henry Joynes and William Boulter as joint Comptrollers. Vanbrugh was later to describe the role of surveyor as 'good Husbandry of the Money . . . [which] lys as entirely upon the Surveyor, as the Designing of the Building'.[15] The building was already under way, and Vanbrugh optimistically wrote to Marlborough that 'the garden wall was set agoing the same day with the House and I hope will be done against your Graces return'.[16] The design for the garden had been finalised as a broderied parterre and the hexagonal Woodwork, illustrated on a plan dated 1719 in the Blenheim archives (Figure 6.6). The existing oaks of Hensgrove that were to be preserved inside the Woodwork are clearly visible on this detailed plan, and the final form of the bridge is depicted with three arches. On the south side of the Woodwork is a round pool which was to be faced with a grotto under the walls, the kitchen garden with its own bastions is visible to the east, and one of the original quarries for building stone to the west.

Although Bridgeman drew the often-reproduced plan in the Great Hall at Blenheim Palace (Figure 6.7), his contribution as anything other than a junior draughtsman has already been discounted. Wise was employed at Blenheim from the beginning of the project and had responsibility for the supply and planting of trees, hedge yews and flowers for the avenues, Woodwork and parterre. The Duke trusted Wise and had no concerns with the advance of the work in the gardens, as he did with the house: 'For the gardening and

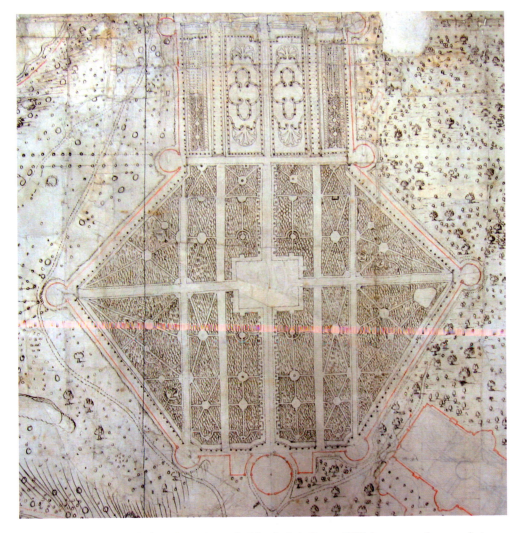

FIGURE 6.6 *Plann of Blenheim*, 1719. Probably dating from 1705 but reused several times after that. Note the design of the parterre and the original oaks of the forest depicted in the Woodwork. Blenheim Palace Archives, by kind permission of His Grace the Duke of Marlborough.

plantations I am at ease, being very sure that Mr Wise will bee diligent', he wrote to the Duchess in 1706.[17] The detail of the parterre was almost certainly of Wise's design, and his contribution to the planting is obvious from the Blenheim accounts. When Green and Whistler were writing in the early 1950s, a bundle of garden plans had just come to light that Green attributed to Wise. Both men subsequently drew the conclusion that Wise had designed the landscape at Woodstock, although Whistler had reservations about the shape of the Woodwork when he wrote that 'surely one mind alone [Vanbrugh] would have imagined the vast military bastions'.[18] But the authorship of Blenheim has been reconsidered in more recent studies, and, although Vanbrugh's contribution as a landscape

FIGURE 6.7 *A Plan of Blenheim*, Charles Bridgeman, 1709. The design for High Park has been simplified to a double row of trees. The Glyme is divided into two – the north stream feeds Mr Aldersea's water engine under the bridge. The bastioned kitchen garden can be seen to the east of the Woodwork. Photo: Richard Craggs, 2007, by kind permission of His Grace the Duke of Marlborough.

architect is still only starting to be understood, Green credits Vanbrugh with the design in *Landscape for a Palace* (2000), as does Downes in his 1987 biography.[19]

Like the garden in Ray Wood, the Woodwork had massive walls sunk into ditches, the earth from the ditches being used to create the internal terrace walk that exposed the surrounding park and countryside. The impact of Vanbrugh's device was described in the third edition of Defoe's *Tour*: '[it is] well contrived by sinking the outer Wall into a Foss, to give a View quite round, and take off the odious Appearance of Confinement, and Limitation to the Eye'.[20] It is not clear whether the ground inside the Woodwork was flat – a geological map suggests that it may have been slightly raised – but the countryside was certainly visible along the many straight avenues of yew hedges and trees from the inner recesses of the garden, and was brought closer by aligning the avenues with interesting distant features that functioned as eye-catchers. Wise may have been responsible for the planting, but Vanbrugh was overseeing the design of the interior of the Woodwork as well as its exterior walls, and he was concerned to align the old trees with the new planting in his geometric scheme:

> I should be glad to know what [Mr Bobart] do's About the Forrest Trees in the Quarters of the Woodwork I mean as to bringing Lines of 'em every where behind the Hedges, for I take that to be the grand point of all.[21]

Contemporary descriptions provide evidence that he was successful: John Macky wrote of the Woodwork that 'you have in these Gardens Nine or Ten different Prospects through Avenues in the Park, which generally terminate in some Steeple at some Miles Distance', and Viscount Percival observed two years later that there were 'private walks cut thro an old wood to which a great deal of new plantation has been added'.[22] The accounts attest to hundreds of pyramid yews and hollies being planted in the Woodwork from 1705 onwards, possibly around the Great Lawn south of the parterre.[23] The landscapes at Blenheim and Castle Howard both owed their overall layouts to Vitruvian principles and they both had military gardens formed from existing woodlands. The Woodwork was different from Ray Wood in that it was a new structure and could therefore be an overt geometrical reference both in its exterior form and, with some judicious reorganisation of the paths, in its interior layout. Vanbrugh created architecture out of trees, hollies and yews in a Woodwork 'after the ancient Roman Manner', as Switzer described it.[24]

Within a year Samuel Travers, the Surveyor General, reported to the Duke that 'the main body of the House is for the most part . . . eight foot high from the cellar floor' and

> the Basin on the south side of the Woodwork is finished up to the coping and partly coped and the Grotto in it 5 foot high. Mr Wise hath made great Magazins of Turfy mold from planting the two Great Avenues in the North and East Approaches to the House.[25]

However, Travers went on to admit that 'your Grace pulls down France much faster than we can build Blenheim Castle and in one month has taken more than one Great Strong City for every foot we have grown'. In fact, the gardens and park were further advanced than the house, possibly because the Duke was always concerned that, for reasons of his age and his choice of career, he might not see the finished result.[26] Macky relates the story that the Duke had told Wise that 'he was an old Man, and could not expect to live till the Trees were grown up', and Thomas Salmon commented on the Woodwork in 1748 that the 'Trees whereof must have been very large when they were planted'.[27] The designed landscapes shown in eighteenth-century plans and engravings would have taken many years to be fully realised, and the use of well-established trees was quite common for this reason; the Blenheim accounts contain an entry in 1705 for 'taking up and loading the Hollys and other Forrest Trees and setts out of the woods and grounds belonging to my Lord Lichfields [at Ditchley] or elsewhere'.[28]

Henry II's old palace soon became a point of disagreement between Vanbrugh and the Duchess of Marlborough who, by 1709, was already exasperated with his strong views on all aspects of the building and landscape design, and the lack of progress on the house. Vanbrugh was lodging in what remained of the old palace, and was putting the cost of renovations to the roof and brickwork through the accounts in 1708.[29] He was to stretch his role as manager of the Blenheim finances a little too far in 1709 when he charged the accounts for repairs to his house in Whitehall.[30] There is an often-quoted letter from Vanbrugh to the Duchess cataloguing his reasons for saving Henry II's 'Manor', which Hart believes was prompted by the associations with the romantic story of Henry and Rosamund, and in particular by Addison's play *Rosamond*, which was staged in 1707.[31] The letter does allude to the story but Vanbrugh's character suggests little that could be interpreted as romantic. He was astute and would use any argument that he thought might win his case. The Duchess took exception to Vanbrugh spending more than £1,000 on renovations to a building that she wanted to be demolished; Vanbrugh needed somewhere to stay.[32] He was interested in the Manor as a balance to Rosamund's Bower on the other side of the bridge and so his letter cleverly combined the argument for the scenic qualities of the Manor with the threat that it would cost more to remove it: '[if] this Building is taken away; there then remains nothing but an Irregular, Ragged Ungovernable Hill, the deformities of which are not to be cured *but by a Vast Expense*'.[33] Before approaching the Duchess he had already tried his point with Godolphin, writing in May 1709:

> I have however taken a good deale of [the Manor] downe, but before tis gone too farr I will desire your Lordship will give yourself the trouble of looking upon a picture I have made of it which will at one view explain the whole design better than a thousand words [see Figure 4.9].[34]

Like Palladio, Vanbrugh wanted to integrate the new building and the surrounding landscape; a broad avenue ran through the house but the north side of the Glyme had 'little Variety of Objects' and the architect needed the Manor to create perspective, to pull the eye out into High Park.[35] He may have had the idea for the Column of Victory in the Grand Avenue as early as 1716, but in 1709 the Manor was the only ornament of note beyond the bridge.[36] Vanbrugh could visualise the finished bridge, the Manor and the Bower as a mathematical composition, offset by his broad canal running perpendicular to the central avenue and sitting deep in the valley. He was irritated by the inability of his contemporaries to see what was obvious to him, and so he resorted, as Palladio had done, to the use of pictures.[37]

Vanbrugh's passion and frustration often led him to argue a point far beyond the limit of what could have been considered acceptable by his employers. The letters between the architect and his client continued in 1709 as Vanbrugh took up the case of the west greenhouse, which he felt was needed to balance the one on the east side of the south front. The Duke thought this second greenhouse would block the view to the west and it was never built, but Vanbrugh was eventually vindicated when in 1724 Viscount Percival wrote of the south front: 'the Green house on one side which stands, in a line with it, having nothing to answer it on the other, looks like a pig with one ear'.[38] It was during the argument about the greenhouse that Vanbrugh first mentioned the lake in the valley to the west of the house (see Figure 6.2).[39] Lancelot 'Capability' Brown's flooding of the valley to create a great lake in the 1760s appears now to be the obvious solution to the problem of the river. In 1705 it meandered to the north and then down the west side of the house and gardens, so far below that it could not be seen, but the early designs are evidence that Vanbrugh always wanted a lake in the Glyme valley, and this is supported by a letter from the Duchess to the Duke of Somerset in 1723, regarding her plans for a lake to the east of the bridge:

> the fine green meadow between the hous & the wood is to remain as it is, & I believe your Grace will think in that, Nature cannot be mended; *tho Sir John formerly sett his heart upon turning that into a lake, as I will do it on the other side*; & I will have swans & all such sort of things in it.[40]

Brown built a cascade on the south end of his lake exactly where Vanbrugh had planned a pond and cascade in his early designs for the valley; thus, Brown's great lake was not an original idea.

In May 1709 Vanbrugh wrote to fellow Kit Cat Thomas Hopkins regarding some statues that had been recommended to Marlborough for the gardens at Blenheim: 'there are twelve of 'em. And they are in the garden of Monsignor Bracci about three miles from Florence', and he also wanted to commission further copies from craftsmen in the city.[41] He was trying to continue with the work at Woodstock despite the gathering political storm. The huge number of Allied casualties at the battle of Malplaquet that year, combined with Louis XIV's refusal to sign a peace agreement, brought the Whigs to a critical point. The Duchess of Marlborough had been a significant ally in the Whig cause, actively promoting the war with the Queen, but she was no longer the favourite, and her power at court had diminished. By early 1710 Vanbrugh was struggling to pay some of the bills, particularly those from Florence, and he was embarrassed for the Duke: 'you may judg how it must sound in the Court at Florence, to hear the Statuarys who are employ'd can't get their money', he told Travers.[42] He was, however, able to reassure Marlborough that the model of the fountain of the Piazza Navona which was already in England 'is of Bernini's doing', and he awaited the yachts bringing 'the bust of the King of France', which would later be erected on the south front.[43] The general election of 1710 led to the fall of the Whig ministry and Robert Harley took power; in November Swift wrote to his friend Esther Johnson that he 'was at Court, where the Queen past by us with all Tories about her; not one Whig'.[44] Vanbrugh continued building that summer, but in August Godolphin lost his post as Lord Treasurer, reputedly saying of Blenheim that they could 'keep their heap of stones', and the Duchess put a stop to all work until further money was received from the Treasury.[45] The following year the Duke and the Duchess were dismissed by the Crown, and they left the country. Despite Vanbrugh's concerns for his own salary, the building and the workmen, which are evident in his continuing entreaties to Marlborough and to Harley, the accounts show that by 1713 the outgoings at Blenheim had decreased to less than £30 each month.

Vanbrugh had always been an admirer and supporter of the Duke; his dismissal in 1713 from the Board of Works was prompted by his letter to the Mayor of Woodstock complaining of Marlborough's 'bitter persecution', which mysteriously ended up in Harley's hands.[46] Their early affiliation was probably strengthened by the Duke's frequent absences abroad; although Godolphin tried vainly to represent Marlborough's interests, Vanbrugh was in command at Blenheim. Marlborough's letter to the Duchess, telling her that Wren had advised that the model of the house in wood should be finished without delay 'for approval, such that no further alterations can be made', suggests that all of those involved felt unable to control their architect.[47] Whilst the Duchess was occupied at Court in the early years of the project, Vanbrugh prioritised the things that were important to him, particularly the Woodwork, the bridge and the kitchen court, as well as his enhancements to the Manor; all of which attracted criticism, by letter, from the Duchess. It was as her power over Queen Anne started to wane that the Duchess took a more active interest in Blenheim, and it was then that the problems with Vanbrugh really began. On the accession of George I, Vanbrugh and Marlborough were reinstated in their posts, but as the work restarted at Woodstock in the summer of 1716 the letters between Vanbrugh and the Duchess are evidence of their rapidly deteriorating relationship. Vanbrugh oversaw the completion of the bridge, without the superstructure he had at first intended, but the Duke was ill and the Duchess questioned the cost of everything. In November that year Vanbrugh wrote to her that 'you have your end Madam, for I will never trouble you more', and he left Blenheim; he would not return.[48] It is notable that after Vanbrugh's departure the Duchess did not appoint a new surveyor; she took control of both the expenditure and the design. No project can have two managers and the Duchess was now in charge.

In 1708 the Duchess had written to the Earl of Manchester, thanking him for his patterns and directions on 'how to proceed with the furnishings at Woodstock', and the Earl subsequently purchased in Venice over 4,700 yards of damask and velvets for Blenheim.[49] It was not until 1719, however, that the Marlboroughs finally moved into the east end of the house, which was still not complete. The Duchess remained enthusiastic about the project; she was worried about the Duke's continuing ill health and wanted the work to be completed. Neglecting the Woodwork in favour of landscaping the Glyme valley, she finally realised the canalisation plans that Vanbrugh had drawn up nearly fifteen years earlier, although she made no mention of his contribution. In a letter to Lady Cairns in 1721 she described the scheme:

> there will be a canal of sixty foot wide which watter will run thro the great Arch of the Bridge, and on each side of this watter under the Arch there will bee a fine grass walk of twenty foot broad, and there will be a room paved that come into this Arch, which will bee very pleasant by the watter to sett in in a very hot day.[50]

William Townesend and Bartholomew Peisley, working under Armstrong's supervision, completed the canals in 1723, when the Duchess wrote to Somerset that 'the Canal & Bason (which is allready don) look very fine' (Figure 6.8).[51]

FIGURE 6.8 *A View of Blenheim Castle from Rosamund's Bower*, 1724. The canal with its terminating circular pond to the right. The Duchess's east lake can be seen centre left. The Bodleian Libraries, University of Oxford MS. Top. Gen. D.14 fol. 14v.

Hawksmoor remained at Blenheim without Vanbrugh, and in 1722 he was probably the originator of the idea for the east lake, as he reminded the Duchess in his usual tentative manner that 'when the Kings of England had the House in their possession there was always a great piece of Water or a Lake, near old Woodstock'.[52] The southern extension to the canal system was completed in 1725; the works are still visible under Brown's lake today (Figure 6.9). In 1723 the Duchess finally got her way and demolished Henry II's Manor. In the letter to Somerset she mentions an obelisk that was planned for the Grand Avenue, in commemoration of Marlborough's victories. The similarities between this obelisk and that at Castle Howard strongly suggest Vanbrugh's authorship, although it was later to be changed to the Column of Victory. The Duchess was thinking about putting the obelisk on the site of the old Manor, perhaps in final recognition that Vanbrugh had been right about the need for an ornament on that 'Ungovernable Hill'. In a reference to their heated argument about the Manor, she remarks that this position 'would please Sr John best, because it would give an opportunity of mentioning that King whose scenes of love he was so much pleas'd with'.[53] The layout of the gardens in the early 1720s is depicted in Campbell's *Vitruvius Britannicus*, Vol. 3 (1725), yet the inaccuracy of the engraving is rarely commented upon (Figure 6.10).[54] This is the only plan in the book that is not signed by Campbell and it shows two lakes joined by the canal under the bridge, the Duchess's lake to the east of the bridge, and a second lake to the west. The west lake could be a reference to Vanbrugh's proposed lake, although it is bigger than the one drawn on the early plans and the source is unknown.

The Frenchman, Fougeroux, included Blenheim in his tour of England in 1728, and his written description and drawing are a valuable record of the landscape (Figure 6.11). Curiously, however, he missed the hexagonal shape of the Woodwork altogether;

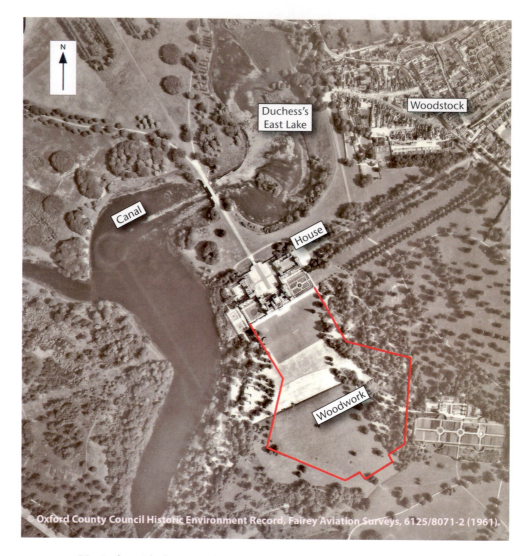

FIGURE 6.9 Vertical aerial photograph of Blenheim, 1961. Annotation: author.

quite how he came to overlook Vanbrugh's huge bastions or to describe the kitchen garden as 'small' is a mystery. The drawing has been corrected later in pencil, possibly by d'Argenville.[55] Fougeroux writes that the Woodwork is 'large but very neglected . . . It is planted in the common (natural) style in woods with walls of yews cut into compartments'.[56] He was more impressed with the park, which was 'infinitely better'. It is surprising that the Woodwork was apparently neglected, but, although Switzer claimed that the garden was 'begun and most part finish'd in three Years time', Viscount Percival recorded in his diary in 1724 that, although the structure of the Woodwork and its planting was complete, 'there is not in the whole garden one fountain, or canal, or arbor or arch'd bench for shelter against the sun or rain but some windsor chairs are placed at distances to restore self when tired'.[57] This aligns with the Duchess's statement during the

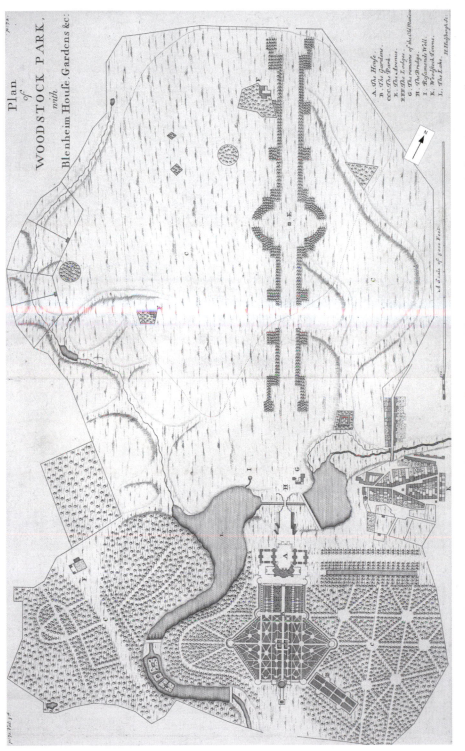

FIGURE 6.10 Plan of Woodstock Park. Colen Campbell, *Vitruvius Britannicus*, Vol. 3, (London: C. Campbell and J. Smith, 1725). Special Collections, University of Bristol.

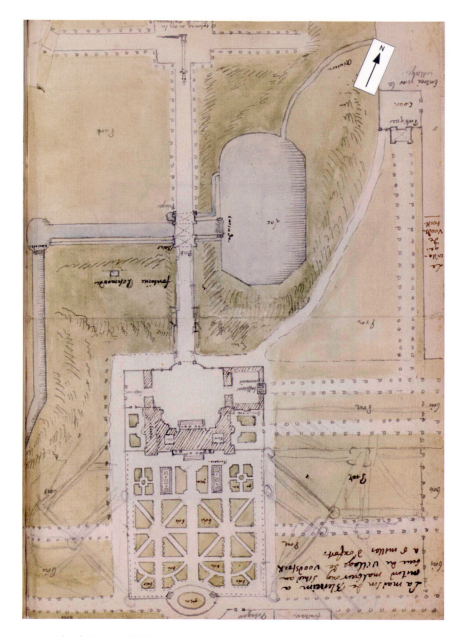

FIGURE 6.11 Blenheim, *c.* 1728. Pierre Jacques Fougeroux, *Voyage d'Angleterre d'Hollande et de Flandre*, manuscript. © V&A Images, Victoria & Albert Museum, London, 86.NN.2.

legal battle over financing the project that 'the gardens were done as forward in 1710 as they were in 1716'; she went on: 'all Woodstock knows that they made Hay in it and sold it [during that time]'.[58] Even when she finally took up residence at Blenheim, the Duchess turned her attention to the canals and lakes rather than to the garden, perhaps because of its association with Vanbrugh.

When he was nearing the end of his life, Vanbrugh bitterly regaled Tonson with the story of his attempted visit to Blenheim with Carlisle and his family in 1725. The Duchess had left orders that neither he nor his wife should be allowed to enter the park, and they were forced to stay at the inn in Woodstock whilst Carlisle and his family viewed the grounds. But Vanbrugh's determination to see how she had implemented his plans had been underestimated by the Duchess, and the gardener John Hughes later reported to her that 'Sir John went to Old Woodstock and there look'd over the wall to see the water and I do believe was in Dr Coxes Garden where he coud see some of the other Works'.[59] Their fight continued until Vanbrugh's death; in October 1725 the architect finally received payment for his work at Blenheim 'in Spight of the Huzzys teeth', as he expressively told Tonson; he was convinced that 'that B.B.B. B. Old B. The Dutchess of Marlb' wished to 'throw me into an English Bastile to finish my days, as I begun them, in a French one'.[60]

After Hawksmoor's Woodstock Gate was completed in 1723, the Duchess's last addition to the landscape was the Column of Victory, begun in 1727. The Duchess took several years to decide on the correct inscription for the monument to her husband; in 1723 she asked the Duke of Somerset if he knew Pope well enough to persuade him to 'add something very right to this'.[61] Pope must have provided some lines as these are mentioned by Vanbrugh in a letter in 1725: 'I am glad your Ldp likes Mr Popes Inscription . . . Every thing proper to be said on the Occasion being express'd in the shortest Compass, and quite in the antique Style and manner'.[62] However, the Duchess eventually rejected Pope's 'antique Style' and opted for the words of Viscount Bolingbroke; an odd choice as Bolingbroke was a Tory who had been Secretary of State in Harley's ministry in 1711, and had been complicit in Marlborough's dismissal. Marlborough was moved to his final resting place in Rybrack's tomb in the chapel in 1733, eleven years after his death. The Duchess now spent more and more time away from Woodstock at her house in London and at the lodge at Windsor, claiming that she 'never design[ed] to see Blenheim again'.[63] Salmon described the Woodwork as finished in 1748, with 'beautiful green Walks planted with Evergreens, Summer-houses, Alcoves, Fountains, and every thing that can render the Place agreeable', yet it was to last only another few years before it was demolished.[64] By the 1760s Vanbrugh's bastioned garden on the south front had been flattened and laid to lawn.

When evaluating the landscape at Blenheim, Hal Mogridge concludes that there is an intrinsic weakness: it is 'simply not possible to see along the Grand Avenue . . . because of the natural slope of the ground' and the features 'failed to fit together'.[65] But Vanbrugh's design merits re-evaluation: the house, the Woodwork, the lake, canals, obelisk, High Lodge and even the Manor were all part of one coherent composition, bound together by the rules of proportion yet sympathetic to an exacting topography. Sight lines were a feature of the landscape in that they drew the eye out of the garden into the countryside beyond, but, as at Castle Howard, they were not important to the underlying layout or the philosophy of the project. Vanbrugh would never have removed the natural slope to the north of the house; he would have used it to partially obscure the obelisk he had intended to place on the Grand Avenue, and to slowly reveal the house on the intended approach from the north. The Duchess eventually completed the landscape mostly to Vanbrugh's original design; the irony cannot have escaped him, and he must have been gratified when he 'look'd over the wall to see the water'.[66]

7

KIMBOLTON, HEYTHROP AND GRIMSTHORPE

Kimbolton, Cambridgeshire

The earliest in Webb's compilation of Vanbrugh's letters is to Charles Montagu, 4th Earl of Manchester, written in December 1699, and it ends with a postscript: 'My Lord Carberry toasts [Lady Manchester] with an Exemplary Consistency'.[1] This reference to the toasts made by the Kit Cat Club demonstrates that Vanbrugh was already on familiar terms with Manchester, who was also a member. Vanbrugh was busy at Castle Howard and at Blenheim when, in the summer of 1707, the south front of Manchester's castle at Kimbolton in Cambridgeshire collapsed. The breach had been predicted and Vanbrugh was on site almost immediately with Hawksmoor at his side. Soon afterwards Vanbrugh wrote to Manchester enclosing a copy of his new design for the front, and raising objections to an alternative tendered by William Coleman, a local architect, who '*had not brought the Door of the House into the Middle of the Front*; Many other great Exceptions there were to it, both within and without'.[2] His attitude towards Coleman was similar to his treatment of Etty, who proposed a design for a spire on the outworks at Castle Howard that Vanbrugh was adamant would 'by no means do'.[3] Vanbrugh often seems to have taken exception to local employees who exceeded their remit by offering unwanted designs for either buildings or landscapes. As a man little disposed towards listening to the opinions of his clients, he would not tolerate interference from his subordinates. He was later to praise Coleman for his contribution as the Clerk of Works at Kimbolton, a vital role that was not a threat to the architect, telling Manchester that if they had such a man at Blenheim 'he'd Save us a Thousand pounds a Year'.[4]

Vanbrugh's observation about the door in his letter to Manchester is the first of many examples in connection with Kimbolton that indicate how important Vitruvian rules of proportion were to his buildings. The castle dated back to the thirteenth century and had last been updated in the 1520s. Manchester was ambassador to Venice in 1707 and he must have seen Palladio's villas in the Veneto; from the correspondence it appears that he requested that his new front was built in Palladian style, and this may explain why Vanbrugh took such care to stress his use of proportions in the final design. The

FIGURE 7.1   The south front of Vanbrugh's redesigned Kimbolton Castle, Cambridgeshire. Photo: author, 2007.

architect had incorporated Palladian elements into the external form of Castle Howard and Blenheim, but for Kimbolton he thought otherwise. He proposed 'something of the Castle Air, tho at the Same time *to make it regular*. And by this means too, all the Old Stone is Serviceable again' (Figure 7.1).[5] He assured the Earl that he should not be 'discourag'd if any Italians you may shew it to, shou'd find fault that 'tis not Roman, for to have built a Front with Pillasters, and what the Orders require cou'd never have been born with the Rest of the Castle'.[6] Classical ornaments were not appropriate for a crenellated roofline, a point that Vanbrugh emphasised by making reference to Alberti: 'tis certainly the *Figure and Proportions* that make the most pleasing Fabrick, And not the delicacy of the Ornaments'.[7] He was reinforcing the idea that overt display could be replaced by a covert application of Vitruvian rules in the design of the building that was equally valid. Vanbrugh sent plans of the new 'noble room' he proposed for the centre of the south front, and drew Manchester's attention to its 'length and breadth', although its height was 'not what in Strictness One wou'd wish'.[8] Between 1708 and 1710 Vanbrugh would remodel the other three fronts of the castle in a similar style to the south. The architect remained adamant about the 'pilasters'; Manchester took an early opportunity once Vanbrugh had left to add the incongruous Doric portico on the east front that he had always wanted.

The castle was situated in a large park that had been laid out with star rides for deer hunting in mediaeval times, and a garden was built within the bounds of the moat to the south of the castle in the sixteenth century.[9] An inventory of 1687 mentions the 'Grat Garden' that was adorned with '66 stone flowerpots on all the walls', which must have been the formal layout of grass plats shown in Thomas Stirrup's map of 1673 (Figure 7.2).[10] Vanbrugh's reference to the 'Canall, wch is now brim full of Water' in March 1708 suggests that a new garden had been only recently laid out; Whistler supports this theory and postulates that London may have designed the garden.[11] Yet in July 1707 Vanbrugh insisted that the noble room was in the centre of the new south front. It was to be positioned 'so right to the Garden, that the Door is in the Middle of the Room, and takes exactly the Middle Walk and the Canall'.[12] This was at the same time that he was designing the south front and only weeks after the collapse of the building. If the canal was not filled until the following spring it suggests that the garden design and construction were coeval with the new front, especially as there is no reference to the renovations to the house causing damage to a garden that was already nearing completion.

FIGURE 7.2 A *True and Exact Plot of all of the West Part of the Lordship of Kimbolton* (detail), Thomas Stirrup, 1673. Huntingdonshire Archives Map 83.

Apart from Vanbrugh's description, Whistler had no visual evidence of the garden, but in 1997 Fougeroux's drawing of Kimbolton was discovered (Figure 7.3).[13] Predictably, Fougeroux has oriented the house and courtyards incorrectly in his drawing, but the garden appears accurate: the canal on the east side has been moved to the centre, and it is now flanked by two planted wildernesses with grass avenues. A terrace fronts the house leading down to a parterre with 'avenues of lime trees to each side, cut underneath

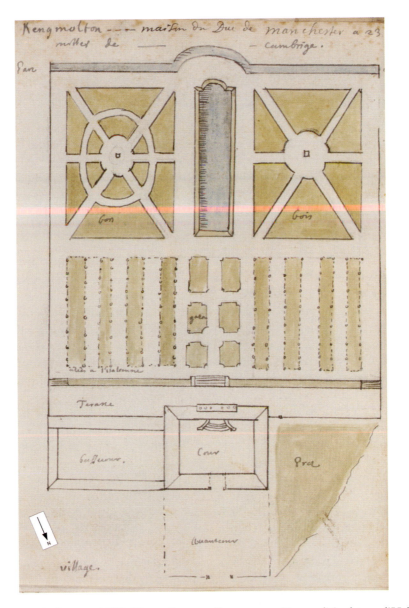

FIGURE 7.3 Kimbolton, *c.* 1728. Pierre Jacques Fougeroux, *Voyage d'Angleterre d'Hollande et de Flandre*, manuscript. © V&A Images, Victoria & Albert Museum, London, 86.NN.2.

in the Italian way, as we can see at Chantilly in front of the chateau'.[14] The statuary was 'poor' but Fougeroux was particularly interested in the use of turf, and he notes that 'all of the grass in the garden is not grown from seed, but is turfed. This is an extravagance usually only found in the gardens of princes'.[15] Fougeroux always depicted the park and garden in his drawings of estates where there were interesting designed landscapes, so the restriction to the area in front of the house at Kimbolton suggests that the remainder of the estate was unchanged from the previous century. He evidently associated Kimbolton with French gardens; in style it appears similar to the plates in James's *Theory* of 1712, but further examination does not support the contention that it was designed by London: it is simply too plain. The garden is a square that is divided in the ratio 2:3 between the rows of limes and the designed woodland and canal at the south end. The geometry, the open aspect of the garden to the south, the strips of grass on the parterre and the allusion to architecture in the rows of lime trees all hint at Vanbrugh's influence. Vanbrugh's effusive assertion that 'the Espalier Hedges will be in great perfection this Year, and the Fruit Trees are now Strong enough to produce abundance: So that I hope yr Ldship will find it Altogether, much improv'd & to your Satisfaction' in a letter to Manchester in 1708 shows that he took an interest in the garden.[16] It was swept away in the 1760s by the 4th Duke of Manchester but a satellite photograph taken during a particularly dry summer has revealed elements of the eighteenth-century layout in parch marks under what is now Kimbolton School's cricket pitch.[17]

Heythrop, Oxfordshire

In 1708 Vanbrugh wrote to Manchester that 'all the World are running Mad after Building, as far as they can reach . . . the Duke of Shrewsbury's house will be About half up this Season'.[18] He was referring to Charles Talbot, 1st Duke of Shrewsbury, and his new house at Heythrop, which was just a few miles north of Blenheim. Shrewsbury had returned from Italy in 1705 where he had procured both an Italian wife and a design for a house by Paulo Falonier; he employed Thomas Archer as his architect, and construction started in 1707.

An estate plan of 1792 (Figure 7.4) shows the house approached by a long avenue of trees in alternating square and round clumps. A broad avenue of grass to the south of the house draws attention to its alignment with the church in the village of Enstone, and to the north a perpendicular avenue runs over a bridge towards Little Tew. Apart from the octagonal bowling green to the north of the house, and the avenues, there is little obvious design here; the remainder of the garden and park is composed of deciduous and evergreen woodland, and fields. Alun Jones contends that the landscape at Heythrop may have been the work of Wise, and he dates the 'classical grove' to the west of the house, with its five-niche alcove, octagon pond and cold bath, to before 1710.[19] Both of these statements are problematic. There is certainly no stylistic evidence that Wise was at Heythrop: the avenue leading up to the house, the geometry of the layout and the ornaments in the classical grove have no obvious antecedents in any of his designs. The date of the grove, which Jones and Mowl believe to be an early example of 'naturalistic' styling, predating Kent's work at Rousham by thirty years, is also questionable. The interior of the house was still not finished in 1724, some six years after Shrewsbury's death, and Viscount Percival described the gardens that year as 'not yet made'.[20] This evidence has to be considered alongside Switzer's 1718 description of a rural garden at Heythrop, of

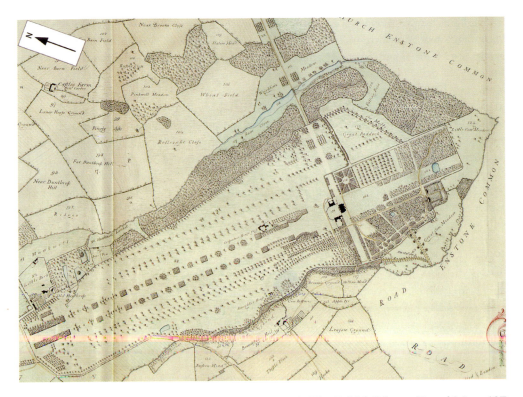

FIGURE 7.4 Plan of the Heythrop Park estate, 1792. © The British Library Board Maps 137 b.1(10).

'Hedge-Rows being mix'd with Primroses [and] Violets' interspersed with fields of cattle and woodlands, which was 'truly delightfully rural, leafy, easy and pleasant'.[21] Rather than design it appears that little work had been done on the landscape. The dukedom became extinct on Shrewsbury's death in 1718, and as he had no children he left his lands to a cousin, George Talbot, who became the 14th Earl in 1743.[22] The Duchess moved to the Shrewsbury property in Warwick Street in London, and Heythrop appears to have been left empty until Talbot inherited the title. Thomas Salmon's description of the gardens just before Talbot took control indicates that that there were few changes since Switzer's visit: the park was a 'perfect Carpet adorn'd with numerous Groves of Forest Trees, intermix'd with Ever-greens'.[23] Talbot was the only Earl to spend any length of time at the estate; it is most likely that he was the instigator of the landscaping of the bridge and the riverside cascade to the east of the house and the classical grove to the west, at a time when neo-classicism in England was gaining renewed vigour from the discoveries at Pompeii and Herculaneum.

The distinctive avenue leading up to the new house formed of clumps of trees was designed before 1712, and it is interesting to consider whether Vanbrugh might have been involved with this aspect of the Heythrop landscape. There is a plan in the Arundel Archives that shows the unusual avenue in its first configuration of square clumps with one pair of circles.[24] The depiction of two quarries, the old park wall and no house suggests that this was drawn up at the beginning of Shrewsbury's new project in 1707. It was normal practice to plant avenues of trees immediately, even before building began on the house, and Heythrop was no exception. Macky visited in 1714/15: 'The Avenue that fronts the House when finished, will certainly be one of the finest in England; for it's large enough for Six Coaches a-breast to come up to the House'.[25] The Duke of Shrewsbury was an astute politician; he had renounced his Catholic faith to avoid the 1678 Test Act, allowing him to take his seat in the Lords in 1680. He was a firm supporter of the Glorious Revolution and the accession of William and Mary, but retained Jacobite sympathies and his politics conveniently switched from Tory to Whig and back again throughout his lifetime. In 1711 Shrewsbury was named by Swift as one of the first members of the Tory Brothers Club, established by Henry St John as a rival to the Kit Cat Club. St John wrote that it would be 'composed of members who have wit and learning or power and influence . . . [where] none of the extravagance of the Kit-Cat Club . . . is to be endured'.[26] Shrewsbury's influence with the Queen at that time would have qualified him for membership, but a year previously he had been close to Godolphin and Marlborough and, it seems, to Vanbrugh: in 1710 the Duchess of Marlborough's secretary, Maynwaring, reported to her that Vanbrugh was often with Shrewsbury.[27] Vanbrugh's letters support this contention; he mentions visits to Heythrop in 1708 and 1709, and in 1716 he offered to act as a mediator between Marlborough and Shrewsbury, who were now estranged, over the purchase of stone from the Heythrop quarries for the building at Blenheim. Other evidence for Vanbrugh's contribution to the landscape is circumstantial and the form of the north approach avenue on the Arundel plan is the most pertinent. From the park gate farthest from the house the clumps of trees are in an arrangement of six squares followed by a circle and a further two squares. Macky noted 'Eight or Nine particular Inclosures of young Wood on each side of the Avenue from its Entrance up to the House, which adds to its Beauty', which align with the nine on the Arundel plan, although by 1792 several more had been added.[28] In 1713 the avenue was finished, and Lord Berkeley commented that he 'was pleas'd with [Shrewsbury's] avenue of a mile and a half long, not of single trees, but square plats of equal bignes and distance which is new and looks very well'.[29] It appears that Berkeley recognised the design as 'new' as in modern and different. Similar clumps of trees forming an avenue appear again in Vanbrugh's design for Eastbury; Shrewsbury was not an admirer of Blenheim Castle but he may have perceived Vanbrugh's flare for landscape design. This is not proof that Vanbrugh was the instigator of the avenue at Heythrop, but the geometrical elements of the layout and his association with Shrewsbury at the time when it was being laid out point to a possible link that has not hitherto been considered.

Grimsthorpe, Lincolnshire

The attribution to Switzer of the early eighteenth-century bastion garden at Grimsthorpe appears to date from Whistler's observation in 1954 that it was of the 'Switzer–Bridgeman type', even though he had already noted that the bastioned Woodwork at Blenheim must have been Vanbrugh's composition.[30] Brogden's assertion twenty years later that Switzer 'remodelled the late 17th century garden and wood [at Grimsthorpe] on the Blenheim model' added to the aura of certainty, and the attribution has been repeated unquestioningly by authors writing about the gardens since that time.[31] The bastion gardens at Castle Howard and Blenheim can now be confidently attributed to Vanbrugh, and as the architect is known to have altered the house at Grimsthorpe Switzer's authorship of the garden should be reconsidered.

The friendship between Vanbrugh and the owner of Grimsthorpe, Robert Bertie, later the 1st Duke of Ancaster and Kesteven, was of long duration. They were distant relations through Vanbrugh's mother and had been together in the service of Lord Abingdon in the 1680s. Vanbrugh was travelling on the Continent with the Bertie brothers when he was arrested in Calais in 1688.[32] In 1715 Vanbrugh drew a plan of the existing Tudor house at Grimsthorpe in preparation for alterations and he finally agreed the design of four new fronts with Bertie in 1722, although only the north front was completed.[33] John Lord has suggested that some of the payments to Vanbrugh between 1703 and 1705 might have been for architectural commissions, particularly for Swinstead House (now demolished) or for the Summerhouse at Swinstead.[34] Further disbursements are in the Lindsey accounts at Child's Bank dated 1711/12; they are relatively small and are unlikely to relate to building work so they may be for a garden plan or design.[35] Evidently Vanbrugh was frequently at the estate; Grimsthorpe was conveniently situated close to the Great North Road and he would have stopped there on his way to and from Castle Howard.[36]

Grimsthorpe was drawn by Kip and Knyff between 1701 and 1705 and their engraving shows the Tudor west front of the house overlooking a deer park and fish ponds. In a second view a broderied parterre separates a wilderness and the house; the new north front (1688) faces onto a courtyard. An avenue in the distance may be that planted by the Countess of Lindsey, who, as Switzer tells us, laid out the gardens 'with Rule, Line etc' before her death in 1669.[37] At some time after 1705, the parterre and the wilderness on the south front were transformed into a bastion garden, which was depicted in a series of sketches by Stukeley in July 1736. Overlaying Stukeley's sketch on modern maps indicates that his outline of the garden, which was based on paced distances, was remarkably accurate (Figure 7.5). His drawing, looking north along Grimes Walk, showed the diamond-shaped bastions with low walls that opened the woodland garden to the rolling countryside to the west. The grass parterre has an outline, possibly drawn in sand, that hints at the old-fashioned *broderie anglaise*, but it has been studded with small obelisks of yew, a reference to James's 'architecture in green' (see Figure 4.20). The walls around a woodland garden, the bastions and the pyramid yews were all elements already seen in Vanbrugh's gardens at Castle Howard and at Blenheim; the mount and the walk out to the edge of the gardens would appear at Eastbury a few years later. The mix of diamond- and square-shaped bastions is also distinctive, but the most convincing evidence for Vanbrugh being responsible for the Grimsthorpe garden lies in the analysis of Stukeley's plan. The outline hexagonal form, the proportions of the bastion section and the parterre and the division of the woodland garden in the ratio 2:3 were the same at Blenheim and Grimsthorpe (Figure 7.6). The resemblance of Switzer's 'Mannour of Paston' to Stukeley's plan is superficial; Paston does not display the same proportions and cannot be construed as evidence of Switzer's authorship of the garden at Grimsthorpe.[38]

Authors who claim that Switzer designed the garden at Grimsthorpe also reference the payments to him between 1710 and 1713 and a letter written by Switzer to Stukeley in 1711 from Eresby in Lincolnshire, another Lindsey estate.[39] The confusion between Eresby and Grimsthorpe is traceable to Whistler, who produced the evidence of the letter but then observed that Switzer 'appears to have worked on the gardens at Grimsthorpe'.[40] The letter gives no clue as to why Switzer was at Eresby but he may have been working as a

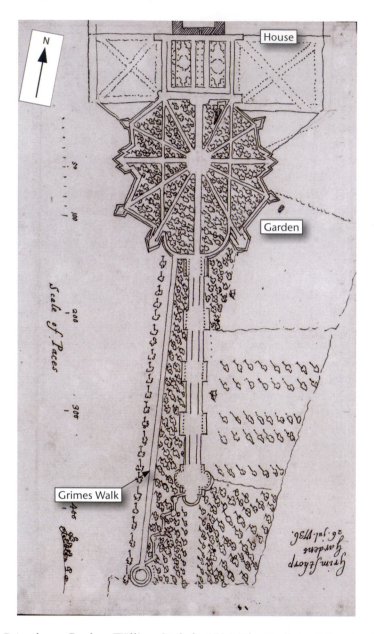

FIGURE 7.5 *Grimsthorpe Gardens*, William Stukely, 1736. The Bodleian Libraries, University of Oxford MS. Top. Gen. D. 14, fol. 36v.

gardener for Robert Bertie's son, Peregrine. The entry in Stukeley's diary for 1 September 1750 which states that Switzer was 'the first promoter of the making of gardens in the present rural taste . . . in the Duke of Ancaster's garden at Grimsthorp' is coeval with an entry that ascribes the Kensington gravel pit to Switzer, even though Addison attributed it to Wise in 1712.[41] Given that he was writing nearly forty years after the event Stukeley may have confused Grimsthorpe with Eresby. Bearing in mind his eagerness to declare

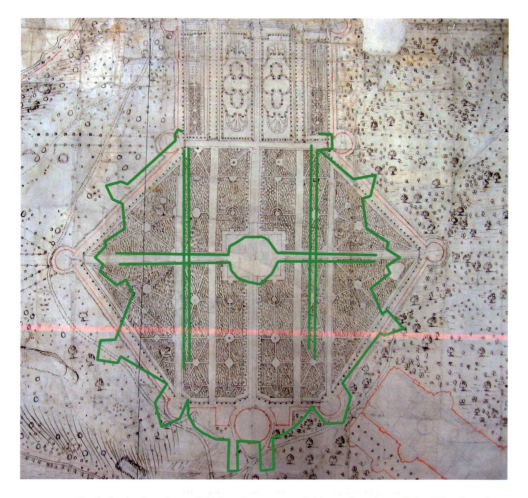

FIGURE 7.6 Stukeley's drawing of Grimsthorpe overlaid on the plan of the Woodwork at Blenheim. The proportions used in the two gardens are identical. The Bodleian Libraries, University of Oxford MS. Top. Gen. D. 14, fol. 36v overlaid on *Plann of Blenheim*, 1719, Blenheim Palace Archives.

ownership of gardens where he had worked, such as Spye Park, it is unlikely that Switzer would not have claimed such an important garden as Grimsthorpe if it really had been of his making.

It is most likely that Switzer was employed on a project for the Bertie family at Eresby from 1711, which lasted three years. He may have visited Grimsthorpe as he described the 'incomparably beautiful Park of his Grace the Duke of Ancaster' in 1718.[42] It is improbable that Robert Bertie would have employed someone who had overseen the planting of hedge yews at Blenheim to design his new garden, in preference to his close friend, who was a proven architect of the innovative bastion gardens that were already attracting the attention of the landscape *cognoscenti*. It may well have been Vanbrugh, and not Switzer, who was the designer of the Grimsthorpe garden.

8

CLAREMONT, SURREY AND NOTTINGHAM CASTLE

In May 1709 Vanbrugh purchased a lease on a house called Chargate (now Claremont) in Surrey to use as a country retreat for himself and possibly as a home for his mother.[1] The house came with sixty acres of land, thirty of which were in Chargate Wood and the remainder in arable and pasture. The lease is evidence that Vanbrugh wanted to rebuild the house and that he already intended to create a garden, for it stipulated that he could 'grub up any Trees in Chargate Wood or on any part of Chargate Farm which should obstruct the visto or prospect of any Building or Walk'.[2] An early layout of the garden was found relatively recently in the Bodleian Library, and was first published by John Harris in 1993 where he describes it as 'Bridgemannic'.[3] Unlike Bridgeman, Vanbrugh was not a draughtsman, and the fact that the plan is hand drawn, together with unusual design and the diamond bastion and the terrace walk on the north boundary of the garden, all support a confident attribution to Vanbrugh of around 1709 (Figure 8.1).[4] Under the terms of the lease, the new house had to be built on the site of the existing building in Chargate Wood towards the eastern edge of the estate. Vanbrugh designed a symmetrical arrangement of predominantly square rooms on two floors, with a castellated roofline; it is shown on the plan centred on an inverted 'A' of grass paths cut through the woodland and running over the steep hill behind the house. To the west of the hill a bowling green leads into a ramp, which runs up the hill to a garden building with a pyramidal roof; both the hill and the building were known as the Mount.[5] The form of the house, its careful positioning with respect to the hill, and the north bastion with its views over the fields are distinctly Vanbrughian.

Harris observed that the house is 'oddly askew to the axial line through the hill'; the new analysis of the geometry of Chargate in Figure 8.2 explains why.[6] Given that the position of the new house was fixed by the terms of the lease and is therefore facing almost due east, the line A–B through the new house and the centre of the hill to the west must have been drawn first. The folds are obvious on this plan and these were used, in conjunction with the lines on the laid paper, to place the rest of the design; it was founded on the inverted 'A' and the division of the main axis E–F in the ratio 3:2 at point X.[7] The geometry is pervasive and characteristic of Vanbrugh, and the later additions (the pond, the Round Temple and the Temple Pavilion) fit with the original scheme.

FIGURE 8.1 Garden plan for Chargate, Surrey, *c*. 1709. The Bodleian Libraries, University of Oxford Gough Drawings a.4 fols. 80–81.

Whistler thought that Claremont was less geometric than Eastbury and observed that 'the choice of site could itself be a contribution to the new gardening', by which he meant the naturalised landscapes associated with Brown.[8] But Chargate illustrates the application of a Vitruvian design to Vanbrugh's own home; it exhibits a precise geometry that was nevertheless entirely sympathetic with the topography of the site.

By 1713 Vanbrugh was heavily in debt; he had lost money on the opera, the work at Blenheim had stopped and he had just been dismissed from his position in the Board of Works. It was perhaps fortuitous that the Earl of Clare had been surveying the estates he inherited from his uncle in 1711 and found them all wanting.[9] He was young but an ardent Whig supporter with political aspirations; his house at Halland was uninhabitable and he needed a country estate that was close to London. Vanbrugh had designed the forty-acre lake at Welbeck for Clare's uncle in 1703 and was a fellow member of the Kit Cat Club, so

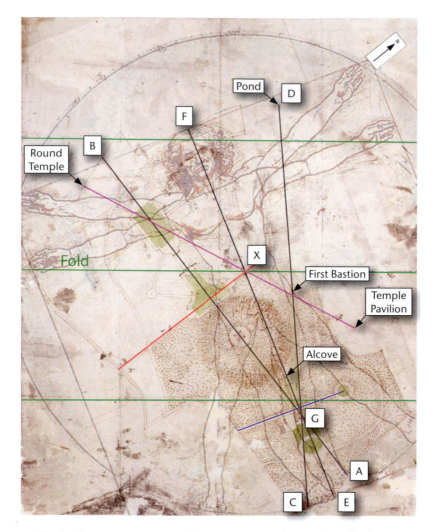

FIGURE 8.2 The landscape geometry at Chargate. Using the rough scale drawn on the plan the black lines are equal (tolerance 1.6 per cent): A–B = 1048', C–D = 1047', E–F = 1031'. The point X divides the line E–F 3:2. The blue line divides the line E–F 1:4. Proportions on other lines are left out for clarity. The angle BGF = the angle FGD = 17°. The pink line joins the later Temple Pavilion to the bowling green and the derived position of the Round Temple. The Bodleian Libraries, University of Oxford Gough Drawings a.4 fols. 80–81. Overlay diagram: author.

it must have been acceptable to both men that, in October 1714, Clare purchased the lease of Chargate, the house and all its contents from Vanbrugh for £1,800.[10] Much of the major landscaping must have been already complete; the nineteenth-century Ordnance Survey map shows significant earthworks on the Mount where Vanbrugh incremented a natural hill to create the viewing mount. The garden building on top of the Mount was finished by October 1715, and two years later the earthworks, and the instigator, were confirmed by Lawrence Eusden's poem: 'the yielding Earth obeys his Vanbrooks Will/Sinks to a Vale, or rises to a Hill'.[11] Vanbrugh built a smooth ramp up the hill from the bowling green that broke through grass ramparts to reach the Mount in a manner reminiscent of the east approach to Palladio's Villa Almerico-Capra. The current brick facade of this building denies its Roman origins but, like the west loggia at Kings Weston and many other Vanbrugh garden buildings, it was originally faced with plaster and painted to look like stone (see Figure 4.15); remnants of the plaster can still be seen. In 1774 it was described as a '*white* summer-house with four little pinnacles [that] rose up finely from behind the trees, and altogether formed a pleasing appearance'.[12] This description does not suggest that it was thought to be mediaeval or Gothick in its original form. Vanbrugh's utilisation of the natural topography at Chargate was inspired: the two cross-avenues afforded glimpses of the countryside from the elevated vantage point of the hill, and there were panoramic views of Surrey from the roof terrace of the Mount, framed by false 'windows' in each of the four towers that mimicked the real windows on the lower floors (Figure 8.3). The framing of views through arches appeared elsewhere in the garden at the Alcove, which was shown on Vanbrugh's first plan and may have been coeval with the Mount.

In 1715 Clare was elevated to the title of Duke of Newcastle, and the commemorative verse by Garth, the Kit Cat's doctor and poet, confirmed that he had changed the name of his Surrey estate to 'Claremont'. Garth was quite clear about the authorship of the gardens when he wrote:

> But say, who shall attempt th'advent'rous Part
> Where Nature borrows Dress from *Vanbrook's* Art.
> If by Apollo taught, he touch the Lyre,
> Stones mount in Columns, Palaces aspire,
> And Rocks are animated with his Fire.
> 'Tis he can Paint in Verse those rising Hills,
> Their gentle Vallies, and those silver Rills:
> Close Groves, and op'ning Glades with Verdure spread,
> Flow'rs sighing Sweets, and Shrubs that Balsam Bleed.[13]

The Newcastle accounts in the British Library start in May 1715 with 'work on the parlour', presaging the extensive building work that left 'Chargate in a rising Claremont lost'.[14] Entries for 'easing Mr Tonson's doors' and to shelves in 'Sir John Vanbrugh's room' are evidence that both men were frequent visitors, Vanbrugh as a friend and as the architect of the new house at Claremont. A 'Necessary House in the wood by the Mount and outworks' in 1717 refers to a toilet by the defensive wall and bastion on the north side of the garden, and a second garden building called the 'round seat' was finished by March 1716.[15] This building in wood on the western extremity of the estate may be the one referenced by Eusden in 1717: 'There, in steep Prospect, Woods and Streams delight/And *Domes*, and distant Turrets fill the Sight'.[16]

Newcastle first started to expand his estate in 1715 when he bought Chargate Farm from Robert Moore.[17] The farm was converted into a laundry and brewhouse, and the land would later be the site of the Kitchen Garden. Chargate House had three orchards, but, given that kitchen gardens were considered to be an essential element of any estate, work may have started on the walls almost immediately, although there is no evidence for it in the accounts. After his marriage to Marlborough's granddaughter in April 1717,[18]

FIGURE 8.3 Vanbrugh framed the views from the roof terrace on the Mount through arches in each of the four towers (left). These mimicked the windows on the lower floors. The window, now bricked up, in the Games Room (right). Photos: author, 2007.

which provided a settlement of £20,000, Newcastle started to extend the garden into the recently purchased Manor of Esher.[19] Pencil additions that appear to be in Vanbrugh's hand annotate the original Chargate plan with designs for the expansion: a rectangular pond and the position of a Temple Pavilion are marked outside the north boundary of the old garden. Newcastle now owned the land to the south and west of the Round Temple, and work started on digging the round Basin with its central obelisk; Vanbrugh would later add a classical 'Seat for the Water side . . . in Brick, not Stone' in 1724.[20] This combination of geometric pond and obelisk, flanked by classical garden buildings, would soon reappear at Stowe, but the date of the amphitheatre remains unclear. Whistler's contention that it was started around 1725 is supported by there being no entries relating to an amphitheatre in the accounts before 1720, and Vanbrugh does not mention it at all in his letters.[21] Even at this late date it would be feasible that it was finished by 1727, when Langley refers to a hill cut into slopes and terraces at Claremont.[22] Campbell's plan of 1725, which shows the pond but no amphitheatre, is, as ever, confusing (Figure 8.4). His depiction of the form of the Great Room (built 1719–20), and Mr Greening's house, which was designed in 1723, is correct as are the alterations to the garden immediately behind the house, which added a bagnio, a flower garden and a double ramp of steps to a piazza. It seems unlikely that Campbell would have missed out such an important feature as the amphitheatre if it had already been constructed, but it is impossible to date features accurately using his plans.

Writing about Carlisle's outworks at Castle Howard in 1723, Vanbrugh hoped that he would 'find the walls at Claremont as much to my satisfaction (and your Graces too) as those are here'.[23] This must be a reference to the outworks and square bastion that were

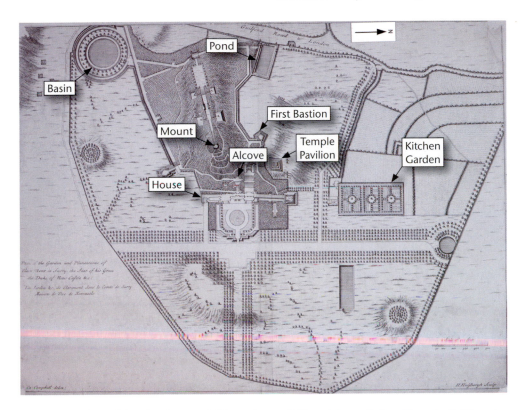

FIGURE 8.4 Plan of the Gardens and Plantations of Clare Mont. Colen Campbell, *Vitruvius Britannicus*, Vol. 3, (London: C. Campbell and J. Smith 1725). Not to scale. Special Collections, University of Bristol.

being built on the south side of the garden, with another terrace walk overlooking Basin Park. Vanbrugh's assurance to Newcastle the following year that he had 'not forgot your seats at Claremont' demonstrates that the architect was still in control of the landscape design, although he was also now occupied with projects at Stowe, Grimsthorpe and Seaton Delaval.[24] There is little doubt, however, that Bridgeman built the amphitheatre next to the Basin; it is ascribed to Bridgeman by Switzer, and by the Duke, who referred to it as 'dear Bridgeman's Hill' in 1752.[25] Much of the hard landscaping was complete by the early 1720s and Bridgeman had been working with Vanbrugh at Sacombe and at Stowe, so he must have taken over and finished the project around 1724.

It is improbable that Bridgeman contributed any more than the amphitheatre to the gardens at Claremont, as Newcastle engaged William Kent in the late 1720s, and his influence is seen in Rocque's plan of 1738 (Figure 8.5). The outline of the round Pond is still visible, but it has been extended with an island and Vanbrugh's 'Seat for the Water side' has been subsumed into Kent's Belisle. The square bastion on the south boundary has been removed although the raised terrace walk that overlooked the park and fields on this side of the garden is still visible today. The classical building at Nine Pin Alley and the bowling green house may be Kent's work as there is no evidence that they were by Vanbrugh, and the later Thatched House and Menagerie may also be attributed to Kent. The 1738 plan

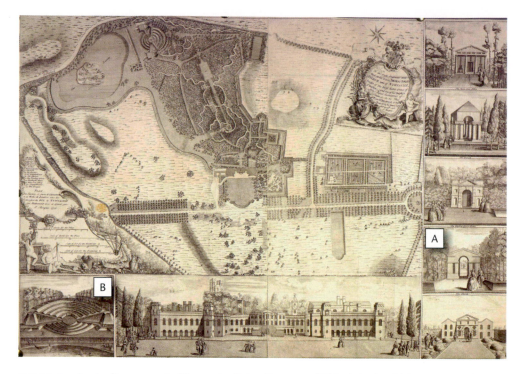

FIGURE 8.5 *Le jardin et parc de Claremont*, John Rocque, 1738. A is the Alcove, an important element of Vanbrugh's original design that framed the view of the west front of the house. B is the Amphitheatre. Newcastle's new house is depicted lower centre with the Mount on the hill behind it. This plan is not to scale. © The British Library Board Maps K. Top. 40 19a.

is not to scale and appears to have used artistic licence in the depiction of the gardens; in particular, the consciously sinuous paths may not have existed, as Rocque's more accurate survey of 1750 suggests. Geo-referencing this plan shows that the underlying geometry of the original design was retained into the middle of the century and highlights how Vanbrugh's original house was engulfed by Newcastle's massive extensions (Figure 8.6). The third edition of Defoe's *Tour* observed that 'as several Persons have had the contrivance of [Newcastle's] Gardens and Buildings, there is not any uniform Taste to be found in either, which is greatly to be regretted', and perhaps it was; Vanbrugh's Vitruvian masterpiece was diluted by Kent's eclectic taste in garden buildings and the removal of the outworks.[26]

When Newcastle inherited the Pelham and Holles estates in 1711–12 he had an annual income of £32,000 (about £4.4m today), yet by the time of his marriage in 1717 he was already short of money, and the dispute with the Duchess of Marlborough over his future wife's dowry went on for some time.[27] Both of his biographers agree that Newcastle was a spendthrift; he spent extravagantly on his buildings and gardens in London, Surrey and at Nottingham Castle, where Vanbrugh was again employed to design the landscape.[28] Concerned to reveal the Beauty of the 'disposition' of the Castle, Vanbrugh wrote to Newcastle in December 1718 that he

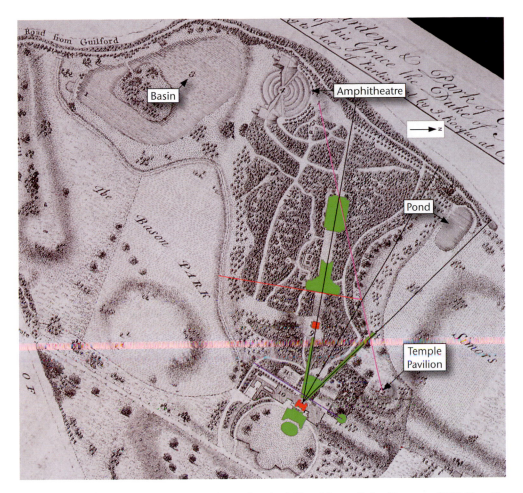

FIGURE 8.6 *A Survey of the House, Garden and Park of Clare Mount,* John Rocque, 1750 (detail). Geo-referenced plan with the elements of Vanbrugh's initial design overlaid in colour (House and Mount in red). This scaled drawing demonstrates that, although slightly distorted by geo-referencing, the ethos of Vanbrugh's underlying Vitruvian grid was retained into the 1750s. Compare with Figure 8.2. © The British Library Board Maps K. Top. 40 19c.

may have as agreable a Castle Garden as you can wish, of near three Acres of ground, And this actually within the Castle Walls & will lye just under the great Terrass in a very right manner. The Park is an extream pretty piece of ground but is all to be planted. There may be a very noble pond in it, with small Expence, And the Views from the upper part of it, are right good.[29]

However, Vanbrugh's allusion to the small outlay for the pond, and his efforts to save money by using brick rather than stone for the garden buildings, may not have been of interest to this particular client. A visitor in 1774 observed that Vanbrugh's Great Room at Claremont 'made the ends of the house not appear similar', but this did not bother

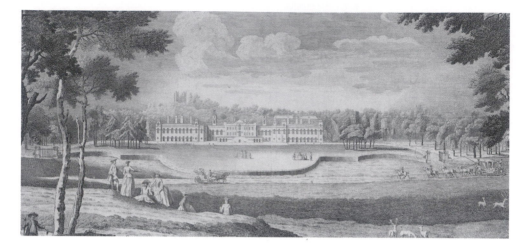

FIGURE 8.7 *Claremont House*, John Rocque, 1750. Newcastle's completed house with the Mount on the hill behind it. The Bodleian Libraries, University of Oxford Gough Maps 30, fol. 59.

Newcastle, who had been intent only on entertaining his guests in lavish style (Figure 8.7).[30] Like Vanbrugh's outworks, the Great Room started a fashion for entertainment rooms; even Chandos, who had previously rejected Vanbrugh as his architect, wanted to see it: 'he talk'd to me of your Graces new Room at Claremont, designing to have such a one in the New house he Builds in London', Vanbrugh reported to Newcastle in 1720.[31] At a time when many men were living beyond their means, Newcastle's spending was reckless. As Ray Kelch points out, other men did not ruin their estates, but Newcastle consistently sold his land to pay debts, and by 1762 his annual income was reduced to only £6,000; after his death in 1768 the Duchess was forced to sell Claremont to Lord Clive.[32] Clive obviously agreed with Defoe's opinion that Newcastle's house was 'very damp', and by January 1771 it had been demolished. Curiously, the architect of both the alterations to the landscape, and the new house a few hundred feet to the north, would be Lancelot 'Capability' Brown.[33]

9

KINGS WESTON, GLOUCESTERSHIRE (NOW AVON)

Edward Southwell was an MP and Secretary of State for Ireland who inherited the family estate at Kings Weston on the death of his father in 1702. He commissioned Vanbrugh to rebuild the house in 1710; this was to be Vanbrugh's western-most project and Southwell was his first Tory client.[1] The connection between Southwell and Vanbrugh is imprecise but Southwell was elected a member of the Royal Society in 1692 and thus entered the intellectual and social circle in London that would have brought Vanbrugh to his attention.[2] Vanbrugh's employment by a number of prominent Whigs had more to do with his talent, his aristocratic connections and his membership of the Kit Cat Club than with politics. He was a staunch supporter of the Whig faction but there is no evidence that he eschewed Tory commissions; three of the fifteen projects considered in this book were for Tories.[3] Vanbrugh made more than one visit to the Tory Duke of Chandos's home at Cannons, observing in a letter of 1720 that Chandos 'has sav'd nothing by not letting me be his Architect'.[4] Both Southwell and Chandos were members of the moderate group of 'Hanoverian' Tories in 1714, but Southwell may have had stronger Tory sympathies than has previously been thought.[5] Kings Weston is therefore the first opportunity to examine whether there was deliberate variation in Whig and Tory designed landscapes in the early eighteenth century.

Whistler's otherwise excellent exposition of Vanbrugh's work as an architect pays little attention to the building at Kings Weston, and none to the landscape. The *Kings Weston Book of Drawings*, now in the Bristol Record Office, was known to Christopher Hussey in 1928 but Whistler references none of the drawings, which are a valuable source of information on the site. A thorough examination of the architecture at Kings Weston is provided by Hart, who notes the niches in the Great Hall as being evidence of the 'known influence of Palladio on Vanbrugh's houses'.[6] Both Hart and Downes mention only two of the garden buildings, Penpole Gate and the Banqueting House Loggia (now known as the Echo), and neither discusses the gardens.[7] Mowl's book on Gloucestershire is the most comprehensive study to date; it draws attention to a survey of 1720 in the British Library that provides important evidence of Vanbrugh's landscape architecture at Kings Weston.[8]

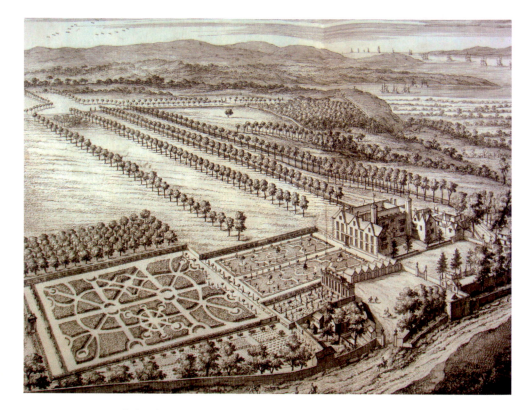

FIGURE 9.1 View of the landscape at Kings Weston, Johannes Kip, *c.* 1710. *The Ancient and Present State of Glostershire*, Sir Robert Atkyns, 1712. Special Collections, University of Bristol.

The layout of the estate just before Vanbrugh's arrival in 1710 is illustrated in an engraving by Kip (Figure 9.1). The Elizabethan house faces south-west along long avenues of trees leading to the River Avon, and the ships in the Severn Estuary can be seen in the distance. The gardens to the side of the house comprise two parterres, one reminiscent of *broderie anglaise* and another with figures cut out in box, and to the north-east is a courtyard flanked by an elevated walkway that terminates in a banqueting pavilion. The lodge at Penpole Point (on a hill, top right) affords extensive views over the park, gardens and river, but is not obviously connected to the landscape design; the whole is a montage of seventeenth-century formality.

The map of 1720 (Figure 9.2) shows how Vanbrugh changed the landscape in the ten years after 1710. He retained the main avenues running south-west from the house and the outline of the two parterres, although the *broderie* has been replaced by grass, but many more avenues at oblique angles and a third parterre laid out as a wilderness have been added. The house has been rebuilt on the footprint of the Elizabethan mansion; bounded by the road and service buildings to the north-east and with a sharp ledge towards the west it would have been difficult to relocate it. Vanbrugh would not have wanted to re-site the house; the opportunities offered by such an interesting topography would have immediately appealed to him. The geological map of the area indicates that the house and the park

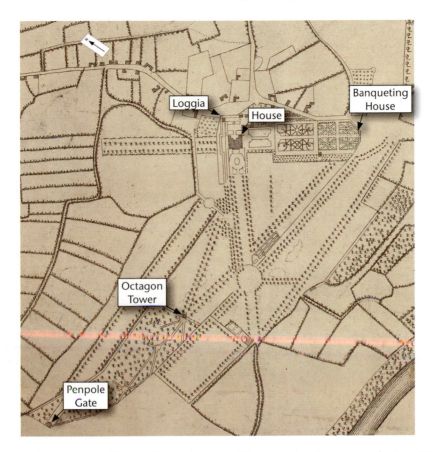

FIGURE 9.2 *The Mannor of Kings Weston*, 1720. © The British Library Board Maps K. Top. 13.

immediately to the south-west of it sit on a bed of sandstone that is surrounded by a raised mudstone bank, extending in an arc towards Penpole Point. To the north the land drops away into the Severn Estuary. In accordance with usual practice, the two seventeenth-century parterres had been restricted to the flat ground next to the house.

Vanbrugh extended the existing parterres up the slope of the mudstone bank creating a new wilderness and placing the Banqueting House Loggia at the far end in the early 1720s. The building became known as the Echo because it reflected the east front of the house (Figure 9.3); the style was similar to Nelson's Seat at Stowe and Vanbrugh's design for a seat in the grove at Cholmondeley in Cheshire dating to 1722.[9] The Banqueting House Loggia sits just below the highest point of the embankment on the eastern extremity of the garden, at the start of an elevated walkway delimited by an avenue of trees that runs west towards Penpole along the mudstone embankment (Figure 9.4). The walkway still affords fine views of the east and south fronts of the house from between the trees, but in the eighteenth century it would also have opened the aspect towards Sneed Park and the Avon. The remains of Vanbrugh's avenue of trees still flank this elevated path; they were aligned with the Banqueting House Loggia even though the building could never have been visible at the end of the avenue through the depths of the wilderness.

FIGURE 9.3 The east front of Kings Weston House. Photo: author, 2008.

FIGURE 9.4 The west loggia (left) and the Banqueting House Loggia or Echo (right). Photos: author, 2008.

The trees provide the first clue to Vanbrugh's new geometrical scheme (Figure 9.5). As at Castle Howard and at Blenheim, sight lines are not the key to understanding Vanbrugh's designs; his use of proportional geometry is not obvious on the ground. The Banqueting House Loggia was carefully placed, not to afford views of the Severn, but to mark the apex of the isosceles triangle that defined the layout. The design was not old-fashioned

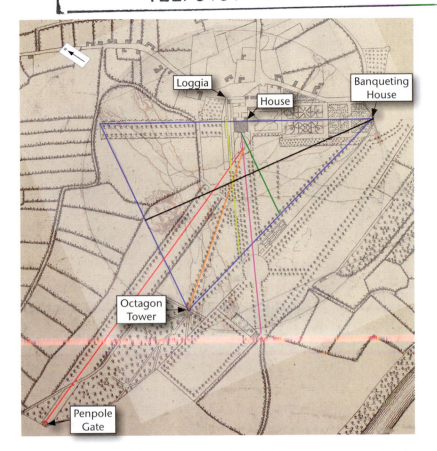

FIGURE 9.5 The geometry of the landscape at Kings Weston, 1720. The pink line marks
the pre-existing avenue associated with the old house. The new geometry is
founded on an isosceles triangle (in blue, with a tolerance of 2.5 per cent). The
orange and yellow lines divide the black line 2:3. The green line divides the
black line in half. Note how the old parterres to the south-east are not centred
on the new house. The new avenue to the north-west is centred. *The Mannor
of Kings Weston*, 1720. © The British Library Board Maps K. Top. 13. Overlay
diagram: author.

as Mowl believes; this was Vanbrugh's Vitruvian grid underlying another demanding
topography.[10] Geo-referencing the 1720 plan and building a three-dimensional computer
model reveals the complexity of the landscape project. The trees along the embankment
and the new double avenue (marked in red) that runs down the side of a hill then back up
into Penpole Wood were inspired.

In October 1713 Vanbrugh wrote to Southwell that he was pleased that the house was
covered, and that his client was willing to wait on a decision about the chimneys until he
could be on site.[11] Although the interior work was still not complete when Southwell died
in 1730, much of the landscaping was finished by 1720. Drawings of a walled enclosure
with a surrounding fosse and a pyramid gate dated 1718 indicate that Vanbrugh designed
mock fortifications for the forecourt very similar to the outworks at Eastbury and Castle

Howard. However, a picture of the south front in 1746 does not show a pyramid gate and it may not have been built.[12]

The Octagon Tower and the west loggia were the earliest garden buildings at Kings Weston; the Tower is shown on the 1720 map, and a plan and elevation in the *Kings Weston Book of Drawings* could be the design for this building.[13] A letter from Southwell to Thomas Coke dated 1719 regarding his 'new Logia on Sir J Van's proposal' is evidence that the loggia at the end of the terraces to the west of the house was being planned in 1719.[14] Vanbrugh had built a two-step terrace here as a means of managing a steep ledge at the boundary between the sandstone and the mudstone at this point. A new avenue of trees ran down from the terraces, pulling the eye towards the Severn Estuary and the Welsh hills beyond, and the effect may have been of an amphitheatre. The west loggia was to provide the north termination of the lower terrace, and was a classical portico hiding the seventeenth-century banqueting pavilion behind it. The pediment with eight Corinthian columns and pilasters supporting an arched opening was meant to complement the south front of the house. The rough brickwork that is now exposed on the side walls of the west loggia indicates that they were originally plastered and painted to match the front stone facade. The last garden building appears to have been the replacement in the early 1720s of the lodge on Penpole Point with a new building of two floors accessed by an external stair. 'Penpole Gate' was demolished in the 1950s, but old photographs indicate that it may have been a double cube (Figure 9.6). The form suggests Vanbrugh although Downes originally thought that it may have been Campbell's work.[15] Located at the highest point at the end of a new avenue this was the obvious place for a belvedere affording fine views of the river and estuary, as well as towards the house. Penpole Wood was turned into a garden, with straight paths, grass cabinets and a terrace walk overlooking the Severn Estuary, in a style very reminiscent of Castle Howard's Ray Wood.[16]

Improvements in the second half of the eighteenth century removed the lines of avenues to the south and west of the house and demolished the lower terrace and the parterres, although the fortified courtyard on the south front is still visible on a map of 1772. A pond to the left of the overgrown path leading up to the Banqueting House Loggia, still visible today, could be a remnant of a fountain in Vanbrugh's eighteenth-century wilderness. The steps from the upper level of the west terrace now lead down to an uneven covering of scrub, and the west loggia faces nothing but the trees of the modern landscaping around the car park. Kings Weston may not have been as extensive as Castle Howard, Blenheim and Stowe, but it ranks in importance with Claremont and Seaton Delaval as an example of Vanbrugh's inspirational landscaping. The underlying geometry pulls together the garden buildings, designed woodland, avenues and terraces into a single unit situated in a stunning topographical site. At the time of writing this landscape is again under threat: the National Trust has recently been able to save Seaton Delaval; the house and grounds of Kings Weston are no less of a deserving cause.

The analysis of this, Vanbrugh's first design for a Tory landscape, indicates that there was no difference between Kings Weston and his layouts for prominent Whigs. Vanbrugh's work at Duncombe in Yorkshire and Sacombe in Hertfordshire further supports the contention that, with the exception of overt political symbolism such as that at Stowe in the 1730s, politics did not directly influence the *form* of designed landscapes during the early eighteenth century. Consideration of the Duke of Chandos's gardens at Cannons, where Vanbrugh was not involved with the landscaping, reinforces this argument.

FIGURE 9.6 Penpole Gate before it was demolished in the 1950s. Bristol Record Office, 33746.

Cannons was reputably the estate that was satirised by Pope as Timon's Villa in his *Epistle to Lord Burlington* (1731):

> His Gardens next your Admiration call,
> On ev'ry side you look, behold the Wall!
> No pleasing Intricacies intervene,
> no artful Wildeness to perplex the Scene:
> Grove nods at Grove, each Ally has a Brother,
> and half the Platform just reflects the other.[17]

There are several correspondences between Pope's verse and a contemporary account by Macky. Macky describes Cannons as a 'Palace' and remarks that in the gardens:

> there is a large Terrass Walk, from whence you descend to the Parterre; this Parterre hath a row of gilded Vases on Pedestals, on each Side down to the great Canal, and in the middle, fronting the Canal, is a Gladiator, gilded also; and through the whole Parterre, Abundance of Statues as big as Life, regularly disposed.[18]

From this description the ornamentation appears to be little different from that at Castle Howard, but it must have attracted criticism long before Pope's *Epistle* because Vanbrugh wrote to Newcastle in 1720 that 'to deal justly with [Chandos's] Magnificence, we found nothing at all Ridiculous or Foppish as many people have Represented'.[19]

If Timon's Villa was a reference to Cannons, Pope had decided to ignore the prevailing fashion for geometry. Fougeroux's depiction of the estate in 1728 bears many similarities to aspects of Burlington's grounds at Chiswick: the house is surrounded by geometric ornamental gardens and a large pond and canal. As Battestin points out: 'at Timon's Villa Pope despised as unnatural, the manifestations of regularity, symmetry and delimitation, of which he otherwise approved'.[20] In the 1720s, the Tory gardens at Cannons and Wanstead (see Figure 4.17) were as extensive and magnificent as the Whig gardens at Stowe and Castle Howard, and Chandos's expenditure was not unusual: Carlisle was spending beyond his means only four years after starting to build Castle Howard and Newcastle was to leave his widow virtually penniless after squandering his considerable fortune on renovations to his houses and gardens, which is perhaps why Vanbrugh was keen to make light of Chandos's profligacy. The Cannons design was flat and uninspiring, so the only obvious difference between this Tory landscape and the designs at Blenheim and Kings Weston is Vanbrugh.

10

DUNCOMBE PARK AND SACOMBE PARK

Duncombe Park, Yorkshire

Sir Charles Duncombe was a Tory MP who established the family fortune as a banker and government financier. In 1711 his nephew Thomas Duncombe inherited his uncle's property in Yorkshire together with his parliamentary seat of Downton in Middlesex, and, although Thomas's parliamentary career is obscure, it is likely that he was also a Tory.[1] Duncombe is only thirteen miles north of Castle Howard, and the Carlisle and Duncombe families were part of the York social circle that met regularly at the York assemblies. Vanbrugh would join them on his visits to Castle Howard and his meeting with his future wife at the assembly was observed by Lady Mary Wortley Montagu: 'his Inclination to Ruins has given [Vanbrugh] a fancy for Mrs Yarborrough'.[2]

In 1713 Thomas Duncombe commissioned a new house near Helmsley, attributed by Campbell to William Wakefield.[3] Whistler ascribes the house to Vanbrugh 'with some confidence', as the ground plan is almost identical to the plan of Eastbury, and the Ionic Temple is 'virtually a replica' of the one at Stowe (Figure 10.1).[4] It is most likely then that Wakefield was a Clerk of Works in a similar role to that of Etty and Smallwell. The estate is situated on a bend of the River Rye, at a point where the river has undercut the limestone platform, creating a natural raised terrace 200 feet above the valley below. The house is aligned so that it is perpendicular to the terrace, and the symmetrical arrangement of rooms about the hall and salon creates a line of sight from the entrance door through the house and over the terrace and the river to the hills on the other side of the valley. In its layout, and its careful integration with the landscape, the house is manifestly Palladian.

The east front of the house faces a sunken parterre that may once have been a bowling green, similar to the one at Castle Howard, and on its eastern boundary is a figure of Father Time holding a sundial of *circa* 1715; it is attributed to Jan Van Nost, who also moulded several of the statues on the Temple Terrace at Castle Howard. The sundial sits on one side of the natural raised terrace that overlooks the river, which is terminated by two temples. On the northern boundary of the gardens, next to a ha-ha, is the Ionic Temple, which affords dramatic views over Helmsley Castle; the overgrown Yew Walk to the west

FIGURE 10.1 The east front of Duncombe Park with Van Nost's sundial in the foreground. The croquet hoops are set up on the original bowling green. Photo: author, 2008.

of the Temple appears to date from the original landscaping. At the south end of the terrace is the Doric Temple, which is attributed to Carlisle's son-in-law Thomas Robinson, and is clearly influenced by Palladio's drawings of Bramante's Tempietto in the *Quattro Libri*. The South Terrace runs west from the Doric Temple to meet the Broadwalk, and it is possible that the area south of the bowling green was originally a wilderness garden. The conservatory and extant statues were added later in the nineteenth century, as were two more sunken parterres next to the house, reputably by Nesfield who, again, worked at Castle Howard.

Analysis of the eighteenth-century landscape reveals that the axis through the house, and the position of the sundial, were the focal points of a design that is founded on two contiguous isosceles triangles (Figure 10.2). The geometry defines the positions of all of the elements of the gardens: the Yew Walk is the base of one triangle, the South Terrace the base of another. The two temples and the sundial are each positioned at a vertex of one of the triangles. The gardens at Duncombe Park appear to be another example of the geometry of triangles that was first evident at Kings Weston. The Van Nost sundial and the Ionic Temple, which was a precursor to the Rotundo at Stowe, date the building of the gardens to between 1715 and 1720. As the position of the Doric Temple was an important part of the composition it must have been part of the original design, even though it was constructed much later. Brogden sees some similarities between the terrace at Duncombe and Switzer's design for Cirencester, and Hussey is tempted to credit the gardens to Switzer, but neither author offers any firm evidence to support these theories.[5] The form and situation of the Ionic Temple is an exact replica of its twin at Stowe; the

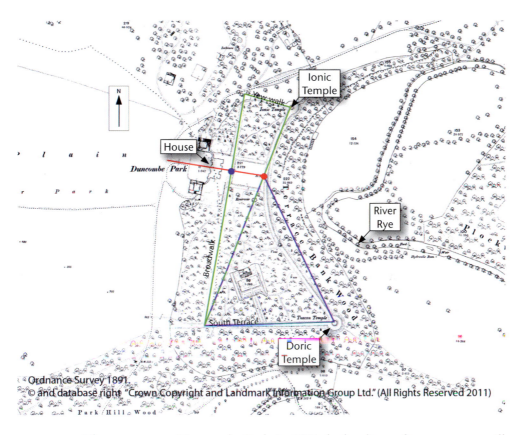

FIGURE 10.2 The geometry at Duncombe Park. In 1891 the key lines of geometry are still evident. The green and the blue lines define two exact isosceles triangles. The red dot is the position of Van Nost's sundial, the blue dot marks the centre front of the house on the Broadwalk. Both the blue and red dots divide the green lines in the ratio 3:2. Overlay diagram: author.

similarities with Castle Howard and the dramatic utilisation of natural topography and Vitruvian geometry suggest Vanbrugh as the most probable architect of the gardens at Duncombe, as Whistler first thought.

In 1774 a visitor described the Rye valley as though it had also been purposefully landscaped:

> the valley is intersected by hedges, which form beautiful inclosures of grass; the meanders of the river are bold and well broken by scattered trees; the cascades almost overhung with pendant trees . . . this view is beheld with a moving variation as you walk along the terrass to the Tuscan [Doric] temple, with fresh objects breaking upon the eye as you advance'.[6]

It is unfortunate that the trees on the edge of the valley have been allowed to grow tall, and have obscured the view from the terrace at Duncombe that was so much admired in the eighteenth century.

Sacombe Park, Hertfordshire

Sacombe Park was purchased by Sir Thomas Rolt in 1688. He had amassed a considerable fortune during his employment by the East India Company, and he was the President of Surat from 1678 to 1682.[7] When Rolt's son Edward inherited the family property in 1710, Vanbrugh was already a celebrated architect, and the Surat connection is a possible explanation for Edward's selection of Vanbrugh as the designer for his new house and gardens at Sacombe Park. Rolt was a Tory MP representing St Mawes in Cornwall between 1713 and 1715; thus, Sacombe was another Tory commission.

It is likely that Vanbrugh introduced Bridgeman to Rolt as the gardener who would realise the project; disbursements from Rolt's accounts at Hoare's and Coutt's total nearly £1,200 (£160,000 today) to Bridgeman from 1715 to 1722, and denote a significant undertaking.[8] An early plan of Sacombe drawn up prior to the improvements appears to be in Bridgeman's hand; the similarities between the handwriting on the legend on this plan and that on one for Down Hall in Essex, where Bridgeman is known to have worked with Gibbs, are notable. The plan shows the existing layout of the estate before work began, to which the axial line of a proposed canal has been added. The known association of Bridgeman with the site appears, however, to have eradicated any doubt that the new landscape was entirely of his design.[9] Analysis of the geometry in a plan showing the updated grounds at Sacombe suggests otherwise (Figure 10.3). According to Whistler the new house 'strongly suggests Vanbrugh' and the massive rectangular kitchen garden was described by Sir Matthew Decker in 1728 as '3 acres, and within walls, with 4 Towers one on each corner so strongly *built by Van Brock* as if they were to defend a city'.[10] Research for this book has found no evidence that Bridgeman was the principal designer on any project on which he worked with Vanbrugh. The landscape at Sacombe displayed many Vanbrughian characteristics apart from the bastioned kitchen garden: the amphitheatre was set in a woodland of 'well-grown Timber' and the canal and its terminating pond extended boldly out into the fields towards the edge of the estate.[11] The canal was flanked by raised walks, and a lightly planted avenue of trees afforded glimpses of the countryside; an effect that was reminiscent of the natural raised terrace at Kings Weston. The octagonal ponds were similar to the 'rectangular circled' pond at Castle Howard that was constructed in 1706.

The geometry is founded on contiguous triangles and inspired by da Vinci's drawing. The amphitheatre, the parterre, the grass cabinet and the *rondpoint* in the centre of the design are defined by an isosceles triangle (blue), and a second isosceles triangle defines the position of the canal and its pond (green). Overlaying the plan of Grimsthorpe, which has already been shown to derive from that of Blenheim, demonstrates that the proportions in the landscape at Sacombe replicate those at Grimsthorpe (Figure 10.4). Sacombe was a classical garden with allusions to Roman architecture in the massive kitchen garden, the octagonal ponds and the amphitheatre. Yet the fussy broderied parterre does not suggest Vanbrugh and Bridgeman's influence must be acknowledged here. The amphitheatre would be consistent with the Roman references in all of Vanbrugh's gardens, and there is no reason to suppose that it was not originally Vanbrugh's idea; it would appear again at Stowe and at Claremont, although the latter was built by Bridgeman. Bridgeman's realisation of the garden at Sacombe is unquestioned, but the underlying geometry that ties the design together is in Vanbrugh's style.

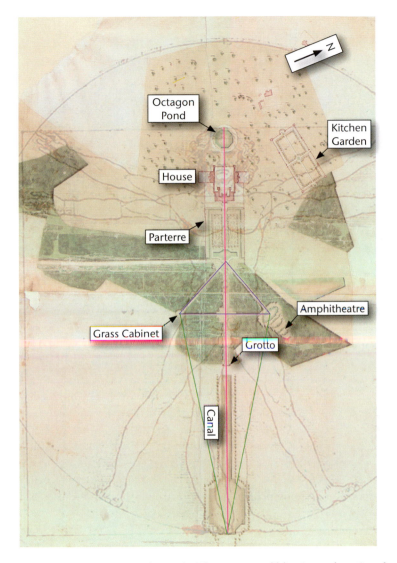

FIGURE 10.3 The geometry at Sacombe Park. The green and blue isosceles triangles link the elements of the plan. The pink axis is divided by the length of the canal 2:3. The angle of the amphitheatre to the pink line is 40°. The Bodleian Libraries, University of Oxford Gough Drawings a.4 fol. 64. Annotation: author.

Rolt had intended to build a new house but he died suddenly in 1722 before his improvements were finished, and Sacombe became an interesting example of a contemporary garden surrounding what Decker described as a 'Little and old' house.[12] The house was let for several years until Edward's son, Thomas, came of age in 1729, which explains why the amphitheatre was complete when Decker and Salmon visited the estate in the 1720s, but the canal and basin were 'only begun'.[13] Overlaying the 1715 plan on a first edition Ordnance Survey map gives the actual positions of the key elements of the early eighteenth-century garden (Figure 10.5). The amphitheatre pond can be seen in Home

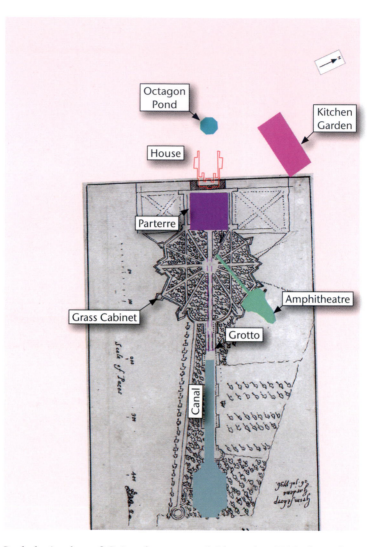

FIGURE 10.4 Stukeley's plan of Grimsthorpe overlaid on the 1715 plan of Sacombe. The proportions used in the two designs are very similar. The Bodleian Libraries, University of Oxford MS. Top. Gen. D. 14, fol. 36v. Annotation: author.

Wood and the raised walk to the canal is traceable through embankments. The extent of Rolt's canal is striking. This was an expensive layout that was meant to impress; as such, it was again little different from the Whig gardens of the time. When George Caswell finally replaced the old house in 1807 with a new one 200 yards to the east, it was built on the site of Bridgeman's parterre. Modern mapping indicates that the amphitheatre pond is extant, and vestiges of the eighteenth-century garden can be seen in the paths; the outline of the foundations of the canal and pond can be seen on an aerial photograph laid out in parch marks under the field to the south of Home Wood.

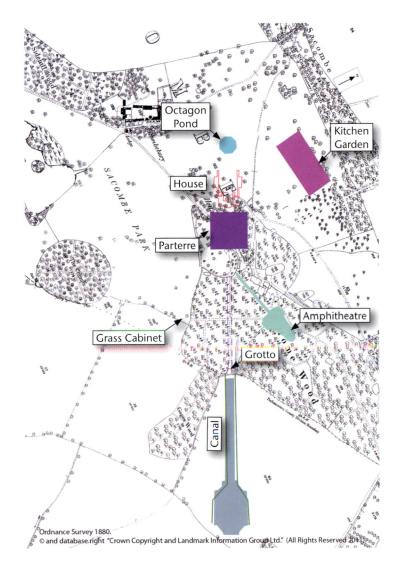

FIGURE 10.5 The 1715 plan of Sacombe, overlaid on the Ordnance Survey map of 1880. This shows exactly where the 1715 garden was located. The positioning is supported by parch marks of the canal visible on an overlaid aerial photograph (dark green lines). Annotation: author.

11

EASTBURY, DORSET

In 1709 George Dodington, a Whig politician, bought the Manor of Tarrant Gunville in Dorset. Dodington was Secretary to the Earl of Orford, and a first cousin of Sir Richard Temple of Stowe. It was through a combination of Orford's influence, his family connections and the money he made from war contracts in the 1690s that he rose to become one of the Lords Commissioners of the Admiralty from 1709 to 1710. Although he was never influential enough in Whig circles to be invited to join the Kit Cat Club, Dodington must have known Vanbrugh through his political contacts, and sometime in 1715 he commissioned the architect to design and build a new house for him at Tarrant Gunville, to be known as Eastbury. Vanbrugh's accounts detail two long visits to Eastbury in July and October 1716, which suggest that work may already have been under way.[1] This view is supported by a statement in Dodington's will of 1718 that 'much money hath been expended already [on the building]', and a letter of 1719 from Thornhill about decoration, addressed to Dodington at Eastbury.[2] The early designs for the house at Eastbury were soon superseded; the plan illustrated in *Vitruvius Britannicus*, Vol. 3 (1725) must have been adopted by 1718 as it incorporated two new octagon rooms on the garden front that were mentioned by Thornhill in his letter. Dodington would have been approaching sixty when he drew up his will in 1718, and was not in good health, for he clearly did not expect to see the work finished when he stipulated that the house and gardens should be 'compleated according to the model made thereof and which model I intend to have fully executed after my decease'.[3]

As Vanbrugh stood on the Dorset Downs in 1715 and surveyed George Dodington's estate he was presented with a new topographical challenge. The village of Tarrant Gunville was one of several along the River Tarrant, a tributary of the River Stour, which must once have been the torrent that its name suggests. Reduced to little more than a brook at Gunville, its many tributaries had long ago disappeared into the ground, creating a rolling chalk landscape of hills and dry valleys. Dodington's estate was to the east of the Tarrant and composed of three hills and two of the dry valleys. Not only did the land fall away to north and south, but also it fell into the Tarrant valley to the west and towards Chettle in the east. Vanbrugh would not have hesitated in placing the house at the highest point and facing west to take full advantage of the open views across Gunville Park and the countryside beyond. The problem was in positioning the gardens; he decided to fix the north–south orientation on the church steeple at Tarrant Hinton, which would be visible from a large mount on the southern boundary. This axis was continued by the avenue of round clumps of trees very reminiscent of Heythrop to the north of the garden.

There are four known garden plans for Eastbury, but only one shows the design for the landscape around the gardens (Figure 11.1). This design must date to around 1718 as it shows the two new octagon towers on the house. The gardens on the east front are composed of formal parterres and wilderness areas and there are two mounts on the north side, and one on the south. The south mount is drawn on a flap of paper overlaying a simpler design, and must have been offered as an option. A canal is situated at the intersection of the two main axes of the design and a second round pond is located at the eastern boundary of the gardens. The landscape appears to have been divided into squares and rectangles, and the geometry is accented by the triangular shape of the stepped groves to the west of the house. It is this plan that provoked Willis's comment that 'even the sight of the deer playing sportively in the fields, cannot compensate for the essential rigidity of

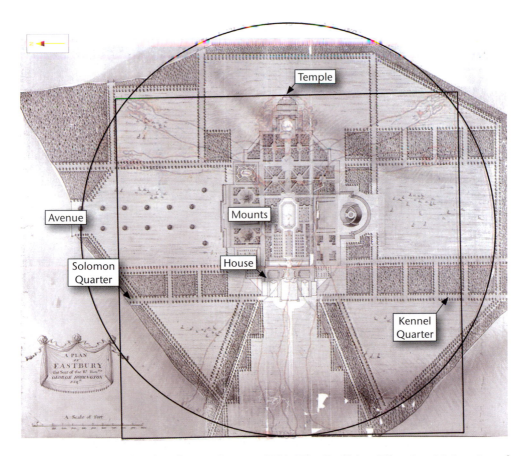

FIGURE 11.1 Landscape plan for Eastbury, *c.* 1718. The Bodleian Libraries, University of Oxford Gough Drawings a.3★ fol. 9. Annotation: author.

the layout', with its implication that straight lines were outmoded by the late 1710s.[4] Even Whistler struggles to categorise Eastbury on the supposed continuum from Art to Nature (Figure 11.2).[5] It is true that the geometry of the layout is more obvious at Eastbury than it is at Castle Howard or at Duncombe, where it underlies an apparently random distribution of garden features, but analysis of the plan uncovers the precise use of the Vitruvian circle and square to create the unusual almost octagonal scheme. All of the elements of the land-scape are in proportion, yet the mathematics are somehow aligned with the complicated

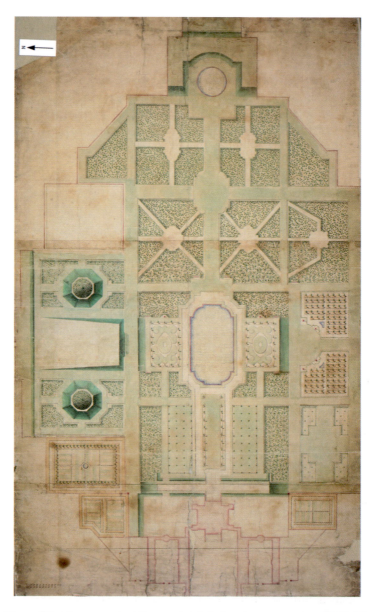

FIGURE 11.2 Plan of Eastbury garden (house in pink, bottom centre), *c.* 1718. The Bodleian Libraries, University of Oxford Gough Drawings a.4 fol. 21.

topography of the site; the positioning of the canal, the round pond, the mounts, the square groves, circular clumps and even the house are all absolutely precise, despite the fact that the land drops away towards the round pond in the east, and the mount to the south. Again, the topography has been incorporated and used to advantage: the garden is opened on the north side by the two mounts, which give views over a high wall, and the avenue of trees pulls the eye towards the hills in the distance. Other designers would have flattened the earth or restricted the design to level ground, and, crucially, they would have enclosed the garden; this garden is open, and the Dorset Downs are part of the scheme. The characteristics of the landscape design are so distinctly Vanbrughian that it must be attributed to him; the grounds for Bridgeman's presence at Eastbury lie only in the draughtsmanship of the landscape plan, and in Campbell's attribution in *Vitruvius Britannicus*, Vol. 3.[6] Bridgeman's role as gardener was nevertheless essential in realising the detail of the garden sections; Eastbury may have been another example of Vanbrugh introducing Bridgeman to his client after he had agreed the commission.

During research for this book an incomplete sketch for the garden at Eastbury was found on the reverse of the 1709 plan of Chargate (Figure 8.1) in Vanbrugh's characteristic rough style. Paper was expensive and often reused, and this suggests that, whilst amending the plans for Claremont in 1717/18, Vanbrugh turned the paper and drew his ideas for the east end of the gardens at Eastbury. The outline of the walls, the round pond and the steps to the temple are clearly visible on this sketch; a second feature is a strong diamond bastion that is apparently related to the dry valley to the south of the gardens (shown by two red lines in Figure 11.3). The diamond bastion is not shown on any other plan but it is still visible today on aerial photographs.[7] The photographs also reveal an extension from this bastion towards the circular grove of trees visible on the 1887 Ordnance Survey but now rooted up. The north and south groves might attest to a later phase of landscaping were they not so obviously linked to the original design; the lack of evidence for the square groves like those still visible in the Kennel and Solomon Quarters on the west side support the theory that the squares were abandoned on the east side and replaced by the bastion and two circular groves. The line leading from the diamond bastion to the south grove appears to have been an elevated walkway similar to Grimes Walk at Grimsthorpe. The Roman road was deliberately preserved and incorporated into this revised scheme. As the 1720s advanced, interest grew in British settlements, but it seems that such relics were not as valued as the Roman at Eastbury: Sir Josiah Banks visiting the site in 1767 recorded somewhat unhappily that part of Chettle Long Barrow on the north-east boundary of the park had been dug up and turned into a grotto.[8]

When George Dodington died in March 1720 it appears that only the offices had been built and that the main part of the house was either not started or at foundation level; Dodington had been living at Eastbury but in the kitchen wing. Work on the gardens would certainly have been under way, but how far it had advanced is unknown. Dodington had no children and had unofficially adopted his young nephew George Bubb after the death of Bubb's father in 1692. Bubb changed his name to George Dodington in 1717, at much the same time as his uncle drew up his will and probably in anticipation of his inheritance of the Dodington estates.[9] Although George Bubb was nearly thirty when his uncle died and the elder man had clearly fostered his career, the strict terms of Dodington's will suggest that he did not trust his nephew to finish the work he had started at Eastbury. Reading the will provides evidence of two things: one is the passion

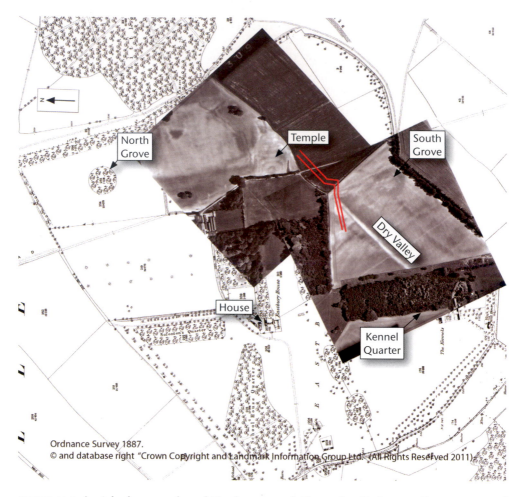

FIGURE 11.3 Aerial photographs of Eastbury overlaid on the Ordnance Survey map of 1887. The red lines mark the feature on the back of the Claremont plan. © Crown Copyright. NMR, 1313/309 ST9312/12 and 13 18 September 1978. Annotation: author.

that Dodington felt for the project he had started so late in his life, the other is a clear belief that Bubb would not complete the building unless other people managed the money. To this end Dodington stipulated that apart from some small annuities the residue of his fortune should be invested by his executors in freehold property in Somerset and Dorset. The income from these purchases was to be used to complete the work at Eastbury for a period of thirty years or until it was finished. The will continues:

> for the better effecting the sayd intentions touching the said buildings and gardens I doe hereby Order that my good friend Sr John Vanbrugh shall direct and order the doeing thereof until the same shall be absolutely compleated in such a manner as I intend the same and of which hee hath been fully informed by my selfe and I order my executors to make him such allowances for his expences and time about the same as they shall think proper'.[10]

This is new evidence that Vanbrugh was managing the project and the design; Bridgeman is not mentioned. Bubb was to be allowed an income from the rents of the Eastbury estate but he effectively had no control over the money under the terms of the will until the building was finished. What he thought of this arrangement can only be guessed but it appears that he immediately tried to overset the will on his uncle's death, as Viscount Cobham (who stood to inherit the property should Bubb have no children) lodged a Chancery Suit to stop him in 1720.[11]

In 1721 the South Sea Bubble burst and must have adversely affected Dodington's legacy. That this was the case is evident from Vanbrugh's letter in 1722 to Lord Carlisle:

> I am now going into Dorsetshire, Mr Dodingtons Trustees having met here in Towne, and adjusted all things for executing the Trust, in regard to the Building, which from this time is to go on without any stop as fast as the Revenue from Southsea has left will allow of, which will be about £1800 a year.[12]

By now Bubb Dodington was an influential politician who had been smart enough to choose the side of Robert Walpole early in the Whig schism of 1717, and he was duly rewarded when Walpole appointed him one of the Lords of the Treasury in 1724. Reputedly an educated man with a deep interest in the classics, he was a patron of Edward Young, James Thomson and other poets. Yet Bubb displayed an eccentricity both in his clothes and his house; Richard Cumberland recorded in his diary an incident when Bubb went to court for the Queen's nuptials:

> he approached to kiss her hand decked in an embroidered suit of silk with lilac waist-coat and breeches, the latter of which, in the act of kneeling down forgot their duty, and broke loose from their moorings in a very indecorous and uncourtly manner.[13]

It seems that he put his clothing to good use in the house: 'round his state bed [Bubb] displayed a carpeting of gold and silver embroidery, which too glaringly betrayed its derivation from coat, waistcoat and breeches by the testimony of pockets, button-holes and loops'.[14] These idiosyncrasies, combined with a tendency to profligacy, may provide an explanation for his uncle's will. It is no wonder that Dodington appointed Vanbrugh to oversee the project at Eastbury, in the expectation that his friend might provide the sense and stability that his heir was clearly lacking. After Vanbrugh's death there were no such restraints, and when Dr Evans visited the house in 1757 he reputedly found a residence 'more like a Royal Palace than a private Gentleman's Country Seat', with rooms 'furnish'd with such a profusion of Expence in gilding &c that they may be call'd rather magnificent than elegant'.[15]

To attract the eye towards the eastern extremity of the garden Vanbrugh had proposed a hexastyle Corinthian 'temple', although this was just a facade; designs for the temple and a bagnio were published with the other plates of Eastbury by Campbell in 1725. Vanbrugh may later have increased the height of the temple over the original design by altering the order to Composite, thus drawing attention to its Roman provenance (Palladio called this order 'Latin'); Thomas Robins's sketch of the 1760s (Figure 11.4) shows the temple approached by a long ramp and two steps reminiscent of the Mount at Claremont.[16] Vanbrugh's aim would have been to create an eye-catcher that would give depth to the

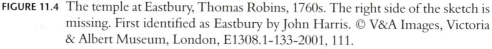

FIGURE 11.4 The temple at Eastbury, Thomas Robins, 1760s. The right side of the sketch is missing. First identified as Eastbury by John Harris. © V&A Images, Victoria & Albert Museum, London, E1308.1-133-2001, 111.

garden in this direction, but it may not have been visible from the east front of the house. Its position in the bottom of the dry valley, although raised on the ramp, suggests that it was deliberately hidden, to be revealed as the visitor started the descent from the parterre and the canal towards the round pond.

Campbell provides the misinformation that the bagnio fronted the bowling green and further confusion is added by Antonio Visentini who painted a bagnio, apparently at Eastbury, in 1746 as part of a set of paintings that Harris believes Bubb Dodington ordered, but never paid for.[17] However, in 1757 Dr Evans recorded that 'the Gardens are not very extraordinary; *nor is there in them any more than one Building* which is a Colonnade or Portico of a Temple facing the Garden Front of the House', and it must be assumed that the bagnio was never built.[18]

In 1723 Vanbrugh finally received the payments for his expenses under the terms of George Dodington's will, which amounted to £700.[19] He spent a month at Eastbury between 1723 and 1725, so work must have been continuing apace on both the house and the gardens.[20] During the long argument with Carlisle over the height of the obelisks on the parterre at Castle Howard, the architect mentioned 'two pretty large' Doric columns at Eastbury that 'succeed[ed] mighty well'.[21] Where the columns were situated is unknown, but these massive ornaments were presumably in keeping with the proportions of the temple. Vanbrugh must have worked on the site up to his death in March 1726, when the shell of the building was apparently complete, according to a comment made by Roger Morris who took over the interior decoration and finished the whole by 1733.[22] A poem by Thomson, written around 1724, indicates that a walk in the gardens could now be enjoyed, although they were not finished. But it is in his description of the view of the Downs and the incorporation of the fields that we find evidence of Vanbrugh's response to Nature:

> Oh lose me in the green delightful walks
> Of, Dodington! Thy seat, serene and plain;
> Where simple nature reigns; and every view;
> Diffusive spreads the pure Dorsetian downs,
> In boundless prospect; yonder shagged with wood,
> Here rich with harvest, and there white with flocks!
> Meanwhile the grandeur of thy lofty dome,
> Far-splendid, seizes on the ravished eye.
> New beauties rise with each revolving day;
> New columns swell; and still fresh Spring finds
> New plants to quicken, and new groves to green.[23]

The landscape at Eastbury was apparently not updated after it was completed, although a painting of the garden front of around 1760 suggests that some simplification had taken place close to the house. In 1756 Jonas Hanway was not impressed with the garden, but he appreciated Vanbrugh's landscape as he wrote:

> the gardens seemed to please you as little as the house. The temple, which stands at the extremity of the lawn, opposite the back front, is indeed heavy; and tho' adorned with the busts of the most celebrated of the antient and modern poets and philosophers, gives no idea of the taste of the founder of it. It must be acknowledged at the same time, that the situation is admirable. The downs and plantations which belong to this house, *take in seven or eight miles in circumference*, and constitute a very pleasing scene.[24]

Bubb Dodington died in 1762 with no immediate heirs, and under the terms of his uncle's will the estate reverted to the Temple family. Richard Grenville, 2nd Earl Temple, found himself saddled with a country estate that he did not need and which was going to be expensive to maintain. Despite offering £200 a year to cover the maintenance of the estate, Temple was unable to persuade anyone to take over the property, and in 1775 work started on the demolition of the house. Both the stables to the north side and part of the kitchens to the south survived until at least 1795 when they featured in a painting, which also shows the outworks to the south of the house (see Figure 4.16). In the nineteenth century the estate was sold to the Wedgwood family and was then purchased in 1807 by John James Farquharson. The Farquharsons still own and farm the estate and, although

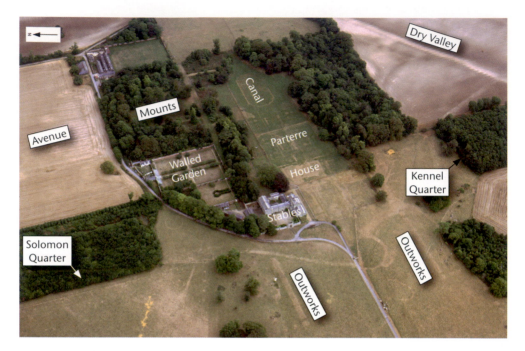

FIGURE 11.5 Oblique aerial photograph showing the outline of the original Eastbury gardens in parch marks. © Crown Copyright. NMR, 15404/10 ST 9312/28 5 September 1995. Annotation: author.

their ancestor intended to redesign the gardens, he did not do so. Today sheep graze the parterres by the canal, the mounts are covered in thick undergrowth and the designed landscape has been veiled by the effects of farming; yet the outline of this important Vanbrugh garden remains in the walls and in the planting, and the detail in parch marks on the ground (Figure 11.5).

12

STOWE, BUCKINGHAMSHIRE

The development of the gardens at Stowe during Vanbrugh's time has been documented in detail by Willis, who draws on both Whistler and the research by George Clarke.[1] A symposium at the Huntington Library in California in 1991 and numerous other articles have discussed the evolution of the landscape.[2] Most of the Stowe archives are now held at the Huntington and this chapter is restricted to a brief history of the landscape and discussion of Vanbrugh's contribution to it. Stowe is the most obviously geometric of the gardens associated with Vanbrugh; although Whistler mentions only the asymmetry of the layout, Clarke was the first to draw attention to the geometry and his analysis was expanded by Steenbergen and Reh in 1996.[3] An evaluation of their work and an alternative explanation for the geometry at Stowe is offered here.

Richard Temple, a soldier and a Whig MP, inherited Stowe in 1697. Temple fought with Marlborough in the War of the Spanish Succession and was promoted to major-general in 1709; but as a Whig he suffered with his fellow members of the Kit Cat Club when Harley took power in 1710. His pro-war stance was a deciding factor in his being cashiered in 1713, soon after Marlborough was dismissed. Like Vanbrugh and Addison, Temple's fortunes were reversed on the accession of George I when he was created Baron Cobham, and his marriage in 1715 resulted in a settlement of £20,000 (£2.6m today), which must have prompted his sudden interest in the house and gardens at Stowe. The house had been rebuilt by his father in 1680 and the gardens were described by Celia Fiennes after a visit in 1694 as a series of terraces 'one below another with low brest walls and Taress walkes . . . beyond it are orchards and woods with rows of trees'.[4] As one of Marlborough's officers and a member of the Kit Cat Club, Cobham's choice of architect for alterations to his house was obvious, but Bridgeman's role remains unclear. Bridgeman may have been at Stowe in 1714 but the evidence is founded on an undated entry in the accounts; the main work began in 1716 when Vanbrugh arrived, after Cobham had received his marriage settlement.[5]

The evolution of the gardens at Stowe is shown in Figure 12.1; in 1716 Cobham started the development of the gardens to the west of the house by laying down the Lime Walk and Nelson's Walk in his father's wilderness. By 1719 Vanbrugh's Nelson's Seat and the

FIGURE 12.1 The evolution of the designed landscape at Stowe. The routes of the original roads and walks are marked in brown. Overlay diagram: author.

Temple of Bacchus were under construction, and work must have started on the alterations to the house. An early account of Stowe by Edward Southwell (of Kings Weston) on 6 August 1724 describes the southern extension to the gardens, now twenty-eight acres 'all in descent'; the three stepped seventeenth-century parterres could still be discerned, but the 'main Parterre is surrounded by an Amphitheatre of Ewe Niches with the Muses etc between them'; an example of Vanbrugh's 'architecture in green'.[6] The statue to the Prince of Wales was forty feet high and the Rotundo with its gilt Venus faced a 'fine canal and amphitheatre of slopes and statues'.[7] It is likely that Southwell visited the estate with Viscount Percival, who gave a more detailed account of the gardens in a letter to his brother-in-law Daniel Dering.[8] Percival's letter is the most complete account of the landscape as Vanbrugh left it:

> The gardens by reason of the good contrivance of the walks, seem to be three times as large as they are. They contain but 28 acres, yet took us up two hours. It is entirely new, and tho' begun but eleven years ago, is now almost finished. From the lower end you ascend a multitude of steps (but at several distances) to the parterre, and from

thence several more to the house, which, standing high, commands a fine prospect. It is impossible to give you an exact Idea of this garden, but we shall shortly have a graving of it. It consists of a number of walks, terminated by summer houses, and heathen Temples of different structure, and adorned with statues cast from the Anticks. Here you see the Temple of Apollo, there a Triumphal Arch. The garden of Venus is delightful: you see her standing in her Temple, at the head of a noble bason of water, and opposite to her an amphitheatre, with statues of Gods and Goddesses; this bason is surrounded with walks and groves, and overlook'd from a considerable height by a tall Column of a Composite order on which stands a statue of Pr: George in his Robes. At the end of the gravel walk leading from the house, are two heathen Temples with a circle of water, 2 acres and a quarter large. In the midst thereof is a Gulio or pyramid, at least 50 foot high, from the top of which it is designed that water shall fall, being by pipes convey'd thro' the heart of it. Half way up this walk is another fine bason, with a pyramid in it 30 foot high, and nearer the house you a meet a fountain that plays 40 foot. The cross walks end in vistos, arches and statues, and the private ones cut thro' groves are delightful. You think twenty times you have no more to see, and of a sudden find yourself in some new garden or walk, as finish'd and adorn'd as that you left. Nothing is more irregular in the whole, nothing more regular in the parts, which totally differ the one from the other. This shows my Lord's good tast, and his fondness for the place appears by the great expense he has been at. We all know how chargeable it is to make a garden with tast; to make one of a sudden more so; but to erect so many Summer houses, Temples, Pillars, Piramids, and Statues, most of fine hewn stone, the rest of guilded lead, would drain the richest purse, and I doubt not but much of his wife's great fortune has been sunk in it. The Pyramid at the end of one of the walks is a copy in mignature of the most famous one in Egypt [Figure 12.2], and the only thing of the kind, I think, in England. Bridgeman laid out the ground and plann'd the whole, which cannot fail of recommending him to business. What adds to the beauty of this garden is that it is not bounded by walls but a Ha-hah which leaves you the sight of the bewtiful woody country, and makes you ignorant how far the high planted walks extend.[9]

A birds-eye view of Stowe in the Bodleian Library of around 1723 is attributed to Bridgeman by Willis (Figure 12.3); its similarity to the plan of Boughton supports this theory.[10] But the authorship of the design is contentious; Percival's observation that 'Bridgeman laid out the ground and plann'd the whole' appears to be substantiated by George Vertue's later comment that the Royal Gardener 'had the direction and disposition of the Gardens'.[11] Bridgeman's authorship is accepted by Willis and Hart but Whistler and Downes contend that both Cobham and Vanbrugh must have been involved in the design process.[12] There are several characteristics of the Stowe layout that suggest Vanbrugh: the plan is clearly geometric, but the main axis through the house is deliberately offset from other axes in the garden and the Rotundo at the centre of this drawing is on the edge of the garden overlooking the Home Park; here, the fields became part of the composition through Vanbrugh's version of the ha-ha. In his statement that 'Nothing is more irregular in the whole, nothing more regular in the parts', Percival deliberately drew attention to the overt geometry of parts of the design that were supported by an underlying geometry. The two mounts, one to the north of the house and one at the southernmost point of the

FIGURE 12.2 *View from the Queen's Statue*, Jacques Rigaud, 1730s (detail). Note the low wall behind the Rotundo that Percival describes as a 'Ha-hah'. The Pyramid is seen top right. © The British Library Board Maps 7.TAB.10, view 15.

estate, the octagon pond with its obelisk spouting water and the careful placing of all of the garden ornaments are all Vanbrughian characteristics. Vanbrugh did not build the original house or define the axes (the Slant Road and Abele Walk) but as he extended the gardens south, down the hill and then back up to the mount on the other side of the valley, he stretched the seventeenth-century design to incorporate the topography of the site. The gentle descent to the octagon pond flanked by two Doric temples suggests Eastbury, and the later extension of the main axis to form the new road to Buckingham, which is so evocative of the approach to Castle Howard, may have originally been Vanbrugh's idea. The contemporary attributions to Bridgeman may be explained by his presence on site, as both gardener and Clerk of Works. If he was building the gardens to Vanbrugh's plans, it is he who would have defined the detail of the sinuous paths in the wildernesses, and directed the labourers as they dug the canals. Further examination of the geometry supports the contention that Vanbrugh was the instigator of the scheme at Stowe.

The following analysis references Sarah Bridgeman's map of 1739, which depicts the completed Vanbrugh/Bridgeman/Kent scheme.[13] In the 1720s the scope for expansion of the Stowe gardens was restricted on the east side of the house by the church and the Hay Way, a public road from Buckingham, and by a Roman road to the north. The designed landscape was therefore extended only to the south and west of the Abele Walk, surrounding the fields in the Home Park. Figure 12.4 shows the underlying grid in 1726;

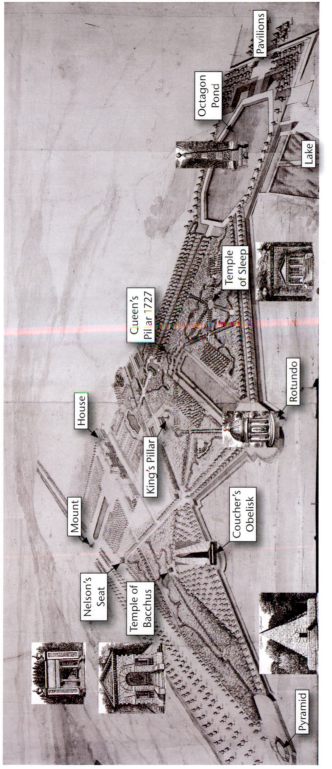

FIGURE 12.3 The landscape at Stowe as Vanbrugh left it, c. 1726. The buildings were all designed by Vanbrugh including the Queen's Pillar, although this was not erected until 1727. The Bodleian Libraries, University of Oxford Gough Drawings a.4 fol. 46. Annotation: author.

it is composed of three nested isosceles triangles with an equilateral triangle (light blue) defining the centre of the design; all of the elements are connected with the exception of Nelson's Seat, which is aligned with the Roman road. In his study Clarke has exposed the continuance of the geometry at Stowe after Vanbrugh's death, but excluding additions after 1726 on the Bridgeman plan helps to identify Vanbrugh's influence. Again, sight lines or obvious paths along existing roads would not necessarily be elements of Vanbrugh's methodology; his intention was to join things that were not visually linked *in* the landscape together in a two-dimensional plan. Like Clarke, Steenbergen and Reh also focus on the roads and assert that *'Bridgeman's* design matrix mediated between the house and the topography [at Stowe]'.[14] In their consideration of the geometry they propose a square grid, but the grid does not link the elements of the design and nothing is

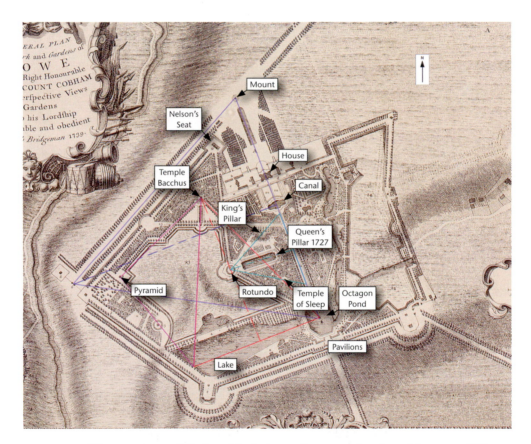

FIGURE 12.4 The geometry of Vanbrugh's design at Stowe can be viewed in many different ways; this is one of them. The design is composed of three isosceles triangles (red, pink, dark blue) that join all of the elements, with the exception of Nelson's Seat. The Rotundo divides the altitude of the red triangle in half and is the focal point for the equilateral light blue triangle that joins it to the Temple of Sleep and the King's Pillar. The Canal divides the blue line from the Mount to the Octagon Pond in half. Other Vitruvian proportions exist. © The British Library Board Maps 7.TAB.10 (detail). Annotation: author.

proportional; the real meaning of mathematics in the Enlightenment designed landscape is lost in their analysis.

The da Vinci figure is left out of the drawing for the sake of clarity, but could be placed in several different positions to expose the many Vitruvian proportions of the scheme. What is interesting is that this exercise implies that Vanbrugh not only devised the scheme depicted in Figure 12.3, but also was responsible for the overall shape of the designed landscape seen in the Bridgeman engraving of 1739. It is quite possible that this was the case, as Cobham would have been anxious to balance his garden on the east side of the Abele Walk and may always have intended to move the public road, the Hay Way. The bastions and the hexagonal form of the finished garden provide supporting evidence for this theory. Consideration of Kent's work on the gardens (Figure 12.5) shows that far from escaping the design matrix the additions of the 1730s simply amplified the existing underlying geometry. Kent used isosceles triangles to connect his new elements such as the Temple of Ancient Virtue, Congreve's Monument and the Shepherd's Cave to existing Vanbrugh buildings such as the Rotundo and the Temple of Sleep. James Gibb's Temple

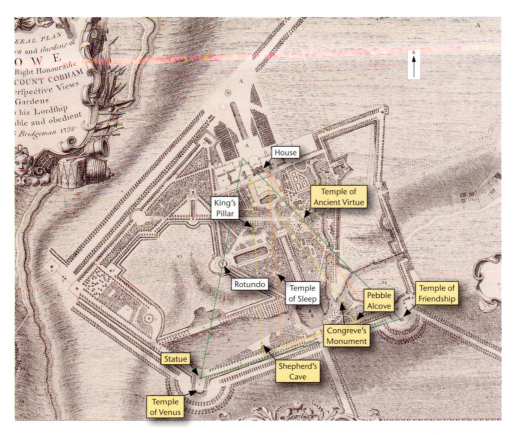

FIGURE 12.5 The geometry of the additions at Stowe. Kent used a similar methodology to Vanbrugh and joined his new elements to Vanbrugh's scheme using isosceles triangles. © The British Library Board Maps 7.TAB.10 (detail). Annotation: author.

of Friendship completed the ornamentation of the two south bastions but it was also connected to the geometry, as was the Gibbs building (marked 5 in Figure 12.4), which clearly sits on Vanbrugh's triangle joining the Pyramid, the Temple of Bacchus and the centre of the termination of the lake.

Benton Seeley's map of 1744 indicates a number of significant changes in the five years after the Bridgeman map was published. Brown was employed at Stowe from 1741 and he was responsible for the extension to the north-east, which included the Grecian Valley. Other alterations included the removal of the parterre and canal and the softening of the outline of the lake. However, Vanbrugh's hexagonal outline and bastions were retained on the south side of the gardens, and the planting seen in modern aerial photographs still alludes to the geometry of the eighteenth century. In July 1725 Vanbrugh wrote to Tonson that he and his wife had been at Stowe for over a fortnight, accompanied by Lord Carlisle and his family: 'a Place now, so Agreeable, that I had much ado to leave it at all'.[15] It was to be his last visit; after he died the following March Lord Cobham inscribed the Pyramid with the following words: 'Among the great number of buildings designed by Sir John Vanbrugh in these gardens, Cobham wished this Pyramid to be sacred to his memory'.[16]

13
SEATON DELAVAL, NORTHUMBERLAND

In October 1710 Swift wrote to Esther Johnson that he had dined at George Delaval's house in London with 'Vanbrug' and Sir Richard Temple.[1] Delaval made his fortune as a diplomat and was an admiral in the navy when he purchased the estate at Seaton Delaval from his impoverished cousin in 1718.[2] That year he told his brother: 'I intend to persuade Sir John Vanbrugh to see Seaton if possible and give me a plan of the house . . . [he] built Castle Howard, and it is from hence I hope to carry him'.[3] Delaval was successful, but Vanbrugh felt unable to modify the Jacobean mansion at Seaton and he proposed building a new house; the work started almost immediately. In October 1719 the Clerk of Works, James Mewburn, wrote to Admiral Delaval that 'the way from the quarry to the house was never so good this summer', and in 1720 the masons were paid just over £426 for 'pulling down Seaton Old House as well as building [the] new Mansion House'.[4] The following year Vanbrugh spent three weeks at Lumley and Seaton: 'since it is not easy, to go there often, I resolv'd to do all the Service I cou'd while I was there now', and he was pleased to find that the Admiral was 'not being dispos'd to starve the Design at all. So that he is like to have, a very fine Dwelling'.[5] On several of his visits the architect was accompanied by William Etty, the Clerk of Works at Castle Howard, who appears to have taken a supervisory role of the work at Seaton in Vanbrugh's absence. It is clear from Mewburn's regular reports to the Admiral that Etty's presence was resented: 'Mr Etty takes the Ordering and Managing of the Draines for himself', he wrote in 1720; however, he felt obliged to point out that they had been 'well advanced *before* [Etty] came to Seaton'.[6]

One evening in June 1723 the Admiral was surveying his new grounds when he was thrown from his horse and killed. His heir was his nephew Captain Francis Delaval who had little interest in the building project that he had inherited; he immediately instructed Mewburn to cover the house and 'do no more than is necessary to preserve what has already been done'.[7] It appears, however, that Delaval's concerns were mostly financial, as his marriage in 1724 to a Herefordshire heiress resulted in the swift resumption of the building work. Vanbrugh was there again with Etty in 1724, when he 'laid in his claim for the fruit at Seaton'; the house was built but undecorated when he died in 1726.[8]

The gardens were constructed in parallel with the house. In November 1720 the 'wherrymen' were paid five shillings to transport 1,200 trees from the ships at Hartley (Seaton Sluice) to the estate, where the gardener John Telford was responsible for planting them along the long avenue that gave access to the estate from the west.[9] Mewburn was concerned that Telford had procured, and planted, 'dead' trees, but was relieved to be able to report to the Admiral that after inspection 'there was only three dead trees in all that west avenue'.[10] The avenue stretched a mile and a quarter from the edge of the estate to the house; two pillars in Vanbrugh's style originally marked the gateway to the estate but were demolished in the twentieth century as the village of Seaton Delaval expanded. The garden was encompassed by a ha-ha wall and ditch and four huge bastions, all of which survive in various states of decay (Figure 13.1); a line of outworks stretched towards the sea to the east. All of this is extant, making Seaton Delaval the most complete example of Vanbrugh's landscape architecture in the country. The kitchen garden remains mostly intact to the north-east of the house, with a grand orangery that appears to be Vanbrugh's work on the north wall. Interestingly, the Church of Our Lady, built by Hubert de la Val in the twelfth century, survives in the vestiges of Vanbrugh's garden. It had originally stood beside the old manor house, and was retained within the new design as the family chapel, hidden in the wilderness. After it became the parish church in 1891, the woodland garden became the resting place for the villagers of Hartley, and now the graves encroach on Vanbrugh's south-west bastion.

The earliest map showing the garden is the recently recovered estate plan of 1808; it depicts the south front of the house facing an open lawn flanked by two areas of designed woodland. Lady Amherst described the prospect from the garden front windows in the

FIGURE 13.1 The north-west bastion on Vanbrugh's garden at Seaton Delaval. Photo: author, 2008.

1760s: 'bordered alleys and pleached walls abound. Pools for lilies and carp entrance the eye'.[11] A visitor in 1778 provides more detail:

> Here are several walks disposed with great taste, some of which are shaded as well by lofty old trees as plantations, through which various vistas are cut, some of them being terminated by elegant stone buildings, and others opening in delightful prospects to the sea towards the east, greatly heightened by ships which are frequently sailing in sight of the windows: to the south there is a fine view over a verdant lawn to another bay of the sea, where frequently 150 sail of colliers may be seen, and enriched with the fine ruin of Tynemouth Priory . . . to the north a view of a great part of Northumberland . . . terminated by the august mountains of Cheviot.[12]

Vanbrugh had oriented the house exactly, to take advantage of the fine views of the sea in two directions and the Cheviots to the north. The sails of the ships and the ruins of Tynemouth Priory pulled the eye out over the ha-ha, and a vast expanse of the county became a part of the garden. Within the bastioned walls a simple grass parterre was flanked by two wildernesses with straight paths and controlled vistas, a simplified version of the geometry of the Blenheim Woodwork; the paths are clearly visible in parch marks on an aerial photograph of 1954.

This was Vanbrugh's last and most obviously Palladian composition, evident in both the structure of the house and its setting (Figure 13.2). The rooms are arranged

FIGURE 13.2 The south front of Seaton Delaval. Photo: author, 2008.

symmetrically about a central axis that runs through the house, linking it to the Cheviots in the north and Tynemouth in the south. The original house was small, consisting of only four rooms on the ground floor, and Vanbrugh built two oval staircases in side towers, following Palladio's advice that they should be used in 'restricted locations because they take up less space'; the similarity between the stair at Seaton and Palladio's oval staircase at the Monastery of the Carità in Venice is striking.[13] The central hall was a square of twenty-five feet, thirty feet high, and was decorated with six life-size statues representing science and the arts, some of which are extant, despite the ravages of a fire in 1822.[14] The statues were an allusion to the taste and learning of the Delavals, but their positioning in niches was a Palladian device, documented in the *Quattro Libri* and used in the Palazzo Thiene in Vicenza.[15] The view from the Ionic portico on the south front was carefully framed by the doors of the hall and the salon beyond it, and the south obelisk in the fields beyond the garden is centred in the picture (Figure 13.3). Seaton Delaval is embedded in its landscape and is the most evocative of Palladio's location of the Villa Emo at Fanzolo.

The south obelisk is one of a pair with the obelisk on the avenue, and there is a legend that one marks the spot where the Admiral fell from his horse and the other the spot to which he was dragged.[16] Only the pedestal of the avenue obelisk remains, but they were important enough to be marked on a county map of 1828, along with a third to the east of the house. The cartographer Greenwood made a mistake here; the third 'obelisk' to the east was in fact the mausoleum, built in 1776 to commemorate John Delaval, Sir Francis's nephew and the only male heir to the estate, who died after an altercation with a kitchen maid to whom he was 'paying his attentions'.[17] With its pedimented Doric portico and cupola, the mausoleum was of classical design but was 'enclosed by a ha-ha wall of 11 feet high and 5 feet thick, so wrought and put together as to have a rocky appearance, giving

FIGURE 13.3 The framed view of the south obelisk through the pillars on the south front of Seaton Delaval. Photo: author, 2008.

the idea of long duration'.[18] The building is now ruined but its situation on what appears to have been a round bastion at the end of Vanbrugh's outworks is suggestive. Vanbrugh was discussing mausoleums with Carlisle and the Duchess of Marlborough during the time that he was building Seaton Delaval, and it is possible that he proposed such a building on this spot. Greenwood's mistake in 1828 may have been caused by an earlier obelisk on the location where the mausoleum was later constructed; further evaluation of this late Vanbrugh landscape supports this theory.

As with all of Vanbrugh's projects the obviously geometric garden immediately surrounding the house contrasts with the apparently dislocated landscape that he constructed around it. The avenue is not perpendicular to the axis that runs through the house and at first sight the mausoleum has no relation to the design. The underlying Vitruvian grid for the Seaton Delaval landscape is shown in Figure 13.4; evidently the positioning of the obelisks and the mausoleum was no accident. The scheme was strictly proportional; three isosceles triangles define the locations of the obelisks, the mausoleum, the Egg Pond and even the central path of the kitchen garden. As the avenue was planted three years before the Admiral's death, the proportions of the design must already have been defined. The obelisk in the avenue may have been built near the point where the Admiral fell from

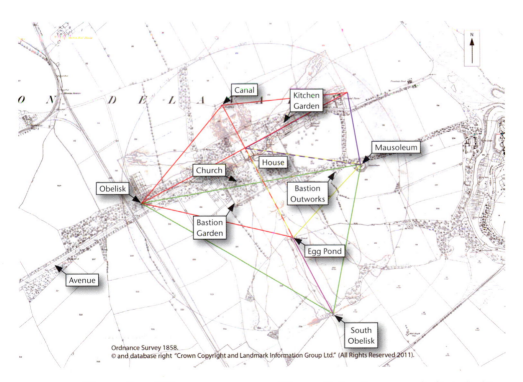

FIGURE 13.4 The perfected Vitruvian geometry of Seaton Delaval composed of interlocking isosceles triangles that tie all of the elements together. The ha-ha at the southern boundary of the garden divides the central pink axis 2:3; the Avenue is 1.5 times the length of this axis. The Mausoleum is an intrinsic part of this design and must have been part of the original plan for the landscape. Overlay diagram: author.

his horse, but it is unlikely that he would have fallen so conveniently as to fit in with the existing geometry of the plan, or that he would have then been dragged to the precise location of the obelisk to the south of the house. This exercise has proved not only that Vanbrugh must have placed a third obelisk where the mausoleum would be, but that the use of proportion continued to be a fundamental characteristic of his landscape architecture throughout his career.

In the 1770s Sir John Delaval added a six-bay extension to the south-east corner of Vanbrugh's building, with a terminating square tower.[19] Although late eighteenth-century paintings show a matching west wing extension it is still unclear whether this wing was only intended or was actually built; at the time of writing geo-physical examination of the site is about to start. A catastrophic fire in 1822 destroyed the new east wing and the central block, and repairs were wiped out by a second fire in 1860 that left the house without a roof; it was subsequently open to the weather for many years. Thus, the later additions have been removed, and now Vanbrugh's nearest approximation to a Palladian villa stands in its original form with its fortified gardens and outworks, embedded in the Northumbrian countryside. It was saved for the nation by the National Trust in 2010.

14

GREENWICH AND LUMLEY CASTLE

Greenwich, London

On 3 March 1718 Vanbrugh signed the lease for a plot of land in Greenwich, with the intention of building a new house to his own design.[1] He was already Surveyor of Greenwich Hospital and had been leasing a property in the area for two years. In 1717 Vanbrugh mentions that he is 'going for a day or two's breath to Greenwich which I stand cruelly in need of', suggesting that the smog in the city must have aggravated his recurrent asthma.[2] Vanbrugh's letters attest to his spending much of the summer of 1718 at Greenwich, when he was overseeing the building of his 'castle'; it was completed in time for the architect and his new wife to take up residence in the spring of 1720. Situated on a hill south of the Thames, the estate at Greenwich offered not only clean air; the views across the city from the summit of Maze Hill, the proximity of Greenwich Park and the nearby Roman entrenchments would also have appealed to Vanbrugh. Vanbrugh Castle was oriented south-east like most of Vanbrugh's buildings, with views across the Blackheath on the south front. It was enclosed by walls and had several outbuildings; a plan in the library at Elton Hall shows the deliberate symmetry of the original Castle, and pencil alterations to the south-west wall suggest that a diamond bastion and a round tower were proposed. Stukeley's early sketch of 1721 depicts a massive gateway flanked by two square towers and substantial castellated outworks, which remained into the nineteenth century, although an engraving of 1798 of the 'Bastile-House', as it was then known, shows that the crenellations had been removed. All of these drawings indicate that the Castle may have originally been plastered and painted white to cover the brick-work, which is now exposed. Soon after the birth of his son Charles, Vanbrugh extended the Castle to the east, adding a tower which, at roof height, had an arched opening that framed the view from the roof terrace; an exact copy of the four 'windows' on the roof of the Mount at Claremont.

In addition to the land on which he built the Castle, Vanbrugh also leased a twelve-acre field immediately to the south of it, and he started construction here in 1719. The first building to be completed was called the Nunnery, and this was occupied by Vanbrugh's brother Philip from the end of 1720.[3] A second house on the north-east corner of the field was rented to another brother, Charles. Vanbrugh House had two round towers with strong rustication, and was labelled in a drawing by Stukeley, *Castellulum Vanbrughiense*, 'little Vanbrugh castle'.[4] Two white towers were to follow, one for each of Vanbrugh's sons, Charles and John; in a letter to Carlisle of 1722 Vanbrugh mentions that Charles 'is much pleas'd with a house I am building him in the field at Greenwich, it being a tower of white bricks only one room and a closet on a floor'.[5] The 'estate', which Whistler believes was modelled on Lord Dartmouth's buildings on the other side of the Heath, was approached through a gateway between two square towers that suggest the entrance to a Roman fort.[6] Rocque's map of London of 1745 gives some indication of the layout (Figure 14.1). Whilst 'Vanbrugh's Field' is bordered by hedges, the outworks around Vanbrugh Castle are evident; within the enclosure some rectangular beds front the house and the area to the east of the house appears to be a kitchen garden. Vanbrugh House, the Nunnery and the two white towers are all arranged on the east boundary facing into the heathland of Vanbrugh Fields; beyond that is Greenwich Park and the River Thames. It is difficult to see any overall plan here apart from the orientation of the buildings to make the most of the rural outlook; an obvious decision for a man who would have appreciated the prospect of the Thames and the fields and hills beyond.

Lumley Castle, County Durham

In August 1721 Vanbrugh wrote to Brigadier Watkins that he had just returned from Lumley Castle, which was

> a Noble thing; and well deserves the Favours Lord Lumley designs to bestow upon it; In order to which I stay'd there near a Week, to form a General Design for the whole, Which consists, in altering the House both for State, Beauty and Convenience, And making the Courts Gardens and Offices suitable to it; All of which I believe may be done, for a Sum, that can never ly very heavy upon the Family.[7]

This is Vanbrugh's most obvious reference to Vitruvius's words on Order, Eurythmy and Economy in building, which must also take into account the 'thrifty balancing of cost and common sense in the construction of the works'.[8]

Lumley Castle was the seat of the 1st Earl of Scarbrough, but the Earl died in December 1721 and it appears that Vanbrugh's reference to 'Lord Lumley' is to his son and heir, Richard. Richard Lumley was a Whig politician and a soldier, who fought against the Jacobites at Preston in 1715; he was also a member of the Kit Cat Club and would naturally have chosen Vanbrugh, who was working at Seaton Delaval at the same time, to be his architect. Vanbrugh was to re-face the west and south fronts of the house and to build the Great Hall, an example of the Palladian double cube that he had wanted to build at Kimbolton.[9] The new hall, on the west front, was designed as an entertainment room similar to Newcastle's room at Claremont, and was approached by a grand double staircase and circular driveway with a central obelisk. This ceremonial entrance to the castle replaced the east front, which had a narrow entrance bounded by a curtain wall and the steep drop into the valley of Lumley Beck (Figure 14.2).

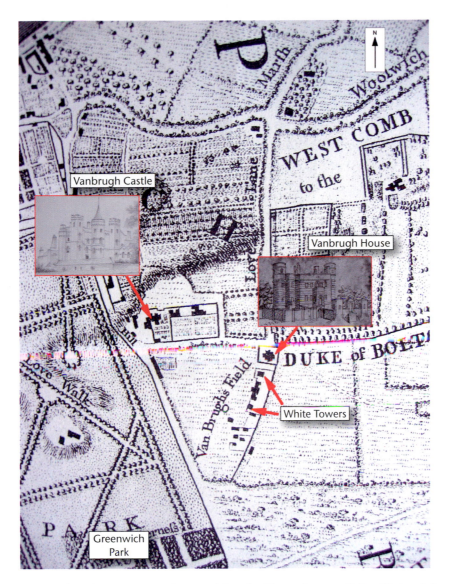

FIGURE 14.1 Vanbrugh's estate at Greenwich. *An Exact Survey of the City's of London Westminster, ye Borough of Southwark and the Country Near Ten Miles Round*, John Rocque, 1746. © The British Library Board CRACE PORT XIX 18. Annotation: author.

Vanbrugh's letter is evidence that he was also to make alterations to the gardens at Lumley, and this was to be one of his most interesting and innovative commissions. It was a project of two halves: the west front of the house faced a gentle decline across fields to the River Wear, the east front towered above the heavily wooded Lumley Beck. A surviving plan in the archive at Sandbeck Park shows the proposed design (Figure 14.3), and is attributed to Bridgeman by Willis, although there is no substantiating evidence.[10] Whistler

FIGURE 14.2 The east front of Lumley Castle, nineteenth century. © The British Library
Board Online Gallery, Add. 42016 f24.

struggles with the authorship of the Lumley gardens, suggesting that Switzer may have
been involved, although Brogden does not support this contention.[11] The Sandbeck plan
depicts a combination of straight lines and winding paths in the Beck valley, with a geometric grove or orchard to the north, an amphitheatre in the centre and a circular grove,
possibly a fruit garden, on the south boundary. This is a woodland garden, and a terrace
walk, as high as the castle on the opposite side of the valley, is punctuated with statues, its
path mirroring the profile of the river below it. The plan gives no clue as to the difficulty
of the site, but a visit to Lumley proves that the design was entirely sympathetic with the
topography, and that it utilised the relatively level ground adjacent to the river meanders
as sites for the three key elements of the scheme.

Whilst the valley comprised a hidden woodland garden, a grand design that involved
damming the River Wear was devised for the west front of the castle. A central axis
focused on one of the statues on the terrace walk; it bisected the castle and formed the
avenue, which was terminated by a large pond in the Wear valley. An unusually shaped
lawn was flanked by a double avenue of trees and two areas of designed woodland with
grass cabinets and sinuous walks. A glance at the plan for Lumley gives no hint of geometry in the valley garden, although there is some allusion to it in the landscape to the
west, but analysis uncovers the underlying framework of a typical Vanbrughian outline.
This, in conjunction with Vanbrugh's letter, suggests that the architect did indeed make

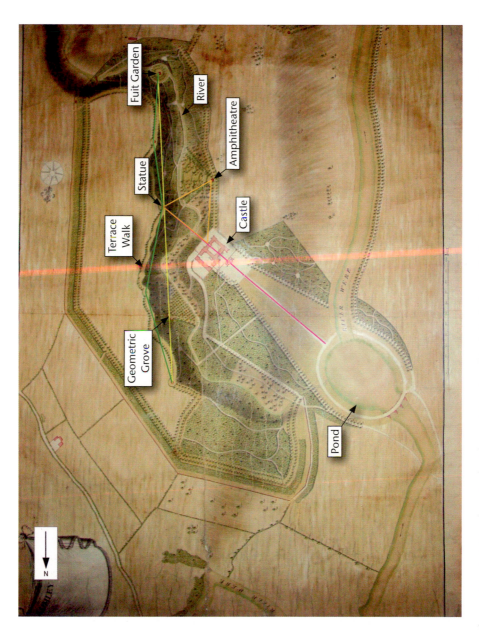

FIGURE 14.3 The geometry at Lumley Castle. Plan *c.* 1721, Sandbeck Park Archive, by kind permission of the Earl of Scarbrough. Annotation: author.

the landscape at Lumley suitable to the Vitruvian proportions of the house. There is no record of the gardeners at Lumley and it must be assumed that local men helped to build the garden according to Vanbrugh's plan.

There is contemporary evidence that the landscape was constructed according to the Sandbeck plan; a drawing by Samuel and Nathaniel Buck of 1728 is annotated: 'stands in a beautiful park on the side of a rising hill curiously planted with trees, at the bottom of wch runs ye River Were, affording a delightful prospect to its pleasant situation'.[12] An engraving of 1779 shows rowing boats on the pond to the west of the castle, and in 1834 the avenue still had its 'fine bason of water'.[13] The path of the terrace walk and the boundary line of trees are shown on the Ordnance Survey map of 1859, and the nursery below the Garden House is clearly the remnant of the geometric grove, but the amphitheatre and the fruit garden are not depicted.

The valley path of the early eighteenth century remains today as part of the Weardale Way, and a site visit in 2008 has proved the remainder of the valley gardens: the steps of the amphitheatre can just be seen amongst the trees next to Lamb's Bridge and the site of the fruit garden is distinguishable on the river meander, although overgrown. Two yew hedges flank the path alongside the river and are old enough to be the remnants of the eighteenth-century gardens. Today, Lumley Castle is a hotel and the grounds have been turned into a golf course. Vanbrugh's west front overlooks the county cricket ground and the large pond has disappeared, but the remains of a lost garden still lie in the valley of Lumley Beck. Walkers on the Weardale Way are unaware that they are following a path through an eighteenth-century garden; another of Vanbrugh's wonderfully empathetic designed landscapes that is neglected and forgotten.

15

VANBRUGH'S LEGACY

Charles Bridgeman and the Vitruvian landscape

Hard evidence of Bridgeman's work as a designer is limited in the period up to 1720 and review of Willis's catalogue of 'Bridgemannic' drawings reveals few proven commissions before then.[1] Willis does note payments to Bridgeman for work at Langleys in Essex in 1719, but his book generally supports the theory that Bridgeman was with Vanbrugh during the 1710s, and was not at that time a well-known designer in his own right. There does, however, appear to have been a radical shift from around 1720, when Bridgeman was established in the coterie of 'Artists or men of superior skill' on the Marylebone Estate, a group that included Gibbs, Thornhill, Prior and Pope.[2] It must have been through these men that Bridgeman gained the commission from Edward Harley, 2nd Earl of Oxford, at Wimpole Hall. Harley had married the daughter of the 1st Duke of Newcastle (uncle of the owner of Claremont) and he was making alterations to the house and gardens he had inherited through his wife. The architect James Gibbs started redesigning the house in 1713; by the 1720s Thornhill was painting the chapel, whilst Gibbs was building summerhouses for the bowling green, and Bridgeman was creating the avenue on the south front. The commission at Wimpole was relatively small, but it does mark the start of Bridgeman's career as an independent gardener and designer without Vanbrugh. The garden at Wimpole is an early example of Bridgeman's use of the sinuous paths that he was to make immensely fashionable during the 1720s, but there are sufficient similarities here to the styles of Grimsthorpe, Eastbury or Duncombe to suggest that he was implementing Vanbrugh's ideas in his own commission. There is little obvious sympathy for the topography of the site, however, and the new avenue that cuts south from the house for over two miles was a bold seventeenth-century statement of Harley's power and status.

Down Hall, Essex

How much influence Gibbs would have had on Bridgeman's design for Wimpole is unknown, but the architect must have been involved in discussions of walls, bastions and garden buildings, taking part of the role that Vanbrugh played in Bridgeman's previous projects. Gibbs was also employed with Bridgeman by the poet and ex-Kit Cat Matthew

Prior, at Down Hall in Essex, where the two men were to design a new house and garden. In 1720 Prior wrote *The Ballad of Down Hall* describing his first visit to the property with his agent John Morley, where he found a 'low, ruin'd white Shed' that was 'until'd and unglaz'd'.[3] Although Prior may have exaggerated the state of the house, he was evidently frustrated by the layout of it, telling Harley in a letter that 'all the cross unmathematical devils on earth first put it together'.[4] By September he had a design: 'Gibbs has built me a house . . . I am going to sup with Dhayl, Wooten and Gibbs . . . to talk of buildings, pictures and maybe . . . politics or religion'.[5] Bridgeman was more elusive than Gibbs; he was working at Wimpole, Stowe and on other commissions, but he was already fashionable enough for Prior to be prepared to wait: 'I shall have a virtuoso grand jardinière to meet me at Down in four or five days; the precise time himself does not know and I must wait for it'.[6] Prior must have met Bridgeman on a visit to Wimpole soon afterwards, and persuaded him to accompany him back to Down, for he wrote to Harley in early October that they had 'talked of nothing but canals, parades and vistas from Wimpole to this place'.[7]

Bridgeman produced two plans for Down, one with and one without his characteristic sinuous paths. Both were designed around Gibbs's new house, which was to be to the west of the existing building, with the entrance front facing south. To the north of the house a wood sloped down towards Pincey Brook, and it was here that Bridgeman was going to construct the new garden (Figure 15.1). On this plan the house is seen flanked by two kitchen gardens, and is cut by a central axis leading from an octagonal pond fed by the brook in the north to Gibbs's new forecourt in the south. A diagonal path off the central axis is terminated by a 'large bason of water and lawne for water fowle', possibly a copy of Harley's duckery at Wimpole; two further ponds, one round and one square, complete the relatively simple design. Prior intended to decorate his woodland garden with references to classical Rome, and he wrote to Harley in 1721 that he loved Down 'more than Tully did his Tusculum, or Horace his Sabine field'.[8]

The positioning of the Jacobean house at Down suggests that any formal seventeenth-century gardens would have been directly to the west of the house, although the condition of the building implies that these may have been derelict. Down is therefore an early example of Bridgeman designing a new garden in pre-existing woodland. The outline is small and not equivalent to Vanbrugh's vast designed landscapes, but it hints at geometry and it is in fact based on nested isosceles triangles with the proportion 2:3 being evident in the scheme. In 1720 Prior wrote to Harley: 'we have laid out squares, rounds and diagonals, and planted quincunxes at Down'.[9] Pincey Brook was clearly to be controlled by geometry, as was the octagonal Great Bason, but in the concession to topography in the gentle decline to the Bason and river on the north boundary Down exhibited characteristics that must have been the result of Vanbrugh's influence during their years of association in the 1710s.

Work in the garden started in 1720, and continued into the following year. A letter to Harley in 1721 indicates that Prior was now intending to renovate his existing house, rather than build to Gibbs's plan, suggesting that he was already in financial difficulties.[10] Prior was not to see the gardens at Down completed; he died of consumption on a visit to Wimpole in August 1721. He had never married, and the purchase of Down Hall with Harley's assistance had been on the understanding that the estate would revert to Harley on Prior's death. Harley's accounts show that Bridgeman continued to be paid for work

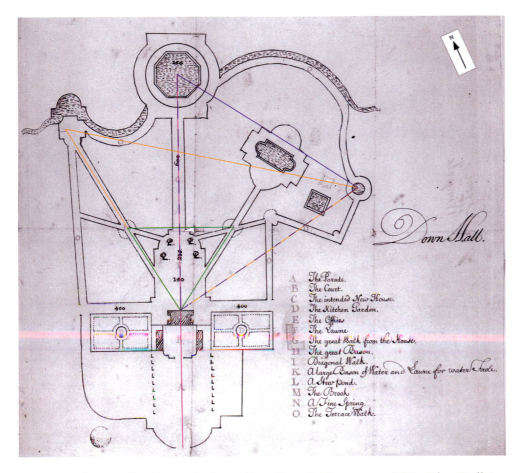

A   *The Parade.*
B   *The Court.*
C   *The intended New House.*
D   *The Kitchen Garden.*
E   *The Offices*
F   *The Lawne*
G   *The great Walk from the House.*
H   *The great Bason.*
I.   *Diagonal Walk.*
K   *A large Bason of Water and Lawne for water Fowle.*
L   *A Stew Pond.*
M   *The Brook.*
N   *A Fine Spring.*
O.   *The Terrace Walk.*

FIGURE 15.1 Design for Down Hall, attributed to Bridgeman, *c.* 1720. The Bodleian Libraries, University of Oxford Gough Maps 46, fol. 262. Annotation: author.

at Down until 1725,[11] but a revised plan in the Gough Collection indicates that the final scheme was further simplified to accommodate the old house once Gibbs's design had been abandoned. Interestingly, this plan shows the addition of two round bastions connected by a terrace walk on the west side of the gardens. The overall layout of the plan corresponds with the evidence of the 1874 Ordnance Survey map, which indicates that the diagonal axes to the canal and the round spring were built, as was one of the bastions. A site visit proves that Bridgeman's garden remains in the wood to the north of Down Hall, which is now a country house hotel. The diagonal avenues are extant, but the statue and obelisk that decorated them have now gone. A temple, almost certainly by Gibbs, is still at the north end of the canal (Figure 15.2) and the west terrace is intact, although covered with moss, nettles and blackberries. An overgrown arch of yew is evidence that the avenue running east from the canal towards the spring was once lined with hedges. A hidden garden, it is fenced off and overgrown, but the design is much as it was when Bridgeman and Gibbs laid it out nearly 300 years ago.

FIGURE 15.2 The canal and the temple in Bridgeman's forgotten garden at Down Hall. Photo: author, 2006.

Hackwood (Spring Wood), Hampshire

Wimpole and Down Hall were the beginning of the partnership of Bridgeman and Gibbs as gardener and architect that was to last into the 1730s. It is notable that, whilst Vanbrugh was working at Lumley Castle and Seaton Delaval with local gardeners and project managers, Bridgeman was with Gibbs at Down, Kedleston Hall in Derbyshire and Hackwood in Hampshire. As landscape architecture succeeded gardening, neither Bridgeman nor Vanbrugh could work without the skills of the other, but it appears that Bridgeman may have deliberately broken away from Vanbrugh's control in the 1720s to forge his own career; his association with Gibbs was necessary for him to be able to do this. Gibbs was employed at Hackwood by the Duke of Bolton in the 1720s and the design of the garden is attributed to Bridgeman by Willis, on the basis of a plan in the Gough Collection.[12] Bolton commissioned Bridgeman to change the star rides in the ancient hunting park of Spring Wood into a garden, and close inspection of a map of the park of *circa* 1720 reveals the designer's pencil marks, as he takes the original shape of the woodland and imposes a strict geometry of canals and bastions on the east boundary. The finished design (Figure 15.3) shows that an amphitheatre and diamond-shaped orchard have been cut out from the original woodland; the sinuous paths still display their geometrical foundations. Spring Wood was a woodland garden with grass cabinets; it was delimited by a raised terrace walk and bastions on the east boundary that suggest Vanbrugh's style.[13]

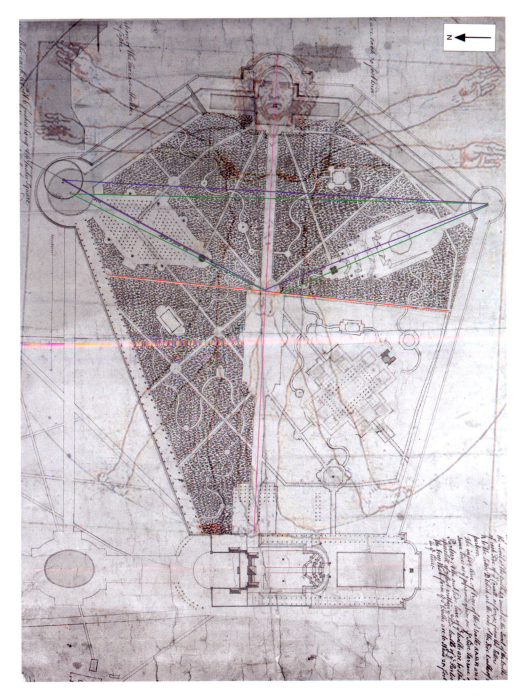

FIGURE 15.3 The Vitruvian layout at Spring Wood (Hackwood), attributed to Bridgeman,
c. 1725. The red and pink lines mark the route of old paths from the original
hunting park that have been incorporated into the new scheme. The Bodleian
Libraries, University of Oxford Gough Drawings a.4, fol. 234.

Overlay of da Vinci's figure (shown here in one of several possible positions) indicates that the canals on the east boundary were deliberately sized to create a Vitruvian garden along the pre-existing central axis of the hunting park. Old and new orientation lines meet at the point where the garden is divided into two and the width of the gardens at the bastions is exactly equal to the length. Even the proposed alteration to the position of the round pond on the north side is kept in proportion with the original design (blue triangle). Such precise geometry could not have been a coincidence and it indicates that proportion was important, even where Bridgeman was altering a pre-existing landscape.

The garden at Spring Wood is extant, and although it has suffered from years of neglect and from the ravages of the 1987 storm, it is now being renovated. It is not possible to gain access to the grounds, but a tour of the boundary reveals the low walls around the amphitheatre, the elevated walkway next to the canal and the south-east bastion enclosing a mount; the countryside merges seamlessly with the garden. Although the gardens at Down and Spring Wood owe much to Vanbrugh in geometry and form, Vanbrugh's 'idea of the beauty of natural gardening' is missing; despite their proportional grid, Bridgeman's early plans are all contiguous and clearly bordered, with each section carefully organised and controlled.[14] At Castle Howard, Stowe and Eastbury, fragments of the agricultural components of the estate were included in the design of the landscape, so grazing animals or fields of crops became part of the composition. Vanbrugh relied on his underlying grid to pull together the beauties of Nature, but Bridgeman does not appear to have had the courage to do this at the initial stages of his career. It was not until after 1728 when he was working at Richmond as Royal Gardener that Bridgeman, as Horace Walpole put it, 'dared to introduce cultivated fields, and even morsels of a forest appearance' into his schemes.[15] The change is evident at Gobions in Hertfordshire, which was designed for Jeremy Sambrooke in the 1730s, and was another alliance with Gibbs.

Bridgeman and Vanbrugh

In reviewing Bridgeman's designs and in considering the influence of Vanbrugh on his career, it is difficult to reconcile the new understanding gained from the research presented in this book with Willis's designation of formal, transitional and progressive features in Bridgeman's compositions.[16] The strong central axis and divergent sub-axes with statues or obelisks at their intersections were a feature of the new Vanbrughian geometry and the underlying Vitruvian grid. They tied the elements of the design together and embedded the house in the surrounding landscape in a way that was completely different from the brash avenues and rectangular formality of the seventeenth century. The 'transitional' mounts and amphitheatres appeared in many of Vanbrugh's designs and the 'progressive' ha-ha and integration of fields and temples at the edges of gardens were all of Vanbrugh's instigation and not Bridgeman's. Horace Walpole's statement that at Gobions Bridgeman had 'many detached thoughts, that strongly indicate the dawn of modern taste' was tele-ological.[17] It was Vanbrugh who had detached the landscape from its formality and moved the geometry underground, but not in anticipation of a future style; it was in response to the philosophy and culture of his time.

Bridgeman was not universally admired by his contemporaries, and Switzer comments on his designs in a section entitled 'Imperfections, Faults and Extravagancies of some Late Designers of Gardens' in the second edition of *Ichnographia Rustica* (1742).[18] Switzer objects to Bridgeman's fondness for great lakes made 'without regard to the Goodness of the Land, which was to be overflowed', and for excessive parterres, which made the 'Mansion-house in the middle look very small, and *by no means proportionable to it*'.[19] Great lakes were already 'the mode' in 1703 when Vanbrugh designed one of forty acres for the Duke of Newcastle.[20] Comparison with the eleven-acre lake at Stowe will give some idea of the scale of this enterprise, but Switzer's remark about proportion is significant. Bridgeman was neither an architect nor an artist; perhaps Vanbrugh's innate ability to compose a background that was suitable to the house was always missing in Bridgeman's work. Vanbrugh's unique combination of Nature and geometry owed little to idealistic pictures; his careful placement of buildings in disguised geometric landscapes came from the science and philosophy of Vitruvius and Alberti, and the artistry of Palladio; it was not a prediction of the late eighteenth-century romantic Picturesque movement. In the 1720s Bridgeman's contiguous gardens exhibited Vanbrugh's green architecture and they were proportional, but his landscapes had none of Vanbrugh's originality; Bridgeman's designs for Tring in Hertfordshire and Spring Wood should be compared with Castle Howard and Claremont. This is why it is difficult to attribute the innovative design of Sacombe in 1715 to Bridgeman. There can be no doubt that Bridgeman, with Gibbs as his architect, was an able and popular successor to Vanbrugh; his work exhibited some of Vanbrugh's geometric style, but it was not until the 1730s that we see in Bridgeman any real understanding of the philosophy of the Enlightenment landscape.

16

CONCLUSION

'An architect who composed like a painter'

In 1708 Vanbrugh observed that 'all the World are running Mad after Building'.[1] Saumarez Smith has highlighted the positive impact that the building of Castle Howard had on the local economy; in the employment of labourers and in the encouragement of the Yorkshire squirearchy to follow suit.[2] The sudden increase in construction was engendered by the relative stability at home and an increase in productivity from land, which was the result of enclosure.[3] To this was added the income from the East India and other trading companies, investment in war contracts, banking, and financial speculation in stocks such as the Mississippi and the South Sea Companies, before their spectacular crashes. Vanbrugh's decision to become an architect in 1699 was therefore a wise one, demonstrating the same good judgement as his decision to become a writer of comedies in 1696. He worked with Hawksmoor on his early projects, but Vanbrugh later established his own office of draughtsmen and used local Clerks of Works to realise his plans. Although he had travelled across England to study existing buildings in 1699, the main source of Vanbrugh's ideas was the writing of the Renaissance architects Palladio and Alberti, as evidenced by his earliest designs for Castle Howard. It was the recovery of Vitruvius's rules on proportion through Alberti and Palladio that would not only direct his building projects, but would also found Vanbrugh's interest in landscape design.

Between 1699 and 1726 Vanbrugh was an architect of landscapes as well as of houses. At his first project at Castle Howard Vanbrugh quickly replaced George London as garden designer, and with Lord Carlisle he created an unusual fortified Ovidian garden out of an existing woodland. By 1710 Castle Howard was already exhibiting the pyramid and octagon pond that presaged Vanbrugh's introduction of obelisks, amphitheatres and temples to his many projects. These allusions to Ancient Rome reinforced the classical iconography of contemporary gardens, but research has shown that none of Vanbrugh's garden ornaments was placed by chance; his obvious interest in the application of Vitruvian proportion to buildings prompted Vanbrugh to use the rules of the Ancients in the construction of landscapes. At a time when gardening treatises were redolent with Euclidian geometry, and with strictures on the correct relationship between the length and the breadth of gardens, it is perhaps not surprising that Vanbrugh brought proportion into the whole landscape; as he wrote to Manchester: 'tis certainly the Figure and Proportions that make the most pleasing Fabrick'.[4] The first design for the Woodwork at Blenheim was Vanbrugh's most conspicuous use of da Vinci's illustration of 'Vitruvian Man'; the squares and circles visible in the plan appear to be a direct reference to the Renaissance drawing. But the obvious geometry of Vanbrugh's gardens, which were a response to Alberti's edict that 'circles, semicircles and other geometric shapes that are favored in the plans of buildings can be modelled out of laurel citrus and juniper', should be contrasted with the hidden geometry of his landscapes, evident from his first design for Castle Howard.[5] Outside the immediate surroundings of the house where 'architecture in green' prevailed, Vanbrugh used the park and features of the surrounding countryside to create landscape compositions that were invisibly tied together by the orientation lines of Vitruvian geometry. Scholars have confused the lack of observable geometry at Castle Howard or Claremont with a move towards the Arcadian landscapes of William Kent and Lancelot Brown. But this is to overlook the innovative style introduced by Vanbrugh, which owed as little to the rectangular formality of the seventeenth century as it did to Brown's sight lines and enclosing shelter belts of the 1760s. Vanbrugh was the first English architect to move into the landscape, and he took the rules of ancient architecture with him.

'Palladian gardening' is a misnomer; Palladio rarely designed gardens, his interest was in building and in the environs of his houses, in setting his villas in the context of the surrounding landscape.[6] The ability to embed a house by orientation, views and long avenues was founded on Palladio's skills as an artist, skills that Vanbrugh also possessed. Despite Swift's jibes about his lack of formal architectural training, this artistic talent, recognised by Whistler (1954) in the title of his book *The Imagination of Vanbrugh and his Fellow Artists*, was of paramount importance. Vanbrugh was able to invoke the rules of perspective, first defined by Vitruvius and documented by Alberti, in the construction of landscapes. His compositions thereby took on some of the aspects of a painting; they were the background for his buildings. Vanbrugh's empathy for Nature, which was founded on the humanist philosophy expressed by Alberti and ultimately derived from Plato and Epicurus, led him to embrace and exploit the topography of his sites. Hills and valleys were used to bring an element of surprise, to hide and reveal ornaments in the landscape. Temples on the edges of parks expressed the wealth and status of Vanbrugh's patrons to those passing by, but they also afforded views over the countryside, as did his bastioned walls and raised terrace walks. By 1706 Vanbrugh's version of the ha-ha was evident in the woodworks at Ray Wood and at Blenheim; these were derived from the Roman fortifications described by Alberti, and had contemporary equivalents in Vauban's fortresses. The effect of the ha-ha is most obvious in the plans of Castle Howard and Stowe, where the low walls exposed the common fields that had been left within the bounds of the design, creating the first *fermes ornées*. Although early eighteenth-century manuals advocated both geometry and the incorporation of Nature into gardens, examination of the work of contemporary designers suggests that, until the late 1720s, Vanbrugh was the only practitioner of this form of Vitruvian landscape. Burlington manifestly understood geometry and he is credited with consulting the 'genius of the place', but at Chiswick there is little evidence that he actually did so. It was Bridgeman who finally adopted Vanbrugh's style, and who used it in his own commissions in the 1730s, when it also appeared in Switzer's designs for Leeswood. Vanbrugh's combination of underlying and overt geometry with empathy for Nature was the product of the Enlightenment, just as Alberti's and Palladio's treatises were the product of the Italian Renaissance; his genre would most aptly be termed 'Vitruvian Landscape Architecture'.

Since Whistler's excellent book of more than fifty years ago, there has been no attempt to re-evaluate all of Vanbrugh's landscape designs. This book has demonstrated how much of his work as a landscape architect has been overlooked in the past, and has proposed that several projects that have previously been attributed to Bridgeman were in fact of Vanbrugh's conception. In conclusion, it is appropriate to quote Joshua Reynolds's thirteenth discourse to the Royal Academy delivered in December 1786. Unlike Walpole, who credited Bridgeman, Reynolds understood Vanbrugh's design philosophy; these are the words of a painter who appreciated the contribution of a fellow artist to the discipline of landscape architecture:

> To speak then of Vanbrugh in the language of a Painter, he had originality of invention, he understood light and shadow, and he had great skill in composition . . . he perfectly understood in *his* Art what is most difficult in ours, the conduct of the back-ground; by which the design and invention is set off to the greatest advantage. What the back-ground is in Painting, in Architecture is the real ground on which the building is erected; and no Architect took greater care than he that his work should not appear crude and hard: that is, it did not abruptly start out of the ground without expectation or preparation.
>
> This is a tribute which a Painter owes to an Architect who composed like a Painter; and was defrauded of the due reward of his merit by the Wits of his time, who did not understand the principles of the composition in poetry better than he; and who knew little, or nothing, *of what he understood perfectly, the general ruling principles of Architecture and Painting.*[7]

APPENDIX A
VANBRUGH'S SITES

Properties referenced in this text are listed below in alphabetical order with their locations. See also Figure A.1.

Property	Owner	New/alteration	Garden	A/E
Blenheim Castle, Oxfordshire	John Churchill, 1st Duke of Marlborough	New house 1705–16 Vanbrugh resigned 1716	1705–16	E
Castle Howard, Yorkshire	Charles Howard, 3rd Earl of Carlisle	New house 1700–13	1700–26	E
Chargate, later Claremont, Surrey	John Vanbrugh Thomas Pelham-Holles, 1st Duke of Newcastle (from 1714)	New house 1710/11 Alterations 1714–20	1709–26	E
Cholmondeley, Cheshire	Sir Hugh Cholmondeley	Alterations 1713	?1722 garden building only	A
Duncombe, Yorkshire	Thomas Duncombe	New house 1713	?1713	A
Eastbury, Dorset	George Dodington George Bubb Dodington (from 1720)	New house 1715–26	1715–26	E
Greenwich, London	Sir John Vanbrugh	New houses 1719–26	1720s	E
Grimsthorpe, Lincolnshire	Robert Bertie, 1st Duke of Ancaster Peregrine Bertie, 2nd Duke of Ancaster (from 1723)	1723–6 north front Designed 1715	?1711–12	A
Heythrop, Oxfordshire	Charles Talbot, 1st Duke of Shrewsbury	House by Thomas Archer	?advised 1707–16	A
Kimbolton, Cambridgeshire	Charles Montagu, 1st Duke of Manchester	Alterations 1707–10	1707–10	A
Kings Weston, Avon	Edward Southwell	1710 new house on existing footprint	1710–23	E
Lumley Castle, Co. Durham	Richard Lumley, 2nd Earl of Scarbrough	Alterations 1721	1721	E
Nottingham Castle, Nottinghamshire	Thomas Pelham-Holles, 1st Duke of Newcastle	Alterations 1719	1719	E

Property	Owner	New/alteration	Garden	A/E
Sacombe, Hertfordshire	Edward Rolt, died 1722	House designed, not built	1715–18	E
Seaton Delaval, Northumberland	Admiral George Delaval Captain Francis Delaval (from 1723)	New house 1718–1726	1719–26	E
Stowe, Buckinghamshire	Richard Temple, 1st Viscount Cobham	Alterations from 1716	1716–26	E

A = gardens and landscapes that may be attributed to Vanbrugh based upon circumstantial evidence;
E = gardens and landscapes known to have been designed by Vanbrugh, or where he had some evidenced influence on the design.

FIGURE A.1 Location map of the Vanbrugh sites in this book. OS Opendata Miniscale. Contains Ordnance Survey data. © Crown copyright and database right (2011). Annotation: author.

APPENDIX B
VANBRUGH'S GARDEN STRUCTURES

Garden structures are listed in chronological order. Dates are 'in construction', from manuscript evidence where applicable.

Date	Estate	Name of building	Order (capitals)
1705	Castle Howard, Yorkshire	'Rustic peer, angular peer with pyramidall top'[1]	
1706	Castle Howard, Yorkshire	'In the brigge in ye Parke – Broacht work under ye pyramids'[2]	
1706	Castle Howard, Yorkshire	'Four Square Summerhouse' and 'rectangular circled' (octagon) pond[3]	
1707	Blenheim, Oxfordshire	Bridge;★ copy of Palladio's unrealised Rialto design	
1712–14	Castle Howard, Yorkshire	Bowling Green House	
1714	Castle Howard, Yorkshire	Obelisk;★ at intersection of approach roads	
1714–15	Chargate/ Claremont, Surrey	The Mount;★ now known as the Belvedere	
1715–16 Appears on a plan *c.* 1709	Claremont, Surrey	The Alcove	Pediment Astylar
1715–16	Claremont, Surrey	Round Seat/Temple; possibly given a temple portico at a later date	Obscured
1715–19	Kings Weston, Bristol	Octagon Tower	
c. 1718	Claremont, Surrey	Temple Pavilion; now known as the Cyprus Temple	Doric
1718	Claremont, Surrey	Round Pond with Obelisk	
1718	Stowe, Buckinghamshire	'Sumer hous', later known as Temple of Bacchus/Brick or Rustick Temple. Viscount Percival's Temple of Apollo?[4]	Pediment Astylar
1719	Stowe, Buckinghamshire	Nelson's Seat	Ionic

Date	Estate	Name of building	Order (capitals)
1719	Stowe, Buckinghamshire	Lake Pavilions★	Doric
1719	Kings Weston, Bristol	West Loggia★	Corinthian
Late 1710s	Duncombe, Yorkshire	Ionic Temple★[5]	Ionic
Late 1710s	Stowe, Buckinghamshire	Octagon Lake with *guglio sudante*	
1720	Stowe, Buckinghamshire	Rotundo	Ionic
1720–6	Seaton Delaval, Northumberland	Three Obelisks★ (one extant) Mausoleum? (built 1776)	
1721–4	Castle Howard, Yorkshire	Obelisk Parterre	
1722–6	Eastbury, Dorset	Temple	Composite: Ionic/ Corinthian
1722	Cholmondeley, Cheshire	Seat	
1722 (built 1729–1740s)	Castle Howard, Yorkshire	Idea for a mausoleum; designed by Hawksmoor after Bramante's Tempietto 1729	Doric
Early 1720s	Kings Weston, Bristol	Banqueting House Loggia (the Echo)★	
Early 1720s	Kings Weston, Bristol	Penpole Gate	
Early 1720s	Stowe, Buckinghamshire	Triumphal Arch; in Percival's account,[6] location unknown, later incorporated into the Doric Arch (extant)	Doric? entablature
Before 1724	Stowe, Buckinghamshire	King's Pillar (as Prince of Wales), Coucher's Obelisk	Corinthian (pillar)
Before 1724	Stowe, Buckinghamshire	Egyptian Pyramid	
1724	Castle Howard, Yorkshire	Temple with the four Porticos;★[7] now known as the Temple of the Four Winds	Ionic
1724	Claremont, Surrey	Seat by the Water; turned into Belisle by Kent	Doric
1724/5	Stowe, Buckinghamshire	Temple of Sleep	Ionic
Before 1726	Castle Howard, Yorkshire	Four Faces and Pyramid in Pretty Wood★	
1726	Stowe, Buckinghamshire	Queen's Column, posthumous. Designed as monument to Princess of Wales	

Buildings marked ★ are extant.

APPENDIX C
COMPUTER METHODOLOGY

Computer software has been used throughout this project to study the maps and plans of early eighteenth-century gardens and to recreate landscapes using three-dimensional modelling. The key method used for the evaluation of all of Vanbrugh's sites was 'overlaying'. This involves loading a base map into a computer program (Adobe Photoshop can be used, also Canvas or ArcGIS), then loading digital pictures of older maps as layers on top of the base map (Figure C.1). The software allows the layers to be moved around and scaled so that they can be correctly positioned. The layers can be made more or less

FIGURE C.1 Visualisation of three maps and an aerial photograph of Castle Howard overlaid using computer software. Each map is stored as a layer on the computer and aligned using landscape features that are visible on all of the maps. Here it is possible to see through the 1744 estate plan to the 1727 plan underneath. Diagram: author.

opaque so that it is possible to see through one layer to the layer below. In most cases the first edition Ordnance Survey maps were used as a base layer, after checking them for accuracy against modern maps. These nineteenth-century maps often have elements of the eighteenth-century schemes extant, or it is possible to see references in remains of lines of trees or ruined buildings that have now disappeared, which allow older maps to be positioned against them more accurately. When positioning older maps the integral scaling function in Photoshop was used so that the maps were not warped; it was not always possible to match every element on the older maps to the Ordnance Survey although some were remarkably accurate; 'best fit' was employed where necessary.

Much of the work presented in this book could have been carried out using Photoshop alone. The software allows custom measurement scales to be set up by copying the scales on the historic maps. Accurate measurements of distances between features on the maps could then be made in pixels; tolerances are given in the text where relevant. The study was focused on proportions and the positions of features of Vanbrugh's landscapes *relative* to other features, all of which were easily established using the ruler tool in Photoshop. Lines, shapes and labels were added using additional layers. The importance of overlaying as a research method is demonstrated by Figure 10.5 (as one of many examples), in which coloured shapes have been drawn to outline features of the 1715 map of Sacombe. This map layer was then 'turned off', leaving the shapes visible on the first edition Ordnance Survey map below. By this method features from the older landscape are accurately positioned on more modern mapping; it is an essential tool for studying the history of the landscape, or for directing survey and other archaeological investigation in the field.

Canvas and ArcGIS use geo-referencing, in which features on maps are located precisely using coordinate systems. All places have geographical coordinates and these can be downloaded with height data from various sites (at a cost), including the Ordnance Survey. A geo-referenced map loaded into ArcGIS becomes a base layer for positioning features on other maps quite precisely. ArcGIS has been used to check a number of theories developed in this book, but the absolute accuracy of such modern mapping methods should be employed with care when working with historic maps; warping old maps so that they 'fit' exactly tells us very little. It is in its ability to create three-dimensional models that ArcGIS has contributed most to this study; Figure 4.8 is a still photograph of the model of Castle Howard. The model itself can be manipulated in real time; the user can be positioned anywhere in the landscape and can move through it at ground level. The calculation of 'viewsheds' allows precise definition of what can, and cannot, be seen from any point in the landscape, thus providing new insights into what it was like to be in the landscape in 1727.

One of the aims of my project on Vanbrugh was to establish how computer software could inform the study of historical geography. Although it is still only a tool that enhances traditional methods of research, twenty-first century computer mapping methodology and model building have contributed substantially to this new understanding of an eighteenth-century landscape architect.

NOTES

Abbreviations used in the notes:

BL, Add.	British Library, London: Additional Manuscripts
BOD	The Bodleian Libraries, University of Oxford
BRO	Bristol Record Office
CHA	Castle Howard Archives
DRO	Dorset Record Office
GRO	Gloucestershire Record Office
HALS	Hertfordshire Archives and Local Studies
HaRO	Hampshire Record Office
HMC	Historic Manuscripts Commission
HRO	Huntingdonshire Record Office
LRO	Lincolnshire Record Office
NA	The National Archive, Kew, London
NRO	Northumberland Record Office
ODNB	*Oxford Dictionary of National Biography* (online edition)
OED	*Oxford English Dictionary* (online edition)
RCW	Royal Commission on the Ancient and Historical Monuments of Wales
SHC	Surrey History Centre
V&A	Victoria & Albert Museum, London.

References to journal articles are shortened in the notes. Full references are given in the bibliography.

Introduction

1 Timothy Nourse, *Campania Fælix* (London: Tomas Bennet, 1700), p. 300, author's emphasis.
2 Sir John Vanbrugh, *The Complete Works of Sir John Vanbrugh*, ed. Geoffrey Webb, Vol. 4 *The Letters* (London: Nonesuch Press, 1928), hereafter Vanbrugh, *Letters*, to the Earl of Manchester December 1699.

3 David Jacques, *Georgian Gardens: The Reign of Nature* (London: Batsford, 1988).
4 See Peter Willis, *Charles Bridgeman and the English Landscape Garden* (Newcastle upon Tyne: Elysium Press, 2002). Quote: Horace Walpole, *Anecdotes of Painting in England*, 2nd edn, Vol. 4 (London: Thomas Kirgate, 1765–71), p. 138.
5 See Quentin Skinner's important article on the reading of history: Skinner, 'Meaning'.
6 Vanbrugh, *Letters*, p. xxxviii.
7 Laurence Whistler, *The Imagination of Vanbrugh and His Fellow Artists* (London: B.T. Batsford, 1954).
8 Kerry Downes, *Vanbrugh* (London: A. Zwemmer, 1977) and Kerry Downes, *Sir John Vanbrugh* (London: Sidgwick & Jackson, 1987); Frank McCormick, *Sir John Vanbrugh: The Playwright as Architect* (University Park, PA: Pennsylvania State University Press, 1991), p. 94.
9 Christopher Ridgway and Robert Williams (eds), *Sir John Vanbrugh and Landscape Architecture in Baroque England* (Stroud: Sutton, 2000).
10 Vaughan Hart, *Sir John Vanbrugh: Storyteller in Stone* (London: Yale University Press, 2008).
11 Whistler, *Vanbrugh*, pp. 212–224.
12 Downes, *Vanbrugh* 1977, p. 124.
13 J. G. A. Pocock, *Barbarism and Religion*, Vol. 1 (Cambridge: Cambridge University Press, 2003). J. C. D. Clark, *English Society 1660–1832*, 2nd edn (Cambridge: Cambridge University Press, 2000). Roy Porter, *Enlightenment Britain and the Creation of the Modern World* (London: Penguin, 2001). See also Robert Mayhew, *Enlightenment Geography: The Political Languages of British Geography, 1650–1850* (Basingstoke: Macmillan, 2000). For a different viewpoint, see Jonathan Israel's most recent book, *A Revolution of the Mind* (2010), which argues for radical and moderate forms of Enlightenment, and disputes the evidence for distinctly national versions.

1 'On ye shoulders of giants'

1 Cato, *On Farming*, reproduced in K. D. White, *Country Life in Classical Times* (London: Book Club Associates, 1978), p. 38.
2 Cicero, *On Old Age*, reproduced ibid., p. 39.
3 Virgil, *The Works of Virgil: Containing his Pastorals, Georgics and Æneis*, Vol. 1 (London: Jacob Tonson, 1709), *Georgics* Book IV.
4 The Younger Pliny, *The Letters of the Younger Pliny* (London: Penguin, 1969), p. 40. There is no modern name for 'Laurentum', which was in the region of Lazio on the coast to the west of Rome.
5 Ibid., p. 144.
6 Ibid., p. 142.
7 Ibid., p. 140.
8 Ibid., p. 140.
9 The villa belonged to Livia Drusill, third wife of the Emperor Augustus (63 BC to AD 14).
10 Kellum, 'Garden Room'. I am indebted to Barbara for helping me with the source of the illustrations in her article.
11 Ibid., p. 215.
12 Myers, 'Gardens in Roman Literature', online.
13 Thorsten Opper, *Hadrian Empire and Conflict: Exhibition Catalogue* (London: British Museum Press, 2008), p. 140.
14 Quoted ibid., p. 155.
15 Ibid., p. 102.
16 Marcus Vitruvius Pollio, *The Ten Books of Architecture* (New York: Dover Publications, 1960), p. 17.
17 Ibid., p. 13.
18 Ibid., p. 15, author's emphasis.
19 Ibid., p. 14.
20 Ibid., p. 72.
21 Ibid., p. 73:

> For if a man be placed flat on his back, with his hands and feet extended, and a pair of compasses centred at his navel, the fingers and toes of his two hands and feet will touch the circumference of a circle described therefrom. And just as the human body yields a circular

outline, so too a square figure may be found from it. For if we measure the distance from the soles of the feet to the top of the head, and then apply that measure to the outstretched arms, the breadth will be found to be the same as the height, as in the case of plane surfaces which are perfectly square.

Therefore since nature has designed the human body so that its members are duly proportioned to the frame as a whole, it appears that the Ancients had good reason for their rule, that in perfect buildings the different members must be in exact symmetrical relations to the whole general scheme.

These words are the source of da Vinci's drawing.

22 Ibid., p. 177: 'using the width to describe a square figure with equal sides, drawing a diagonal line in this square, and giving the atrium the length of this diagonal line'. An irrational number is one that cannot be expressed as a fraction of whole numbers.

23 'A line is said to have been cut in extream and mean ratio when, as the whole line is to the greater segment, so is the greater to the lesser'; see Euclid, *Euclides Elements of Geometry* (London: Richard Tomlins and Robert Boydell, 1651), Book VI, Proposition 30.

24 For historical uses of Fibonacci see Birkett and Jurgenson, 'Practical Geometry and Proportion'. $\Phi = 1.618033\ldots$

25 See Markowsky, 'Golden Ratio'.

26 Vitruvius, *Architecture*, p. 14.

27 Anthony Grafton, *Leon Battista Alberti* (New York: Hill & Wang, 2000), p. 245. See George Saliba, *Islamic Science and the Making of the European Renaissance* (Cambridge, MA: MIT Press, 2007) and Jim Al-Khalili, *Pathfinders* (London: Allen Lane, 2010) on the history of Arabic science.

28 Al-Khalili, *Pathfinders*, p. 157.

29 Saliba, *Islamic Science*, p. 224; Copernicus could not speak Arabic.

30 H. W. Turnbull, J. F. Scott and A. R. Hall, *The Correspondence of Isaac Newton* (Cambridge: Cambridge University Press, 1959), p. 416.

31 *Il Saggiatore*, 1623, translated by Stillman Drake, *Discoveries and Opinions of Galileo* (New York: Anchor Books, 1957), pp. 237–238.

32 Jana K. Schulman (ed.), *The Rise of the Medieval World, 500–1300: A Biographical Dictionary* (London: Greenwood Press, 2002), p. 181.

33 Martin Kemp, *Leonardo da Vinci* (Oxford: Oxford University Press, 2006), p. 12.

34 Peter Ackroyd, *Venice Pure City* (London: Chatto & Windus, 2009), p. 96.

35 Syson, 'Holes and Loops'.

36 Leon Battista Alberti, *De re aedificatoria* (Florence: Magistri Nicolai Laurentii Alamani, 1486). Note that the date is corrected to 1486 'by modern reckoning' in Leon Battista Alberti, *On the Art of Building in Ten Books* (London: MIT Press, 1988), p. xxii. Lorenzo asked for each page of Albert's book to be sent to him as it was being printed (from woodcuts).

37 See the excellent description of Renaissance humanism in Grafton, *Alberti*, Chapter 2.

38 John Bury quoted in Baron, 'Querelle', p. 4.

39 Quoted ibid., p. 19.

40 Alberti, *Building*, p. 155.

41 Grafton, *Alberti*, p. 125.

42 Cosgrove, 'Prospect, Perspective'.

43 See Liane LeFaivre, *Leon Battista Alberti's Hypnerotomachia Poliphili* (Cambridge, MA: MIT, 1997), who attributes the work to Alberti.

44 Stewering, 'Architectural Representations'.

45 Alberti, *Building*, p. 305.

46 For an explanation of harmonic proportion see Erickson, 'Art and Geometry'.

47 Donata Mazzini and Simone Martini, *Villa Medici a Fiesole Leon Battista Alberti e il Prototipo di Villa Rinascimentale* (Firenze: Centro Di, 2004), pp. 130–131. Their work references Clemens Steenbergen and Wouter Reh, *Architecture and Landscape: The Design Experiment of the Great European Gardens and Landscapes* (Munich: Prestel, 1996).

48 Roy Strong, *The Renaissance Garden in England* (London: Thames and Hudson, 1998), p. 15.

49 Grafton, *Alberti*, p. 320.

50 *c.* 1490. Da Vinci includes a standard scale underneath the drawing; the proportions that can be derived from this figure are all whole number fractions: (⅓, ⅔, ¼ &c), not irrational numbers.

51 Quoted in Geoffrey Scott, *The Architecture of Humanism: A Study in the History of Taste* (London: Constable, 1929), p. 221.

52 Quoted in Kemp, *da Vinci*, p. 243.

53 Grafton, *Alberti*, p. 270.

54 Andrea Palladio, *The Four Books on Architecture*, translated by R. Tavernor and R. Schofield (London: MIT Press, 2002), p. 94.

55 Ibid., p. 57; the seven most beautiful room proportions were the circle, the square, and length to breadth of √2:1, 2:1, 5:3, 3:2 and 4:3. Palladio visited Rome five times between 1541 and 1554 to survey antiquities. But many Roman buildings did not exhibit the rules of proportion documented by Vitruvius: James Ackerman, *Palladio* (London: Penguin, 1991), p. 161. Palladio's understanding of proportion must have come from other sources, including Alberti and Vitruvius.

56 Howard and Longair, 'Harmonic Proportion'. For Renaissance architectural theory see Rudolf Wittkower, *Architectural Principles in the Age of Humanism* (London: Warburg Institute, 1949), Part IV, pp. 89–135.

57 Alberti, *Building*, p. 145.

58 Alberti, *Building*, p. 300, author's emphasis.

59 Palladio's involvement in the nymphaeum at Maser is unproven; see Howard Burns, *Palladio: Exhibition Catalogue* (Venice: Royal Academy of Arts, 2008), p. 136 cat. 75a and 76.

60 Quoted in Howard, 'Literature on Palladio', p. 232.

61 Denis Cosgrove, 'The geometry of landscape: practical and speculative arts in sixteenth-century Venetian land territories', in Denis Cosgrove and Stephen Daniels (eds), *The Iconography of Landscape* (Cambridge: Cambridge University Press, 1988), pp. 254–276.

62 Ibid.

63 Claudia Lazzaro, *The Italian Renaissance Garden* (London: Yale University Press, 1990), p. 109.

64 Lazzaro maintains that paths in the *barco* were always straight and that only watercourses were allowed to wind or curve; ibid., p. 55.

65 David Starkey, 'England', in Roy Porter and Mikulas Teich (eds), *The Renaissance in National Context* (Cambridge: Cambridge University Press, 1994), pp. 146–163.

66 Homer quote: Sir Roger Askham, 1545; Karl Erik Elmquist, 'An Observation on Chaucer's Astrolabe', *Modern Language Notes* (1941), Vol. 56, No. 7, pp. 530–534, p. 533.

67 Starkey, *England*.

68 Inigo Jones, *The Most Notable Antiquity of Great Britain, Vulgarly Called Stone-Heng on Salisbury Plain Restored by Inigo Jones* (London: Daniel Pakeman, 1655). His assessment written *c.* 1620 was not published until after his death in 1652.

69 He goes on: 'a good Historian, a diligent hearer of Philosophers, well experienc'd in Physick, Musick, Law and Astrologie'; ibid., p. 4.

70 Ibid., p. 79. William Stukeley surveyed Stonehenge in the 1720s and decided that it was a Celtic monument, thus agreeing with John Aubrey's earlier assessment.

71 Burns, *Palladio*, p. 386.

72 Sir Henry Wotton, *The Elements of Architecture* (London: John Bill, 1624), p. 4.

73 Ibid., pp. 53, 21.

74 On variety in gardens see John Dixon Hunt, *Garden and Grove, The Italian Renaissance Garden in the English Imagination 1600–1750* (Philadelphia: University of Pennsylvania Press, 1996), pp. 83–89. See also Strong, *Renaissance Garden*.

75 Skinner, 'Meaning'; see also Clark, *English Society*, in which he discusses the contextual meaning of words with reference to Samuel Johnson's 1755 dictionary.

76 Francis Bacon, *The Essayes or Counsels, Ciuill and Morall, of Francis Lo. Verulam, Viscount St. Alban* (London: Hanna Barret, 1625), p. 273.

77 Wotton, *Architecture*, p. 6.

78 Luke Morgan, 'Isaac de Caus *invenit*', *Studies in the History of Gardens & Designed Landscapes* (2009), Vol. 29, No. 3, pp. 141–151.

2 The early Enlightenment in England

1 Skinner, 'Thomas Hobbes'.

2 Peter Millican (ed.), *David Hume: An Essay Concerning Human Understanding* (Oxford: Oxford University Press, 2008), introduction.

3 Quote: Sir William Temple, *Miscellanea: The Second Part. In Four Essays, 2nd edn*, Vol. 2 (London: R. Simpson, 1960), p. 57. Swift suspected Epicurus of atheism, but Epicurus did not believe that all pain was to be avoided in pursuit of pleasure. Temple blamed the negative view of Epicurus on the 'Stoicks'. Ibid., p. 86.
4 Sir William Temple, *Miscellanea*, 2nd edn, Vol. 2 (London: Ri. and Ra. Simpson, 1690), pp. 82–83.
5 J. D. Davies, 'Sir William Temple', ODNB.
6 For *Sharawadgi* see John Harris, 'The Artinatural Style', in Charles Hind (ed.), *The Rococo in England* (London: Victoria & Albert Museum, 1986), pp. 8–20. See also Ciaran Murray, *Sharawadgi: The Romantic Return to Nature* (London: International Scholars Publications, 1999) and Charles Saumarez Smith, *The Building of Castle Howard* (London: Pimlico, 1997), p. 128, in which he attributes the layout of Ray Wood at Castle Howard to Carlisle's personal association with Temple.
7 John Kersey, *A New English Dictionary* (London: Henry Bonwicke, 1702).
8 Joseph Addison, *The Spectator*, Nos 411–421 (London: R. Steele and J. Addison, 1712), No. 414, 25 June.
9 Joseph Addison, *The Lucubrations of Isaac Bickerstaff, Esq*, Vol. 1 (London: John Morphew, 1710–11), No. 179.
10 See Martin C. Battestin, *The Providence of Wit: Aspects of Form in Augustan Literature and the Arts* (Oxford: Oxford Clarendon Press, 1974), p. 15, Daniel Carey, *Locke, Shaftesbury and Hutcheson: Contesting Diversity in the Enlightenment* (Cambridge: Cambridge University Press, 2006), p. 118, and Townsend, 'Shaftesbury's Aesthetic Theory'. All discuss the equivalence of some of Shaftesbury's ideas with those of the Cambridge Platonists.
11 Anthony Ashley Cooper, Earl of Shaftesbury, *Several Letters Written by a Noble Lord to a Young Man at the University* (London: J. Roberts, 1716), p. 22.
12 Anthony Ashley Cooper, Earl of Shaftesbury, *Characteristicks of Men, Manners, Opinions, Times*, Vol. 3 (London, 1711), p. 180; Addison, *Spectator*, No. 412, 23 June.
13 John Dixon Hunt and Peter Willis (eds), *The Genius of the Place* (Cambridge, MA: MIT Press, 1988), p. 9.
14 Leatherbarrow, 'Character, Geometry'.
15 Ibid., p. 353.
16 Shaftesbury, *Characteristicks*, pp. 184–185.
17 Anthony Ashley Cooper, Earl of Shaftesbury, *The Life, Unpublished Letters, and Philosophical Regimen of Anthony, Earl of Shaftesbury*, ed. B. Rand (London: Swan Sonnenschein, 1900). Notes on 'The Beautiful' (*to Kalon*), p. 244.
18 Anthony Ashley Cooper, Earl of Shaftesbury, *The Moralists* (London: J. Wyat, 1709), p. 205.
19 Shaftesbury, *Unpublished Letters*, pp. 246–247.
20 'the Word Tory was entertained, which signified the most despicable Savages among the Wild Irish', Roger North in *Examen* (1740), OED, entry for 'Tory'.
21 Pocock, *Barbarism*, p. 15.
22 Stephen Pincus, *1688: The First Modern Revolution* (Yale: Yale University Press, 2009), p. 393.
23 Ibid., p. 485.
24 For political landscape history see Tim Richardson, *Arcadian Friends* (London: Transworld Publishers, 2007), p. 164 *et passim*; Nigel Everett, *The Tory View of Landscape* (London: Yale University Press, 1994).
25 Stasavage, 'Partisan Politics'.
26 Philip Ayres, *Classical Culture and the Idea of Rome in Eighteenth-Century England* (Cambridge: Cambridge University Press, 1997), p. 20.
27 Pocock, *Barbarism*, p. 105.
28 Ibid., p. 105.
29 Lake and Pincus, 'Public Sphere'.
30 Jurgen Habermas, *The Structural Transformation of the Public Sphere* (Cambridge: Polity Press, 2008), p. 32.
31 Fraser, 'Public Sphere'. Clark in *English Society* considers 'middle class' to be a modern retrospective interpretation. Both Habermas and Pincus refer to a middle class although the term was not used in the eighteenth century.
32 Clark, *English Society*, p. 9.

33 Samuel Johnson, *A Dictionary of the English Language*, Vol. 1, 2nd edn (London: J. and P. Knaptor, T. and T. Longman, C. Hitch and L. Hawes, A. Millar, and R. and J. Dodsley, 1755). See Israel, *Revolution*, for a different approach.

34 Habermas, *Sphere*, p. 36.

35 Pocock, *Barbarism*, pp. 106–108.

36 Donald Bond (ed.), *The Spectator* (Oxford: Clarendon Press, 1965), pp. lxxxvii–xcv.

37 Louis Kelly, 'The Eighteenth Century to Tytler', in Stuart Gillespie and David Hopkins (eds), *The Oxford History of Literary Translation in English. Vol. 3: 1660–1790* (Oxford: Oxford University Press, 2005), pp. 67–78. The 'modernisation' of older texts was common practice in the early eighteenth century; see Mayhew, 'Shakespeare'.

38 Howard Erskine-Hill, *The Augustan Idea in English Literature* (London: Edward Arnold, 1983), p. 214.

39 Quoted in Weinbrot, *Britannia's Issue*, pp. 61–62.

40 Erskine-Hill, 'Medal against Time'.

41 *Dialogues upon the Usefulness of Ancient Medals* in Joseph Addison, *Works* (London: Jacob Tonson, 1721), pp. 443–444.

42 Quoted in John M. Gray, 'Memoirs of the Life of Sir John Clerk of Penicuik, Baronet', *Publications of the Scottish Historical Society* (1892), Vol. 13, p. 126.

43 Alexander Pope, *The Guardian*, No. 173 (London: R. Steele, 1713) 29 September.

44 Joseph Addison, *The Spectator*, No. 477 (London: R. Steele and J. Addison, 1712) 6 September; Joseph Addison, *The Spectator*, No. 583 (London: R. Steele and J. Addison, 1714) 20 August.

45 Addison, *Spectator*, No. 414, 25 June.

46 See Tom Williamson, 'Estate Management and Landscape Design', in Christopher Ridgway and Robert Williams (eds), *Sir John Vanbrugh and Landscape Architecture in Baroque England* (Stroud: Sutton, 2000), pp. 12–30.

47 Arthur Earl of Anglesey, *Memoirs of the Right Honourable Arthur Earl of Anglesey* (London: Sir Peter Pett Knight, 1693).

48 Dixon Hunt, *Garden and Grove*, p. 153 *et passim*.

49 Gray, 'Penicuik', p. 236.

50 John Macky, *A Journey through England*, Vol. 1, 1st edn (London: J. Hooke and T. Caldecott, 1714), p. 30.

51 Switzer, *Ichnographia*, Vol. 3, p. xvi.

52 HMC, *Bath*, Vol. 3, Matthew Prior to Edward Harley, June 1721.

53 Robert Castell, *The Villas of the Ancients Illustrated* (London: Robert Castell, 1728).

54 Pliny, *Letters*.

55 The Younger Pliny, *Les plans et les descriptions de deux des plus belles maisons de campagne de Pline le Consul*, Vol. 6, translated by Jean-François Félibien des Avaux (Paris: Florentin & Pierre Delanine, 1699). Carlisle had three copies in his library in 1716.

56 See, for example, Dixon Hunt and Willis, *Genius* and Hart, *Storyteller*; both follow English garden literature through time.

57 BL, Sloane. 3881; Moses Cook, *The Manner of Raising, Ordering, and Improving Forrest-Trees* (London: Peter Parker, 1676).

58 Jean de la Quintinie, *The Compleat Gard'ner*, 1st edn, translated by John Evelyn (London: M. Gillyflower, 1693), p. 33.

59 Vanbrugh, *Letters* to Tonson, July 1703.

60 Ibid., to the Earl of Manchester, July 1707.

61 Dézallier d'Argenville, *The Theory and Practice of Gardening*, translated by John James (London: printed by G. James, 1712), p. 80.

62 Vitruvius, *Architecture*, p. 301.

63 Stephen Switzer, *The Nobleman, Gentleman, and Gardener's Recreation* (London: B. Barker, C. King, 1715), p. 21, author's emphasis.

64 Ibid., p. 221, author's emphasis.

65 D'Argenville, *Gardening*, 2nd edn, translated by John James (London: B. Lintot, 1728), p. 91.

66 Ibid., p. 20; he continues: 'but to make it twice or thrice its breadth, makes the place look disagreeable'.

67 Richard Bradley, *A Survey of the Ancient Husbandry and Gardening* (London: B. Motte, 1725), p. 359.

68 Ibid., p. 359.
69 Batty Langley, *New Principles of Gardening* (London: A. Bettesworth and J. Batley, 1727), pp. 193, 198 and 201.
70 Ibid., p. 194.
71 Ibid., Problem XII.
72 Willis, *Bridgeman*, p. 48.
73 D'Argenville, *Gardening* 1712, pp. 7 and 13.
74 Ibid., p. 13.
75 Switzer, *Ichnographia*, Vol. 1, p. xxviii.
76 Ibid., p. xvi.
77 Alexander Pope, *An Essay on Criticism* (London: W. Lewis, 1713), p. 11.
78 Battestin, *Literature*, p. 26. Morris was still writing about proportion in building in the 1730s.
79 Battestin, *Literature*, p. 35.
80 William Hogarth, *The Analysis of Beauty* (London: Hogarth, 1753), p. 45.
81 Phibbs, 'Projective Geometry', p. 13.
82 Switzer, *Ichnographia*, Vol. 1, p. xxviii.
83 Pliny, *Letters*, p. 142. It is a common misconception that Pliny's gardens contained temples, statues and other forms of architecture; he refers only to stone seats, pools and fountains.
84 To avoid associations with Roman religion, Palladio claimed that the temple portico appeared on antique houses as well as religious buildings; Ackerman, *Palladio*, p. 61.
85 Switzer, *Ichnographia*, Vol. 3, p. 8.
86 Saumarez Smith, *Castle Howard*, p 99.
87 See, for example, Stapleford and Potter, 'Velazquez'.
88 See Dixon Hunt, *Garden and Grove*, for a discussion of the influence of travel on the seventeenth-century garden.
89 'Warsiles [Versailles] is the noblest house in the world and the beauty of the Parter and Parcke and water workes is inexpresable', quoted in Black, 'Grand Tour'.
90 John Locke, *Some Thoughts Concerning Education*, quoted in Mark Wenger (ed.), *The English Travels of Sir John Percival and William Byrd II: The Percival Diary of 1701* (Columbia: University of Missouri Press, 1989), p. 12.
91 John Churchill, quoted ibid., p. 22.
92 Mayhew, *Enlightenment Geography*, p. 141.
93 Dixon Hunt, *Garden and Grove*.
94 Pincus, *Revolution*, p. 382.

3 John Vanbrugh (1664–1726)

 1 For chronological detail this chapter draws on the work of Vanbrugh's most important biographers: see Whistler, *Vanbrugh*, Downes, *Vanbrugh* 1977, Downes, *Vanbrugh* 1987, and most recently Hart, *Storyteller*.
 2 In Robert Williams, 'Vanbrugh's India and his mausolea for England', in Ridgway and Williams, *Vanbrugh*, pp. 114–130, Williams proved that Vanbrugh had been in India in the early 1680s.
 3 For house building at this time see Saumarez Smith, 'Country House Building'.
 4 Vanbrugh, *Letters*, to the Duke of Newcastle, *c.* 1718.
 5 CHA, G2/2/11–20.
 6 Vanbrugh, *Letters* to Henry Joynes, March 1706; David Green, *Blenheim Palace* (London: Country Life, 1951), p. 301; BL, Add. 61353, Vanbrugh to the Duke of Marlborough, August, 1705.
 7 Vanbrugh, *Letters*, to Earl Stanhope, September 1719.
 8 BL, Add. 61353, Nicholas Hawksmoor to the Duchess of Marlborough, 1725.
 9 BL, Stowe 748, Sir Godfrey Copley to Thomas Kirke, June 1703.
10 Jonathon Swift, *Miscellanies in Prose and Verse* (London: J. Morphew, 1711), p. 370.
11 Jonathon Swift, *The History of Vanbrug's House (1706)* (London: B. Motte, C. Bathurst, 1736), p. 176.
12 Vanbrugh, *Letters*, to Manchester, December 1699.

13 John Churchill, 1704, quoted in Mark Wenger (ed.), *The English Travels of Sir John Percival and William Byrd II: The Percival Diary of 1701* (Columbia: University of Missouri Press, 1989), p. 22.
14 Swift, *Vanbrug's House*, p. 175.
15 Swift, *Vanbrug's House*, p. 177.
16 Jonathan Swift, *Journal to Stella*, ed. Harold Williams, Vol. 1 (Oxford: Clarendon Press, 1948), pp. 83–85.
17 Edward Ward, *The Secret History of Clubs* (London, 1709), pp. 361–362.
18 Ibid.
19 Vanbrugh, *Letters*, to Tonson, July 1703.
20 Nicolas Tindal, *The Continuation of Mr Rapin's History of England*, Vol. 6 (London: T. Osborne, J. Hodges et al., 1758), p. 170.
21 Walpole, *Anecdotes*, p. 111.
22 Calhoun Winton, 'Richard Steele', ODNB.
23 Joseph Spence, *Anecdotes, Observations and Characters of Books and Men*, ed. Samuel Singer (Centaur Press, 1964), 'Mr Pope, 1730', p. 197.
24 Vanbrugh, *Letters*, to Tonson in Amsterdam, July 1703. Both Edmund Dunch and John Dormer were club members. Dormer's later marriage to Diana Kirk ended in a notorious divorce case. Lord Wharton was convinced he was dying and summoned Kit Cat doctor Samuel Garth to his side at Winchington.
25 Ibid., to Carlisle, November 1721; ibid., to Manchester, February 1708. He later bemoaned 'the Curst Difficulty that Haymarket undertaking involved me in' in a letter to Tonson in 1719.
26 Carlisle accounts: four payments in 1704 total just over 100 guineas + £50 in 1708. Ancaster: £143 in 1703 + £53.15.0 in 1704.
27 Saumarez Smith, *Castle Howard*, p. 75.
28 Carlisle may have used his position as Earl Marshal to advance the interests of his friends.
29 Vanbrugh wears the insignia of the Clarenceux Herald on a chain. Vanbrugh aspired to be Garter but the post was conferred on John Anstis after a long battle between them.
30 Vanbrugh, *Letters*, to Tonson, November 1719.
31 BL, Add. 19594. Vanbrugh, *Letters*, to Carlisle, September 1725: he had 'prevail'd with ye Treasury, to Issue Farther . . . a Sum just enough to pay [him], being about £1700'.
32 Quoted in Downes, *Vanbrugh* 1987, p. 461.
33 For the South Sea Bubble see Malcolm Balen, *A Very English Deceit* (London: Fourth Estate, 2003).
34 Vanbrugh, *Letters* to Tonson, February 1720; a reference to the spectacular rise (and fall) of the Mississippi Company in Paris in 1720.
35 Ibid., to Carlisle, March 1721.
36 Ibid., to the Duke of Newcastle, December 1718.
37 Ibid., to Newcastle, January 1719.
38 A letter from Lady Mary Wortley Montagu, quoted in Downes, *Vanbrugh* 1987, p. 375.
39 Vanbrugh, *Letters*, to Tonson, June 1722.
40 Ibid., to Carlisle, July 1722.
41 Ibid., to Tonson, August 1725.

4 Influences on Vanbrugh's landscape style

1 Vanbrugh, *Letters*, to Tonson, July 1703; ibid. to Henry Joynes, February 1711.
2 John Dixon Hunt, 'Castle Howard Revisited', in John Dixon Hunt (ed.), *Gardens and the Picturesque* (London: MIT Press, 1992), p. 24; Levine, 'Castle Howard'. Both authors describe Castle Howard as Palladian.
3 Quote from Vanbrugh, *Letters*, to Manchester, December 1699.
4 Palladio devised a small number of standard room sizes that appeared again and again in his designs.
5 Vanbrugh, *Letters*, to Manchester, July 1707, author's emphasis.
6 Although Palladio wrote that 'usually I do not make halls longer than two squares which are derived from the breadth'; Palladio, *Architecture*, p. 57.

7 Ackerman, *Palladio*, p. 31.
8 Barlow, 'Vanbrugh's Queen's Theatre'.
9 Burns, *Palladio*, p. 246.
10 Cibber, quoted in Hart, *Storyteller*, p. 43.
11 Burns, *Palladio*, p. 247.
12 BL, Add. 61353, Vanbrugh to the 1st Earl of Godolphin, May 1709.
13 Vanbrugh, *Letters*, to the Duke of Marlborough, September 1710.
14 Although the plans were often outdated; see Colen Campbell, *Vitruvius Britannicus, or the British Architect*, Vol. 1 (London: s.n., 1715), plates 55–71.
15 Lang, 'Vanbrugh's Theory'; Alberti, *aedificatoria*.
16 Palladio, *Architecture*, p. 5.
17 Vanbrugh, *Letters*, to Manchester, November 1707; Alberti, *Building*, p. 156.
18 Vanbrugh, *Letters*, to Lord Poulet, September 1710; ibid., to Brigadier Watkins, August 1721.
19 Vanbrugh wrote to fellow Kit Cat Arthur Maynwaring in 1708: ''tis very Seldom That I am not Earnestly Employ'd, in Studdying how to make this [Blenheim] the Cheapest, as well as (it possibly) the best Hous in Europe'; Vanbrugh, *Letters*, to Arthur Maynwaring, July 1708. See also Vitruvius on economy: *Architecture*, p. 16.
20 Alberti, *Building*, p. 156.
21 Vanbrugh, *Letters* to Henry Joynes, November 1708.
22 BL, Add. 33064, Vanbrugh to Newcastle, August 1721.
23 Alberti, *Building*, p. 158.
24 Geoffrey Scott, *The Architecture of Humanism: A Study in the History of Taste* (London: Constable, 1929), p. 220.
25 Lang, 'Vanbrugh's Theory'.
26 Quote from Vanbrugh, *Letters*, to Carlisle, February 1724; the 'Temple with the four Porticos' at the south-east corner of Ray Wood is now known as the Temple of the Four Winds.
27 See Levine, 'Castle Howard'; he is unable to explain the offset of the pyramid. See also Saumarez Smith, *Castle Howard*, p. 148.
28 See Emilia Daniele (ed.), *Leon Battista Alberti Firenze e la Toscana: Exhibition Catalogue* (Firenze: Maschietto Editore, 2006), p. 41, where the Villa Fiesole is described as a perfect cube.
29 Alberti, *Building*, p. 307; Mazzini and Martini, *Medici*, pp. 130–131.
30 Steenbergen and Reh, *Architecture*, p. 52.
31 Ibid., p. 16.
32 Nourse, *Campania*, p. 299.
33 Steenbergen and Reh, *Architecture*, p. 271; Worsley, 'Campagna'; Whistler, *Vanbrugh*, p. 67.
34 Steenbergen and Reh, *Architecture*, p. 253.
35 Vanbrugh, *Letters*, to the Duchess of Marlborough, June 1709.
36 Ibid., to the Duchess of Marlborough, June 1709.
37 Hart, *Storyteller*, p. 109.
38 BL, Add. 33064, Vanbrugh to Newcastle, August 1721.
39 Saumarez Smith, *Castle Howard*, p. 148; Levine, 'Castle Howard'; Neckar, 'Castle Howard', p. 25.
40 CHA, G2/1/1, entries for October 1706: 'In ye wall of Wray Wood being 7ft high, Broach work in ye Butrasses and Bastions, Flagging at ye summerhouse in ye wood'.
41 Vanbrugh, *Letters*, to Carlisle, November 1724: 'a Cap is all that those sort of Towers shou'd have, and I have seen one upon a round Tower on the Walls of Chester, that I thought did extreamly well'; Alberti, *Building*, p. 133.
42 Nicholas de Fer, *Les Forces de l'Europe, ou Description des Principales Villes* (Paris, 1694).
43 Alberti, *Building*, p. 134.
44 LRO, 3ANC5/97/5 and HRO, M1B/3–1.
45 LRO, 3ANC5/97/6. As Comptroller of the King's Works Vanbrugh would have been consulted on the design of any new fortifications.
46 Switzer, *Ichnographia*, Vol. 2, p. 164. Vanbrugh was reinstated as Comptroller of the King's Works in 1715 and also made Surveyor of Gardens and Waters in the same year.
47 Ibid., p. 164.
48 D'Argenville, *Gardening* 1712, p. 77.
49 Ibid., p. 25.

50 Switzer, *Ichnographia*, Vol. 2, p. 174, author's emphasis.
51 Willis, 'Charles Bridgeman's "Capital Stroke"'.
52 BL, Add. 47030, to Daniel Dering, August, 1724.
53 BL, Maps 7.TAB10.
54 Christopher Duffy, *The Fortress in the Age of Vauban and Frederick the Great 1660–1789* (London: Routledge, 1985), p. 40.
55 Vanbrugh, *Letters*, to Lord Carlisle, November 1724.
56 Hart, *Storyteller*, p. 45; Mowl, *Early Mediaevalism*.
57 Downes, *Vanbrugh* 1987, p. 364; Hart, *Storyteller*, p. 234.
58 The Mount is shown in white in Kneller's Kit Cat painting of Newcastle and the Earl of Lincoln (*c.* 1717) in the National Portrait Gallery in London. Palladio often used this device as a means of controlling expense.
59 BL, Add. 33442; BRO, 33746: 'Sir John Vanbrugh's project for the front wall of the Great Court at Kings Weston February 1718'. The outworks were not built.
60 Vanbrugh, *Letters,* to Lord Carlisle, March 1726.
61 Quoted in Strong, *Renaissance*, p. 123.
62 BL, Sloane. 3881, f29: 'To fortifie a square piece of ground or to make a square fort according to Mr Gunter'.
63 Vanbrugh, *Letters*, to the Duke of Newcastle, December 1718.
64 Ibid., to Newcastle, September 1720.
65 Lazzaro, *Garden*, p. 130.
66 Michel de Montaigne, *Michel de Montaigne's Travel Journal* (San Francisco: North Point Press, 1983); Lazzaro, *Garden*, Appendix 3.
67 CHA, G2/1/1, entry for October 1706: 'Flagging at ye summerhouse in ye wood'.
68 GRO, D391.
69 CHA, G2/2/31–40.
70 Celia Fiennes, quoted in Timothy Mowl, *Gentlemen and Players* (Stroud: Sutton, 2004), p. 56.
71 Alberti, *Building*, p. 145.
72 Hart, *Storyteller*, p. 185.
73 The Temple at Castle Howard was possibly a dining parlour or games room. Both buildings had a practical purpose.
74 Lawrence Eusden, *A Poem on the Marriage of His Grace the Duke of Newcastle to the Right Honourable the Lady Henrietta Godolphin* (London: Jacob Tonson, 1717).
75 Vanbrugh, *Letters*, to Lord Carlisle, April 1724, author's emphasis.
76 Alberti, *Building*, p. 194, author's emphasis.
77 Palladio, *Architecture*, p. 215.
78 The temple at Eastbury may have been one exception; future three-dimensional modelling will confirm this.
79 Alberti, *Building*, p. 199. Measurements from digital photographs indicate that Vanbrugh's Temple is a perfect cube. 'The Ceiling will do very well flat, because it will shape the room just to a Cube', Vanbrugh, *Letters*, to Carlisle, March 1724. See Daniele, *Leon Battista Alberti*, p. 41, who refers to a '*perfetto cubo pitagorico*' (perfect Pythagoran cube) at Fiesole.
80 Alberti, *Building*, p. 199. Measurements from digital photographs.
81 Alberti did not reproduce Vitruvius exactly on this point but only alludes to the Orders; see ibid., p. 195.
82 CHA, J8/1/554–573, Hawksmoor to Lord Carlisle, January 1724, author's emphasis.
83 Letter, Hawksmoor to Lord Carlisle, July 1735, quoted in Saumarez Smith, *Castle Howard*, p. 147.
84 Ibid., pp. 179–180.
85 Worsley, 'Nicholas Hawksmoor'.
86 Alexander Pope, *Letters of Mr Pope, and Several Eminent Persons, from the Year 1705, to 1735, Vol. I* (London: T. Cooper, 1735), p. 142; Vanbrugh, *Letters*, to Brigadier Watkins at Claremont, August 1721, author's emphasis.
87 Hawksmoor to Lord Carlisle, 1724, quoted in Downes, *Vanbrugh* 1987, p. 469.
88 Ibid., p. 465.
89 Palladio, *Architecture*, p. 94.
90 BL, BLEN G-1–16.

91   BL, Add. 19593, entry January 1710.
92   Edward Southwell, August 1724, quoted in G. Clarke, *Descriptions of Lord Cobhams Gardens at Stowe* (Aylesbury: Buckingham Record Society, 1990), p. 19.
93   Vanbrugh, *Letters*, to Lord Carlisle, June 1722.
94   Robert Williams, 'Vanbrugh's India and his Mausolea for England', in Ridgway and Williams, *Vanbrugh*, pp. 114–130.
95   Howard Colvin, *Architecture and the Afterlife* (London: Yale University Press, 1991), pp. 200, 290.
96   Ibid., p. 315.
97   Surrounding walls were added by Lord Burlington's protégé David Garrett.
98   Vanbrugh was made Herald Extraordinary in June 1703. He did not become King of Arms until March 1704.
99   Hart, *Storyteller*, pp. 106–108, 54.
100 Downes, *Vanbrugh* 1987, p. 241.
101 Vanbrugh, *Letters*, to Tonson, July 1703.
102 Ibid., to Tonson, October 1725.
103 Ibid., to Carlisle, September 1725.
104 McCormick, 'Vanbrugh's Architecture'. Repeated in Hart, *Storyteller*, p. 43; Steenbergen and Reh, *Architecture*, p. 249.
105 Vanbrugh, *Letters*, to Tonson, July 1703; Graham F. Barlow, 'Vanbrugh's Queen's Theatre in the Haymarket, 1703–9', *Early Music* (1989), Vol. 17, No. 4, pp. 515–521.
106 McCormick, *Playwright as Architect*, pp. 94–95.
107 Switzer, *Ichnographia*, Vol. 2, p. 198.
108 CHA, H1/1/4 and H1/1/5.
109 CHA, J8/35/51.
110 John Churchill, 1st Duke of Marlborough, *The Marlborough–Godolphin Correspondence*, ed. Henry Snyder (Oxford: Clarendon Press, 1975) Duke of Marlborough to the Duchess, May 1706.
111 Vanbrugh, *Letters*, to Manchester, August 1708.
112 Neckar, 'Castle Howard'; Dixon Hunt, 'Castle Howard'.
113 Whistler, *Vanbrugh*, p. 64.
114 Downes, *Vanbrugh* 1987, p. 461.
115 Whistler, *Vanbrugh*, p. 68.
116 See Batey, 'Pleasures of the Imagination'; Neckar, 'Castle Howard'; Hart, *Storyteller*, p. 91.
117 Tracy Chevalier (ed.), *Encyclopedia of the Essay* (London: Taylor & Francis, 1997), p. 805; quote from Porter, *Enlightenment*, p. 195.
118 Habermas, *Sphere*, p. 43.
119 Addison, *Spectator*, No. 414, 25 June.
120 Vanbrugh frequently mentions Essex, Garth and visits to John Dormer at Rousham in his correspondence.
121 Alberti, *Building*, p. 295.
122 'I have been so taken up with killing Hares and Partridges that I have scarce time to do anything else. I have planted a great many Trees all about me and intend to make up the number a thousand before I shall think I have done my years work', Addison, 1713, quoted in Walter Graham (ed.), *The Letters of Joseph Addison* (Oxford: Clarendon Press, 1941), Addison to Ambrose Philips, November 1713.
123 Dorothy Kingsbury, *Bilton Hall: Its History and Literary Association* (London: Mitre Press, 1957), p. 17, author's emphasis.
124 Addison, *Spectator*, No. 414, 25 June. In 1714 Addison's steward Edward Addison wrote that he had restocked the fish ponds, but that his pigeons were 'much thinned'; there is later mention of the orchard and a nursery for young trees, BL, Egerton MSS. 1971.
125 Peter Smithers, *The Life of Joseph Addison* (Oxford: Clarendon Press, 1954), p. 248.
126 Graham, *Addison*, Edward Addison to Joseph Addison, November 1714.
127 Smithers, *Addison*, p. 310.
128 Addison, *Spectator*, No. 414, 25 June.
129 Pope, *Guardian*, No. 173, 29 September.
130 Ibid.

131 Switzer, *Ichnographia*, Vol. 3, p. 46.
132 Switzer, *Ichnographia*, Vol. 2, p. 191; Stephen Switzer, *An Introduction to a General System of Hydrostaticks and Hydraulicks*, Vol. 1 (London: T. Astley, S. Austen, L. Gilliver, 1729).
133 William Brogden, *Stephen Switzer and Garden Design in the Early Eighteenth Century*, PhD thesis, University of Edinburgh (1973).
134 Alexander Pope, *The Guardian*, No. 4 (London: R. Steele, 1713), 16 March.
135 BL, Add. 19592, entry November 1705.
136 Switzer, *Hydrostaticks*, Vol. 1, p. 10.
137 BL, Add. 19608, Samuel Travers to William Boulter, March 1708.
138 Brogden, *Switzer*, p. 175. The contract for Caversham in Berkshire is not signed. HaRO, 63M84/190.
139 BOD, MS Eng. Misc. C. 114.
140 Brogden, *Switzer*, p. 57. Brogden's attribution is repeated widely by Willis, Williams, Dixon Hunt, Downes and most recently Hart.
141 Ibid., p. 197.
142 David Jacques and Jane Furse, *Report of the Historical Interest of the Gardens and Grounds at Leeswood Hall, Clwyd*, Garden History Society (1981).
143 Hoare's Bank, payment of £53.05.0. *Archaeologia*, quoted in Jacques and Furse, *Leeswood Hall*, p. 2.
144 See RCW, D/HE/313. Switzer was expecting further payments, which had not materialised.
145 Flintshire, *Leeswood Hall Garden Site Report*, RCW.
146 Howard Erskine-Hill, 'Alexander Pope', ODNB.
147 Bond, *Spectator*, p. lxxxvii.
148 Erskine-Hill, 'Alexander Pope', ODNB.
149 Alexander Pope, *An Epistle to the Right Honourable Richard Earl of Burlington* (London: L. Gilliver, 1731), p. 7; Joseph Addison, *The Guardian*, No. 101 (London: R. Steele, 1713), 7 July.
150 See, for example, Dixon Hunt and Willis, *Genius*.
151 Alexander Pope, *The Works of Alexander Pope*, Vol. 8 (London: J. & P. Knapton, 1753), Pope to Edward Blount, June 1725.
152 Brownell, 'Pope's Twickenham', p. 21.
153 David Green, *Gardener to Queen Anne* (London: Oxford University Press, 1956), p. 143.
154 'Where My Lord Burlington is building a lovely house . . . There is a canal which borders the garden on one side with two other smaller pieces of water formed in the woods. Everything is covered in grass. At the end is a high terass covered in grass from which one can see the Thames', National Art Library, 86.NN.2.
155 Tom Williamson, *Polite Landscapes* (Stroud: Sutton, 1998), p. 43.
156 Pope, *Epistle*, p. 7.
157 Ackerman, *Palladio*, p. 185.
158 Vanbrugh, *Letters*, to Tonson, November 1719.
159 See Appendix B.
160 This style emerged as Vanbrugh's work with Bridgeman progressed.
161 However, Willis, *Bridgeman*, p. 109, n. 14 refers to an undated account for Bridgeman at Stowe that has been filed in the '1714' packet.
162 Hoare's Bank, *Private Accounts for Edward Rolt*, 1714–20: Ledger 17 folio 33913 June 1715, Ledger 18 folio 2662 July 1715 and June 1716, Ledger 20 folio 615 June 1717 and September 1717, Ledger 20 folio 4364 August 1718.
163 Nathaniel Salmon, *The History of Hertfordshire* (London: s.n., 1728), Sacombe, p. 225.
164 Willis, *Bridgeman*, p. 60.

5 Castle Howard, Yorkshire

1 Downes, *Vanbrugh* 1987, p. 276.
2 Dixon Hunt, 'Castle Howard', p. 24: 'ultimately a Palladian house, on which a classical dome has been placed'; Levine, 'Castle Howard'.
3 Ralph Freman visited Castle Howard in 1736/37: 'There are three fine visto's one thro the depth of the house, & two very long ones thro the whole length which terminate in the same room at end, one is a library the other a parlour', from Anne Rowe (ed.), *Garden Making and the*

Freman Family: A Memoir of Hamels 1713–33 (Hertford: Hertfordshire Record Society, 2001), p. 69.

4 Vanbrugh, *Letters*, to Manchester, December 1699.
5 Ibid.
6 Hart, *Storyteller*, p. 78.
7 See Hawksmoor's drawings for the west front of the Great Cabinet 1707, BL, Maps K.Top.45.
8 V&A, E432.1951; attached notes: 'The Prick Line Markt with R is Wray Wood Wall as is now standing, the lines Markt S S S is more of the Old Wall. The lines Markt with T T is the new Wall which is built'. CHA, G2/1/1.
9 CHA, G2/2/11–20: 'work don att the Brest Wall or Low South Tarass', May 1705.
10 CHA, G2/1/2. The remains of Vanbrugh's ditch can be seen to the north of the path from the Temple of Venus to the white gate. The wall was removed in the late eighteenth century.
11 Vanbrugh, *Letters,* to Carlisle, December 1724, including a reference to the walls to the north of the entrance court.
12 Neckar believes this to be a design for waterworks in Ray Wood; Neckar, 'Castle Howard'.
13 Entry for carving of the 'Satyr gate in ye garding', CHA, G2/1/2.
14 CHA, G2/2/21–30.
15 CHA, G2/2/31–40.
16 Saumarez Smith, *Castle Howard*, p. 80; Vanbrugh, *Letters*, to Manchester, July 1707.
17 CHA, G2/2/11–20.
18 GRO, D391. Dated by his reference to 'The house is now Building of which the body and one wing is up, towards the garden front, are windows' and Vanbrugh's letter to Manchester, July 1708: 'My Ld Carlisle has got his whole Garden Front up'. Neckar recreates the garden in the 1730s using accounts by Player, Irwin and Atkyns; Neckar, 'Castle Howard'.
19 CHA, J8/35/51.
20 GRO, D391.
21 Saumarez Smith, *Castle Howard*, p. 107.
22 GRO, D391.
23 Venus, Book 14; Bacchus, Book 11; Diana and stag, Book 3; a Satyr, Book 6; and a shepherd with his dog, Book 1.
24 GRO, D391.
25 Player did not comment on the allegorical theme in his diary.
26 CHA, H2/3/1. Carlisle's Grand Tour notes are partly in Italian. He had copies of Ovid in French and English.
27 CHA, G2/2/21-30 and CHA, G2/2/51-60.
28 Lady Anne Irwin, *Castle-Howard, the Seat of the Right Honourable Charles Earl of Carlisle* (London: E. Owen, 1732).
29 Dixon Hunt, 'Castle Howard'.
30 Lazzaro, *Garden*, Appendix 3.
31 Switzer, *Ichnographia*, Vol. 2, p.199.
32 Switzer, *Ichnographia*, Vol. 3, p. 46.
33 Switzer, *Nobleman*, p. 64.
34 John Tracy Atkyns, 1732, quoted in Saumarez Smith, *Castle Howard*, p. 127.
35 Switzer, *Ichnographia*, Vol. 1, p. xxviii.
36 Brogden, *Switzer*, p. 149; Neckar, 'Castle Howard'; Dixon Hunt, 'Castle Howard'; Whistler, *Vanbrugh*, p. 64.
37 CHA, H1/1/4 and H1/1/5.
38 At Caversham.
39 Reservoir in Ray Wood in CHA, G2/2/41–50, and Atkyns 1732, quoted in Saumarez Smith, *Castle Howard*, p. 127.
40 According to Atkyns 1732, quoted ibid.
41 Whistler, *Vanbrugh*, p. 114, quoting BL Add. 19591 and 19606.
42 He also worked at Chatsworth and the Father Time statue at Duncombe (1715) is also attributed to him.
43 CHA, J8/5.
44 CHA, G2/2/41–50. Two references to work on a 'pedestal on the stairs down to the bowling green' and a 'doore head in the bowling green house', No. 43.

45 Ibid.
46 Ibid., 45 and 47.
47 Ibid., 46, entry 1720/1721 'pedestal at end of the terrass entering Wray Wood'.
48 Ibid., 46 and 48.
49 Vanbrugh, *Letters*, to Carlisle, February 1721.
50 Ibid., to Carlisle, May 1722.
51 CHA, J8/1/554–573.
52 CHA, G2/2/41–50. Vanbrugh, *Letters*, to Carlisle, April 1722.
53 BL, Add. 33064. 'I hope I shall find the walls at Claremont as much to my satisfaction (and your Graces too) as those are here. I find the more my Lord Carlisle sees of them the more he is pleas'd with them, And I think all that come here are surpris'd at their Magnificent Effect', Vanbrugh, *Letters*, to Newcastle, August 1723. The new outworks at Claremont must have been to the south of the Mount, as northern outworks were already built.
54 Vanbrugh, *Letters*, to Carlisle, March 1726.
55 BL, Add. 70405.
56 Neckar, 'Castle Howard'.
57 BL, Stowe 748.
58 Switzer, *Ichnographia*, Vol. 1, p. 305; Vanbrugh, *Letters*, to Carlisle, February 1724.
59 In 1719 there were payments for 'Securing ye Canall [at Chatsworth]' with further payments promised provided it 'doth not loose water', quoted from Tom Williamson and John Barnatt, *Chatsworth: A Landscape History* (Macclesfield: Windgather Press, 2005), p. 72.
60 CHA, J8/1/554–573.
61 Vanbrugh, *Letters*, to Carlisle, February 1724.
62 Downes, *Vanbrugh* 1987, p. 469; Whistler, *Vanbrugh*, p. 76.
63 Mazzini and Martini, *Medici*, pp. 171–172.
64 Whistler, *Vanbrugh*, p. 75.
65 Irwin, *Castle-Howard*, p. 13.
66 Vanbrugh, *Letters*, to Carlisle, December 1725.
67 Vanbrugh, *Letters*, to Carlisle, December 1725.
68 CHA, G2/2/51–60.
69 Ibid., entry 1729.
70 Saumarez Smith, *Castle Howard*, p. 147.
71 'Drawing several Plans & Uprights for the Octagon Turrett', December 1731, quoted ibid., p. 147.
72 Quoted ibid., p. 147.
73 Quoted ibid., p. 169.
74 BL, Add. 33064, Vanbrugh to the Duke of Newcastle, August 1721.

6 Blenheim, Oxfordshire

1 Vanbrugh, *Letters,* to Manchester, December 1699.
2 Quoted in Grafton, *Alberti*, p. 319.
3 Vanbrugh, *Letters*, to Manchester, December 1699.
4 Vanbrugh, *Letters*, to Lord Poulet, September 1710. The Blenheim model had two functions: as a design to be approved by the monarch, and as a way of controlling the architect.
5 James Bond, 'Woodstock in the sixteenth and seventeenth centuries', in James Bond and Kate Tiller (eds), *Landscape for a Palace*, 2nd edn (Stroud: Sutton, 2000), pp. 55–66.
6 Ibid.
7 BOD, MS Wood 276B.
8 Willis, *Bridgeman*, p. 49 and Hart, *Vanbrugh*, p. 109; both describe Blenheim as 'Picturesque'.
9 Reference to the kitchen court in 1707: Vanbrugh, *Letters*, to the Duchess of Marlborough, June 1709.
10 See David Green and James Bond, 'Blenheim after Vanbrugh', in Bond and Tiller, *Landscape*, pp. 80–89.
11 See Whistler, *Vanbrugh*, Appendix 3 for a copy of Wren's proposal.
12 Designed and built by Robert Aldersea in 1706.
13 Downes, *Vanbrugh* 1977, p. 73. The dimensions are actually given in two contemporary accounts by Fougeroux, National Art Library, 86.NN.2, and the Duchess: 'There will be a

canal of sixty foot wide which watter will run thro the great Arch of the Bridge and on each side of this watter under the Arch there will bee a fine grass walk of twenty foot broad', totalling 100 feet, BL, BLEN G-1–16.

14 Green, *Blenheim Palace*. See BL, Add. 19601.
15 Vanbrugh, *Letters*, to Maynwaring, July 1708. Maynwaring was secretary to the Duchess of Marlborough and a fellow member of the Kit Cat Club.
16 BL, Add. 61353, Vanbrugh to the Duke of Marlborough, June 1705.
17 Churchill, *Marlborough–Godolphin Correspondence*, Duke of Marlborough to the Duchess, May 1706.
18 Green, *Blenheim Palace*, p. 68; Whistler, *Vanbrugh*, p. 117.
19 David Green, 'Blenheim: The Palace and Gardens under Vanbrugh, Hawksmoor and Wise', in Bond and Tiller (eds), *Landscape*, p. 73; Downes, *Vanbrugh* 1987, p. 282.
20 Daniel Defoe, *A Tour thro' the Whole Island of Great Britain*, 3rd edn, Vol. 2 (London: J. Osborn, S. Birt, D. Browne, J. Hodges, A. Millar, J. Whiston and J. Robinson, 1742), p. 232.
21 Vanbrugh, *Letters*, to Henry Joynes, November 1708.
22 John Macky, *A Journey through England*, Vol. II, 1st edn (London: J. Pemberton, 1722), p. 117; BL, Add. 47030, Viscount Perceval to Daniel Dering, August 1724.
23 BL, Add. 19592, entry December 1705; BL, Add. 19595, reference to the Great Lawn in the Woodwork, December 1708.
24 Switzer, *Ichnographia*, Vol. 2, p. 174.
25 Churchill, *Marlborough–Godolphin Correspondence*, Samuel Travers to the Duke of Marlborough, June 1706.
26 Green, *Blenheim Palace*, p. 67.
27 Macky, *Journey*, Vol. II, 2nd edn (London: T. Caldecott, 1724), p. 108. He goes on: 'Accordingly Mr Wise transplanted thither full grown trees in Baskets, which he bury'd in the Earth, which look and thrive the same, as if they had stood there 30 or 40 years'. Thomas Salmon, *The Foreigner's Companion through the Universities of Cambridge and Oxford, and the Adjacent Counties* (London: William Owen, 1748), p. 6.
28 BL, Add. 19592, entry payment to Wise, December 1705.
29 BL, Add. 19595, entry July 1708.
30 BL, Add. 19596, entry May 1709.
31 Hart, *Storyteller*, p. 145.
32 His lack of salary must have prompted the desire for free lodging in the Manor.
33 Vanbrugh, *Letters*, to the Duchess of Marlborough, June 1709, author's emphasis.
34 BL, Add. 61353, Vanbrugh to Godolphin, May 1709.
35 Vanbrugh, *Letters*, to the Duchess of Marlborough, June 1709.
36 Green, *Blenheim Palace*, p. 163.
37 Lecture 'Making a New Architecture, Palladio as Innovator', Howard Burns, Royal Academy of Arts, 13 March 2009. Burns believes that Palladio's use of orthogonal projections in *Quattro Libri* made it possible for architects to study proportions for the first time.
38 BL, Add. 47030, Viscount Perceval to his brother Daniel Dering, August 1724.
39 'The water (where it will appear to best advantage, whether Lake or River)', BL, Add. 61353, Vanbrugh to the Duke of Marlborough, July 1709.
40 BL, Add. 61457, author's emphasis.
41 BL, Add. 61523, Vanbrugh to Thomas Hopkins, May 1709.
42 Vanbrugh, *Letters*, to Travers, undated, early 1710.
43 Ibid., to the Duke of Marlborough, April 1710.
44 Swift, *Stella*, pp. 83–85.
45 Quoted in Green, *Blenheim Palace*, p. 121; possibly the source of Pope's quote, attributed to Shrewsbury, that Blenheim was 'a great pile of stones above ground', see Pope, *Letters*, p. 142.
46 See Vanbrugh, *Letters*, pp. 54–55.
47 Churchill, *Marlborough–Godolphin Correspondence*, Marlborough to the Duchess, November 1705.
48 Vanbrugh, *Letters*, to the Duchess of Marlborough, November 1716.
49 HMC, *Manchester*, Duchess of Marlborough to Manchester, August 1708.
50 BL, BLEN G-1–16, Duchess of Marlborough to Lady Cairns, 1721.
51 BL, Add. 61457, Duchess of Marlborough to Somerset, August 1723.
52 BL, Add. 61353, Hawksmoor to the Duchess of Marlborough, April 1722.

53 BL, Add. 61457, Duchess of Marlborough to Somerset, August 1723.
54 Alan Crossley and C. R. Elrington (eds), *History of the County of Oxford: Volume 12* (London: Victoria County History of the Counties of England, 1990), pp. 460–470. Steenbergen and Reh also note the discrepancy.
55 On the evidence of the handwriting; see John Harris (ed.), *The Palladian Revival: Exhibition Catalogue* (London: Royal Academy of Arts, 1994).
56 Excerpts translated from French:

> The garden is large but very neglected . . . It is planted in the common (natural) style in woods with walls of yews cut into compartments which are not bad. At the end is a small kitchen garden. The outer park is infinitely better. Opposite the chateau is a large piece of water in a valley forming a lake, which falls by a very beautiful waterfall of five steps to a broad canal which curves very far and then falls into a small river. The canal is crossed by a very beautiful bridge with a single arch of 100 feet . . . a mill with six pumps which provides the water to the house reservoir. There are parapets furnished with iron balustrades on both side of the road.
>
> . . . At the end of the canal is a large round pool from which the water tumbles by a beautiful waterfall into another channel which winds around the park. There is no better view than into a valley, but this canal is so deeply entrenched and the lovely waterfall cannot be seen from the palace. It is necessary to be on the parapet of the bridge to look at it across the water of the canal. (National Art Library, 86.NN.2, section on Blenheim)

57 Switzer, *Ichnographia*, Vol. 1, p. 84; BL, Add. 47030, Viscount Percival to Daniel Dering, August 1724.
58 During the 1719 court case Vanbrugh did not support the Duchess's contention that the debt was the Crown's. Webb believes that the Duchess's hatred of Vanbrugh dates from this time. Vanbrugh, *Letters*, p. xxv; quote from BL, Add. 38056.
59 BL, Add. 61354, John Hughes to the Duchess of Marlborough, July 1725.
60 Vanbrugh, *Letters*, to Tonson, October 1725.
61 BL, Add. 61457.
62 Vanbrugh, *Letters*, to Lord Carlisle, September 1725.
63 Sarah Duchess of Marlborough, *The Opinions of Sarah Duchess-Dowager of Marlborough. Published from Original MSS*, eds Sir David Dalrymple and Lord Hailes (Edinburgh: s.n., 1788).
64 Salmon, *Companion*, p. 6.
65 Hal Mogridge, 'Capability Brown at Blenheim', in Bond, *Landscape*, p. 91.
66 BL, Add. 61354, John Hughes to the Duchess of Marlborough, July 1725.

7 Kimbolton, Heythrop and Grimsthorpe

1 Vanbrugh, *Letters*, to the Earl of Manchester, December 1699.
2 Ibid., to Manchester, July 1707, author's emphasis.
3 Ibid., to Carlisle, November 1724.
4 Ibid., to Manchester, July 1708.
5 Ibid., to Manchester, July 1707, author's emphasis. Reuse of old stone was an example of Vitruvian 'economy'.
6 Ibid., to Manchester, July 1707.
7 Ibid., to Manchester, September 1707, author's emphasis.
8 Ibid., to Manchester, July 1707.
9 John Stratford, 'The Lost Gardens of Kimbolton Castle', *Kimbolton Local History Journal* (1998), Vol. 3, pp. 21–30.
10 Kimbolton Castle, Bedfordshire, *Inventory of Goods of Charles, Earl of Manchester about the Castle of Kimbolton*, 1687.
11 Vanbrugh, *Letters*, to the Earl of Manchester, March 1708; Whistler, *Vanbrugh*, p. 142.
12 Ibid., to Manchester, July 1707.
13 First published by Stratford, 'Kimbolton Castle'. I am indebted to Norah Butler, who drew my attention to Fougeroux's travel diary in the National Art Library.
14 Translation from French: 'On the garden side one sees a large portico with columns . . . The garden is very lovely. At the end of the parterre is a canal edged with embankments, and

woodland on both sides interspersed with avenues of grass. On descending from the terrace to the parterre there are avenues of lime trees to each side, cut underneath in the Italian way, as we can see at Chantilly in front of the chateau. There are some poor examples of statuary. Copies after the antique style are placed at the intersections of the avenues in the woods'. National Art Library, 86.NN.2.

15 National Art Library, 86.NN.2.
16 Vanbrugh, *Letters*, to Manchester, March 1708.
17 Not printed: Google Earth licensing is restrictive.
18 Vanbrugh, *Letters*, to Manchester, July 1708.
19 Jones's plan of Heythrop is reproduced in Timothy Mowl, *The Historic Gardens of England: Oxfordshire* (Stroud: Tempus, 2007), p. 57.
20 BL, Add. 47030, letter to Daniel Dering, August 1724: 'much is yet wanting to be done within the house, tho built 18 years ago'.
21 Switzer, *Ichnographia*, Vol. 3, pp. 87–88.
22 Shrewsbury deliberately left his lands to the younger George fearing that his elder brother Gilbert would give the estates to the church; see Stuart Handley, 'Charles Talbot', ODNB.
23 Thomas Salmon, *The Present State of the Universities and of the Five Adjacent Counties* (London: Thomas Salmon, 1743), p. 13.
24 Arundel Castle, TP 133.
25 Macky, *Journey*, Vol. II, 1st edn, p. 119. The visit is dated from a comment in the first edition of Vol. I of his *Journey*, published in 1714.
26 Swift, *Stella*, entry June 1711, n. 2.
27 'But one thing I heard this very day which I never suspected before that [Vanbrugh] is often with [Shrewsbury]', quoted in Green, *Blenheim Palace*, p. 248.
28 Macky, *Journey*, Vol. II, 1st edn, p. 119.
29 Thomas Wentworth, *The Wentworth Papers 1705–1739*, ed. J Cartwright (London: Wyman and Sons, 1883) Lord Berkeley to the Earl of Strafford, July 1713.
30 Whistler, *Vanbrugh*, p. 63, n. 1 and p. 117.
31 Brogden, *Switzer*, p. 57. Grimsthorpe attributed to Switzer by Willis, *Bridgeman*, p. 134; Robert Williams, 'Fortified Gardens', in Ridgway and Williams, *Vanbrugh*, pp. 48–70; Hart, *Storyteller*, plate 294; Steffie Shields, 'The Magnificence of Grimsthorpe', *Lincolnshire Life* (2006), August, pp. 16–20.
32 Robert Bertie was Earl of Lindsey in 1701, Marquis of Lindsey in 1706 and 1st Duke of Ancaster and Kesteven in 1715. Referred to as 'Bertie' in this section. His brother Peregrine (died 1711) was also a friend of Vanbrugh.
33 Howard Colvin, 'Grimsthorpe Castle: The North Front', in Howard Colvin and John Harris (eds), *The Country Seat* (London: Allen Lane, 1970), pp. 91–93. After Bertie's death in 1723, Vanbrugh completed the work for his son Peregrine.
34 Lord, 'John Vanbrugh'.
35 26 October 1711 £18.12.0 and 22 November 1712 £39.6.0, RBS Group Archives, CH/194/12.
36 Vanbrugh made further visits in 1718 and in 1720, Borthwick Institute, YM/VAN/1.
37 Switzer, *Ichnographia*, Vol. 1, pp. 54–55.
38 Switzer, *Ichnographia*, Vol. 2, p. 115.
39 Downes referred to the Switzer payments; Tim Connor directed me to Child's Bank. December 1710 £100, January 1711 £19.0.10, March 1712 £100, April 1713 £24.10.9, August 1713 £20, September 1713 £44.2.9, RBS Group Archives, CH/194/12. The letter is in the Bodleian Library: MS Eng. Misc. C. 114.
40 Whistler, *Vanbrugh*, p. 63.
41 Addison, *Spectator*, No. 477, 6 September.
42 Switzer, *Ichnographia*, Vol. 2, pp. 203–4.

8 Claremont, Surrey and Nottingham Castle

1 See Downes, *Vanbrugh* 1987, p. 339.
2 'A licence from the Lord of the Manor to Robert Moore to Lease said premises to John Vanbrough Esq for a term of 70 years from Michaelmas next./And to pull down Chargate House and the outhouses or buildings thereto belonging – building in the same place some

other Brick House Tenement Outhouses or buildings as large good substantial &c./And to grub up any Trees in Chargate Wood or on any part of Chargate Farm which should obstruct the visto or prospect of any Building or Walk which said John Vanbrough should build or make on the premises'. SHC, K176/14/2.

3 Harris, 'Beginnings of Claremont', p. 225; albeit with Vanbrugh 'in design control'.
4 Vanbrugh wrote to Maynwaring from Chargate in October 1710, BL, Add. 61353.
5 Subsequent references to 'the Mount' refer predominantly to the building.
6 Harris, 'Beginnings of Claremont', p. 224.
7 Laid paper was formed by pressing linen pulp on a sieve – the lines from the grids are discernible on the finished paper and are distinguishing marks for production before 1750.
8 Whistler, *Vanbrugh*, p. 154.
9 Reed Browning, *The Duke of Newcastle* (London: Yale University Press, 1975), p. 6.
10 SHC, K176/14/2.
11 Eusden, 'Poem', p. 11.
12 Anon., *The Ambulator*, 1st edn (London: J. Bew, 1774), p. 36, author's emphasis.
13 Samuel Garth, *Claremont* (London, J. Tonson, 1715), p. 5, author's emphasis. Vanbrugh was also known as Vanbrook.
14 BL, Add. 33442, entry May 1715; Eusden, 'Poem', p. 11.
15 BL, Add. 33442, entries 1715–17. The account entries for a 'house of office', one by the bowling green, one at the end of a walk in the wood, were also for toilets.
16 Eusden, 'Poem', p. 12, author's emphasis.
17 SHC, K176/14/2.
18 Vanbrugh was instrumental in arranging this marriage.
19 Purchased in January 1717.
20 Vanbrugh, *Letters*, to Newcastle, August 1724.
21 Whistler, *Vanbrugh*, p. 153.
22 Langley, *Gardening*, p. vii.
23 BL, Add. 33064, Vanbrugh to Newcastle, August 1723.
24 Ibid., Vanbrugh to Newcastle, August 1724.
25 Switzer, *Hydrostaticks*, Vol. 2, p. 405; The National Trust, *Claremont* (London: Centurion Press, 2000), p. 21.
26 Daniel Defoe, *Tour*, 3rd edn, Vol. 1, p. 228. Defoe died in 1731; his *Tour* was revised and reprinted after his death.
27 Browning, *Newcastle*, p. 6.
28 See ibid. and Ray Kelch, *Newcastle, a Duke without Money: Thomas Pelham-Holles, 1693–1768* (London: Routledge & Kegan Paul, 1974).
29 BL, Add. 33064, Vanbrugh to the Duke of Newcastle, December 1718.
30 Anon, *Ambulator*, p. 36.
31 Vanbrugh, *Letters*, to Newcastle, September 1720.
32 Kelch, *Newcastle*, p. 12.
33 Defoe, *Tour*, 3rd edn, Vol. 1, p. 227.

9 Kings Weston, Gloucestershire (now Avon)

1 D. W. Hayton, 'Edward Southwell', ODNB.
2 Notes by an unknown author found in BRO (POL/HM/3/10) suggest a connection with the Marlboroughs. The Duchess of Marlborough accused the Duke of having an affair with Lady Southwell in 1704. The Marlboroughs visited Kings Weston in 1716; see Vanbrugh, *Letters*, to the Duchess of Marlborough, August 1716.
3 Kings Weston, Sacombe and Duncombe.
4 Vanbrugh, *Letters*, to Newcastle, September 1720.
5 Hanoverian Tories supported the protestant succession. Southwell was secretary to the 2nd Duke of Ormond, who was one of the founding members of the Tory Brothers Club; he was also a close friend of Jonathan Swift.
6 Hart, *Storyteller*, p. 171.
7 Ibid., pp. 171–85. Downes, *Vanbrugh* 1987, p. 343.
8 Timothy Mowl, *The Historic Gardens of England: Gloucestershire* (Stroud: Tempus, 2005), pp. 57–63.

9 Downes, 'Kings Weston Book of Drawings', p. 18; the drawing appears to be annotated by Southwell.
10 Mowl, *Gloucestershire*, p. 60.
11 Vanbrugh, *Letters*, to Edward Southwell, October 1713.
12 See Mowl, *Gloucestershire*, p. 60, n. 3.
13 Downes, 'Kings Weston Book of Drawings', p. 79
14 BL, Add. 69965.
15 Downes, *Vanbrugh* 1977, p. 79. Southwell was a patron of Campbell.
16 Mowl, *Gloucestershire*, p. 60.
17 Pope, *Epistle*, p. 10.
18 Macky, *Journey*, Vol. II, 1st edn (London: J. Pemberton, 1722), p. 9.
19 Vanbrugh, *Letters*, to Newcastle, September 1720.
20 Battestin, *Literature*, p. 37.

10 Duncombe Park and Sacombe Park

1 David Hayton, Eveline Cruickshanks and Stuart Handley, *The House of Commons, 1690–1715* (Cambridge: Cambridge University Press, 2002), p. 945.
2 Quoted in Downes, *Vanbrugh* 1987, p. 375.
3 *Vitruvius Britannicus*, Vol. 3.
4 Whistler, *Vanbrugh*, p. 21. The dome on the temple at Stowe was lowered during the eighteenth century. Whistler considers Cholmondeley, Duncombe and Eastbury as a 'single period of inspiration', see ibid., p. 160.
5 Brogden, *Switzer*, p. 9; Christopher Hussey, *English Gardens and Landscapes 1700–1750* (London: Country Life, 1967), p. 78.
6 Anon., *A New Display of the Beauties of England*, Vol. 1 (London: R. Goadby, 1774), p. 152.
7 Milledge, 'Sacombe Park'.
8 £654 between 1715 and 1718, Hoare's Bank, Private Accounts for Edward Rolt; Coutt's £534 in 1720, from Milledge, 'Sacombe Park', p. 42.
9 Willis, *Bridgeman*, p. 60.
10 Quoted in Whistler, *Vanbrugh*, p. 152, author's emphasis. Van Brock is another version of Vanbrugh.
11 Salmon, *Hertfordshire*, p. 225.
12 Sir Matthew Decker, 1728, quoted in Milledge, 'Sacombe Park', p. 39.
13 Ibid., p. 42.

11 Eastbury, Dorset

1 Borthwick Institute, YM/VAN/16.
2 NA, PROB 11/573. Thornhill, quoted in Whistler, *Vanbrugh*, p 164. Whistler surmises that Dodington lived in the kitchen wing.
3 NA, PROB 11/573.
4 Willis, *Bridgeman*, p. 48.
5 Whistler, *Vanbrugh*, p. 164.
6 Whistler highlights the similarity between this plan and that for Amesbury, which is signed by Bridgeman and dated 1738; ibid., p. 164.
7 According to the present owner, Jim Farquharson, a well is situated in the diamond (June 2008).
8 'A small part of one end was within the pail that had been opend, and a grotto made in the hollow. We were told that when it was opend a number of Bones were found', Sir Josiah Banks, *Journal of an Excursion to Eastbury*, pp. 143–149.
9 'Bubb' will be used here to avoid confusion.
10 NA, PROB 11/573.
11 A. Hanham, 'George Bubb Dodington', ODNB.
12 Vanbrugh, *Letters*, to Carlisle, July 1722.
13 Richard Cumberland, *Memoirs of Richard Cumberland* (New York: Brisban and Bannan, 1806), p. 143
14 Ibid., pp. 142–3.

15 DRO, PH843.
16 Palladio, *Architecture*, p. 48.
17 Harris, 'An English Neo-Palladian Episode'.
18 DRO, PH843, author's emphasis.
19 Borthwick Institute, YM/VAN/16.
20 Ibid.
21 Vanbrugh, *Letters*, to Lord Carlisle, March 1724.
22 Whistler, *Vanbrugh*, plate 75: a drawing by Roger Morris dated 1733 annotated: 'this Building was built by Sir John Vanbrugh . . . I finished the inside by contract for £9000'.
23 Thomson, *Autumn* (Dublin: George Rise, 1730), written 1724/5.
24 Jonas Hanway, *A Journal of Eight Days Journey* (London: H. Woodfall, 1756), pp. 60–61, author's emphasis.

12 Stowe, Buckinghamshire

1 Willis, *Bridgeman*, pp. 106–127; Whistler, *Vanbrugh*, Chapter 7; Clarke, 'Sir Richard Temple's House'.
2 See, for example, 'The Landscape and Buildings of Stowe', Symposium, and Gibbon, 'Stowe, Buckinghamshire'; also Mowl, *Gentlemen*, pp. 73–76.
3 For Clarke's work see plates 114 and 115 in Willis, *Bridgeman*, and 'Landscape and Buildings of Stowe', Symposium; Steenbergen and Reh, *Architecture*, p. 281 *et seq*.
4 Quoted in Whistler, *Vanbrugh*, p. 181.
5 The undated account entry is noted in Willis, *Bridgeman*, p. 109, n. 14. Vanbrugh made several visits to Stowe often accompanied by other Kit Cat members.
6 Edward Southwell, 6 August 1724, quoted in G. Clarke, *Descriptions of Lord Cobham's Gardens at Stowe* (Aylesbury: Buckingham Record Society, 1990), p. 19.
7 Ibid., p. 19.
8 BL, Add. 47030, Percival to Daniel Dering, 14 August 1724. Percival had been raised at Kings Weston by Robert Southwell after the death of his own father.
9 Ibid.
10 Willis, *Bridgeman*, p. 110. It may be the engraving that Percival refers to in his letter of 1724: 'we shall shortly have a graving of it', BL, Add. 47030.
11 BL, Add. 47030; quoted in Whistler, *Vanbrugh*, p. 65.
12 Willis, *Bridgeman*, p. 110; Hart, *Storyteller*, p. 208; Whistler, *Vanbrugh*, p. 181; Downes, *Vanbrugh* 1987, p. 464.
13 BL, Maps 7.TAB.10.
14 Steenbergen and Reh, *Architecture*, p. 281, authors' emphasis.
15 Vanbrugh, *Letters*, to Carlisle, August 1725.
16 Quoted in Whistler, *Vanbrugh*, p. 186.

13 Seaton Delaval, Northumberland

1 Swift, *Stella*, entry 31 October 1710. Delaval was at that time envoy to Portugal.
2 He was promoted to vice admiral in 1722. Delaval was also MP for West Looe; Swift's comments suggest that he was a Whig.
3 Quoted in Francis Askham, *The Gay Delavals* (London: Wyman, 1955), p. 22.
4 Letter from James Mewburn to George Delaval, 12 October 1719, in Seaton Delaval House. I am indebted to Martin Green who provided a copy of this paper.
5 Vanbrugh, *Letters*, to Brigadier Watkins, August 1721.
6 NRO, 1DE/13/6, author's emphasis.
7 Askham, *Delavals*, p. 24.
8 Letter Sir Francis Delaval to his brother Edward, July 1724, in Seaton Delaval House.
9 Planting account November 1720, in Seaton Delaval House.
10 NRO, 1DE/13/6.
11 Quoted in Askham, *Delavals*, p. 18.
12 William Hutchinson, *A View of Northumberland*, Vol. 2 (Newcastle: W. Charnley, and Messrs Vesey & Whitfield, 1779), p. 332.

13 Palladio, *Architecture*, p. 70.
14 'Music', 'Painting', 'Geography', 'Sculpture', 'Architecture' and 'Astronomy', according to Hutchinson, *Northumberland*, p. 331.
15 Palladio, *Architecture*, p. 91.
16 William Garson, *Old Seaton Sluice and Seaton Delaval Hall* (North Shields: Private, 1930).
17 Askham, *Delavals*, p. 166.
18 Hutchinson, *Northumberland*, p. 333.
19 The rooms in this wing are described ibid., pp. 331–332.

14 Greenwich and Lumley Castle

1 Downes, *Vanbrugh* 1987, p. 381.
2 Vanbrugh, *Letters*, to Newcastle, July 1717.
3 Downes, *Vanbrugh* 1987, p. 434.
4 Ibid., p. 434.
5 Vanbrugh, *Letters*, to Carlisle, July 1722.
6 Whistler, *Vanbrugh*, p. 200.
7 Vanbrugh, *Letters*, to Brigadier Watkins, August 1721.
8 Vitruvius, *Architecture*, p. 13.
9 Sixty feet long, thirty feet wide and proportionate height.
10 Willis, *Bridgeman*, p. 432.
11 Whistler, *Vanbrugh*, p. 63; Brogden, *Switzer*, p. 145.
12 BOD, Gough Maps 7, fol. 22b.
13 E. Mackenzie and M. Ross, *View of the County Palatine of Durham* (Newcastle upon Tyne: Mackenie, Dent, 1834), p. 124.

15 Vanbrugh's legacy

1 Willis, *Bridgeman*, pp. 173–186. More detail is available after 1728, when Bridgeman was made Royal Gardener.
2 Ibid., p. 70
3 HALS, D/EHx/F92.
4 HMC, *Bath*, Vol. 3, p. 483.
5 Ibid., p. 488.
6 Ibid., p. 488.
7 Quoted in Willis, *Bridgeman*, p. 74.
8 Quoted ibid., p. 75.
9 HMC, *Bath*, Vol. 3, Prior to Harley, September 1720.
10 Ibid., Prior to Harley, June 1721.
11 Willis, *Bridgeman*, p. 76.
12 BOD, volume a.4, Gough Drawings, 1700–40. f. 4.
13 I am indebted to Valerie Joynt, who brought Spring Wood to my attention.
14 Joseph Spence, *Observations, Anecdotes and Characters of Books and Men*, ed. James Osborn (Oxford: Clarendon Press, 1966), No. 1067, including a comment regarding the oaks left in the Woodwork at Blenheim.
15 Walpole, *Anecdotes*, p. 136.
16 Willis, *Bridgeman*, p. 132.
17 Walpole, *Anecdotes*, p. 136.
18 Stephen Switzer, *Ichnographia Rustica*, Vol. 1, 2nd edn (London: J. and J. Fox, B. and B. Barker, D. Browne and F. Gosling, 1742), p. 12
19 Ibid., pp. 11–12, author's emphasis.
20 BL, Stowe 748.

16 Conclusion

1 Vanbrugh, *Letters*, to Manchester, July 1708.
2 Saumarez Smith, *Castle Howard*, p. 87.

3 W. G. Hoskins, *The Making of the English Landscape* (London: Penguin, 1985), p. 178.
4 Vanbrugh, *Letters*, to Manchester, September 1707.
5 Alberti, *Architecture*, p. 300.
6 Dixon Hunt, *Garden and Grove*, chapter 11; John Harris, 'Is Chiswick a "Palladian" Garden?', *Garden History* (2004), Vol. 32, No. 1, pp. 124–136; both authors refer to Palladian gardening.
7 Joshua Reynolds, *The Works of Sir Joshua Reynolds, Knight*, Vol. 2 (London: T. Cadell, Jun. and W. Davies, 1798), pp. 141–142, author's emphasis in the concluding sentence.

Appendix B Vanbrugh's garden structures

1 CHA, G2/2/11–20, entry October 1705, either in Ray Wood or in the kitchen garden.
2 Ibid., entry October 1706.
3 Ibid.
4 BL Add. 47030.
5 This temple is an exact copy of the original form of the Rotundo at Stowe (before the roof was altered). Attributed by Whistler.
6 BL Add. 47030.
7 '[I] am very glad to find your Ldship at last incline to the Temple with the four Porticos'; Vanbrugh, *Letters*, to Carlisle, February 1724.

SELECT BIBLIOGRAPHY

Manuscripts

Arundel Castle, Sussex, TP 133, *Talbot Papers.*
Bodleian Library, University of Oxford, *Volume a3★, a.4, Gough Drawings.*
Bodleian Library, University of Oxford, *MS Wood 276B.*
Bodleian Library, University of Oxford, MS. Top. Gen. D14.
Bodleian Library, University of Oxford, MS. Top. Oxon. A37★.
Bodleian Library, University of Oxford, Gough Maps Volume 17, 30, 46.
Bodleian Library, University of Oxford, *MS Eng. Misc. C. 114, English Letters.*
Borthwick Institute, York, YM/VAN/1, *Yarburgh Muniments.*
Borthwick Institute, York, YM/VAN/16, *Yarburgh Muniments.*
Bristol Record Office, Bristol, 33746, *Kings Weston MS.*
British Library, London, *Blenheim Papers*:
    BLEN G-1–16.
    Add. 19592, 19593, 19594, 19595, 19596, 19597, 19601, 19608, 61354, 61457, 61353, 61523.
British Library, London, Sloane. 3881, *Thomas Brush: Application of Arithmetic and Geometry to the Art of Making Garden Plots.*
British Library, London, Add. 69965, *Coke Papers.*
British Library, London, Add. 47030, *Letter Book of Lord Egmont.*
British Library, London, Add. 70405, *Letters of Edward Harley, Earl of Oxford.*
British Library, London, Add. 33064, *Newcastle Papers.*
British Library, London, Add. 33442, *Newcastle Papers.*
British Library, London, Stowe 748, *Stowe Papers.*
British Library, London, Maps 7.TAB.10, *A General Plan of the Woods, Park and Gardens of Stowe.*
British Library, London, Maps K.Top.13, *Kings Topography.*
Castle Howard Archives, Yorkshire:
    Carlisle MS: G2/1/1, G2/1/2, G2/2/11–20, G2/2/21–30, G2/2/31–40, G2/2/41–50, G2/2/51–60, H1/1/4 and H1/1/5, H2/3/1, J8/1/554–573, J8/5.
    Misc. Letters: J8/35/51.
Department of Prints and Drawings, Victoria & Albert Museum, London, E432.1951, E433.1951, E434.1951, *Bute Collection.*
Dorset Record Office, Dorchester, PH843, *Diary of Dr Evans, Archdeacon of Worcester (attrib.).*

Gloucester Record Office, Gloucestershire, D391, *An Account of a Journey into Norfolk and Back on the South Sea Coast into Somersetshire.*

Hampshire Record Office, Winchester, 63M84/190, *Heathcote Family of Hursley.*

Hertfordshire Archives and Local Studies, Hertford, D/EHx/F92, *The Ballad of Down Hall.*

Hoare's Bank, Fleet Street, London, Private Accounts, *Vols 17, 18 and 20.*

Hoare's Bank, Fleet Street, London, Private Accounts, *Vols 23–50.*

Huntingdon Record Office, Cambridgeshire, M1B/3–1, *Manchester MS.*

Kimbolton Castle, Bedfordshire, *Inventory of Goods of Charles, Earl of Manchester about the Castle of Kimbolton.*

Lincolnshire Record Office, Lincoln, 3ANC5/97/5, *Ancaster MS.*

Lincolnshire Record Office, Lincoln, 3ANC5/97/6, *Ancaster MS.*

National Art Library, London, 86.NN.2, Special Collections, *Voyage d'Angleterre d'Hollande et de Flandre fait en l'annee 1728 par Mr Fougeroux Pierre Jacques.*

Northumberland Record Office, Ashington, 1DE/13/6, *Delaval Family Papers.*

RBS Group Archives, London, CH/194/12, *Private Account, Robert Bertie, Marquess of Lindsay.*

Royal Commission on the Ancient and Historical Monuments of Wales, Aberystwyth, D/HE/313, *Correspondence.*

Surrey History Centre, Woking, K176/14/2, *Abstract of Title to the Manors of Esher and Waterville Esher, the Capital Mansion House called Claremont, Chargate Farm and Stony Hill Close.*

The National Archive, London, PROB 11/573, *Will of George Dodington.*

Primary sources

Anon., *A New Display of the Beauties of England*, Vol. 1 (London: R Goadby, 1774).

Anon., *The Ambulator; Or, the Stranger's Companion in a Tour Round London; within the Circuit of Twenty-Five Miles*, 1st edn (London: J. Bew, 1774).

Addison, Joseph, *The Lucubrations of Isaac Bickerstaff Esq*, Vol. 1 (London: John Morphew, 1710–11).

Addison, Joseph, *The Spectator*, Nos. 411–421 (London: R. Steele and J. Addison, 1712).

Addison, Joseph, *The Guardian*, No. 101 (London: R. Steele, 1713).

Addison, Joseph, *The Works of the Right Honourable Joseph Addison, Esq*, in four volumes (London: Jacob Tonson, 1721).

Alberti, Leon Battista, *De re aedificatoria* (Florence: Magistri Nicolai Laurentii Alamani, 1486).

Alberti, Leon Battista, *On the Art of Building in Ten Books*, translated by Joseph Rykwert, Neil Leach and Robert Tavernor (Cambridge, MA: MIT Press, 1988).

d'Argenville, Dézallier, *The Theory and Practice of Gardening*, translated by John James (London: printed by G. James, 1712).

d'Argenville, Dézallier, *The Theory and Practice of Gardening*, 2nd edn, translated by John James (London: B. Lintot, 1728).

Arthur, Earl of Anglesey, *Memoirs of the Right Honourable Arthur Earl of Anglesey* (London: Sir Peter Pett Knight, 1693).

Bacon, Francis, *The Essayes or Counsels, Ciuill and Morall, of Francis Lo. Verulam, Viscount St. Alban* (London: Hanna Barret, 1625).

Banks, Sir Josiah, Journal of an Excursion to Eastbury and Bristol &c in May and June 1767, *Proceedings of the Dorset Natural History Field Club*, Vol. 21, July 1901, pp. 143–149.

Bradley, Richard, *A Survey of the Ancient Husbandry and Gardening* (London: B. Motte, 1725).

Campbell, Colen, *Vitruvius Britannicus, or the British Architect*, Vol. 1 (London: s.n., 1715).

Campbell, Colen, *Vitruvius Britannicus, or the British architect*, Vol. 3 (London: C. Campbell and J. Smith, 1725).

Castell, Robert, *The Villas of the Ancients Illustrated* (London: Robert Castell, 1728).

Churchill, John, 1st Duke of Marlborough, *John Duke of Marlborough, Appellant. Edward Strong, Senior, and Edward Strong, Junior, Respondents. The Duke of Marlborough's Case* (London: s.n., 1721).

Churchill, John, 1st Duke of Marlborough, *The Marlborough–Godolphin Correspondence*, ed. Henry Snyder (Oxford: Clarendon Press, 1975).

Colonna, Francesco, *Hypnerotomachia Poliphili* (Venice: Aldi Manutii, 1499).

Cook, Moses, *The Manner of Raising, Ordering, and Improving Forrest-Trees* (London: Peter Parker, 1676).

Cooper, Anthony Ashley, Earl of Shaftesbury, *Characteristicks of Men, Manners, Opinions, Times*, Vol. 3 (London, 1711).

Cooper, Anthony Ashley, Earl of Shaftesbury, *Several Letters Written by a Noble Lord to a Young Man at the University* (London: J. Roberts, 1716).

Cooper, Anthony Ashley, Earl of Shaftesbury, *A Letter Concerning the Art or Science of Design, Characteristicks*, Vol. 3 (London: John Darby, 1732).

Cooper, Anthony Ashley, Earl of Shaftesbury, *The Life, Unpublished Letters, and Philosophical Regimen of Anthony, Earl of Shaftesbury*, ed. B. Rand (London: Swan Sonnenschein, 1900).

Cumberland, Richard, *Memoirs of Richard Cumberland* (New York: Brisban and Bannan, 1806).

Defoe, Daniel, *A Tour thro' the Whole Island of Great Britain*, Vol. 1, 3rd edn (London: J. Osborn, S. Birt, D. Browne, J. Hodges, A. Millar, J. Whiston and J. Robinson, 1742).

Defoe, Daniel, *A Tour thro' the Whole Island of Great Britain*, Vol. 2, 3rd edn (London: J. Osborn, S. Birt, D. Browne, J. Hodges, A. Millar, J. Whiston and J. Robinson, 1742).

Euclid, *Euclides Elements of Geometry: The First VI Books, in a Compendious Form Contracted and Demonstrated*, translated by Thomas Rudd (London: Richard Tomlins and Robert Boydell, 1651).

Eusden, Lawrence, *A Poem on the Marriage of His Grace the Duke of Newcastle to the Right Honourable the Lady Henrietta Godolphin* (London: Jacob Tonson, 1717).

de Fer, Nicholas, *Les Forces de l'Europe, ou Description des Principales Villes* (Paris: s.n., 1694).

Garth, Samuel, *Claremont* (London: J. Tonson, 1715).

Gentil, Francois, *The Solitary Gard'ner*, translated by George London and Henry Wise (London: Tooke, 1706).

Hanway, Jonas, *A Journal of Eight Days Journey from Portsmouth to Kingston upon Thames* (London: H. Woodfall, 1756).

Hogarth, William, *The Analysis of Beauty. Written with a View of Fixing the Fluctuating Ideas of Taste* (London: Hogarth, 1753).

Hutchinson, William, *A View of Northumberland with an Excursion to the Abbey of Mailross in Scotland*, Vol. 2 (Newcastle: W. Charnley, and Messrs Vesey & Whitfield, 1779).

Irwin, Lady Anne, *Castle-Howard, the Seat of the Right Honourable Charles Earl of Carlisle* (London: E. Owen, 1732).

Johnson, Samuel, *A Dictionary of the English Language*, Vol. 1, 2nd edn (London: J. and P. Knaptor, T. and T. Longman, C. Hitch and L. Hawes, A. Millar, and R. and J. Dodsley, 1755).

Jones, Inigo, *The Most Notable Antiquity of Great Britain, Vulgarly called Stone-Heng, on Salisbury Plain, restored by Inigo Jones* (London: Daniel Pakeman, 1655).

Kersey, John, *A New English Dictionary* (London: H. Bonwicke and R. Knaplock, 1702).

Kip, J. and L. Knyff, *Britannia Illustrata* (London: D. Mortier, 1707).

Langley, Batty, *New Principles of Gardening* (London: A. Bettesworth and J. Batley, 1727).

Mackenzie, E. and M. Ross, *An Historical, Topographical and Descriptive View of the County Palatine of Durham* (Newcastle Upon Tyne: Mackenzie and Dent, 1834).

Macky, John, *A Journey through England*, Vol. I, 1st edn (London: J. Hooke and T. Caldecott, 1714).

Macky, John, *A Journey through England*, Vol. II, 1st edn (London: J. Pemberton, 1722).

Macky, John, *A Journey through England*, Vol. II, 2nd edn (London: T. Caldecott, 1724).

de Montaigne, Michel, *Michel de Montaigne's Travel Journal*, translated by Donald M. Frame (San Francisco: North Point Press, 1983).

Morris, Robert, *Lectures on Architecture. Consisting of Rules Founded upon Harmonick and Arithmetical Proportions in Building* (London: J. Brindley, 1734).

Nourse, Timothy, *Campania Fœlix*, 2nd edn (London: Thomas Bennet, 1706).

Palladio, Andrea, *The Four Books on Architecture*, translated by Robert Tavernor and Richard Schofield (Cambridge, MA: MIT Press, 2002).

Pollio, Marcus Vitruvius, *The Ten Books of Architecture*, translated by Morris Hicky Morgan (New York: Dover Publications, 1960).

Pope, Alexander, *The Guardian* (London: R. Steele, 1713).

Pope, Alexander, *An Epistle to the Right Honourable Richard Earl of Burlington* (London: L. Gilliver, 1731).

Pope, Alexander, *Letters of Mr Pope, and Several Eminent Persons, from the Year 1705, to 1735*, Vol. I (London: T. Cooper, 1735).

Pope, Alexander, *The Works of Alexander Pope*, Vol. 8 (London: J. & P. Knapton, 1753).

de la Quintinie, Jean, *The Compleat Gard'ner*, translated by John Evelyn (London: M. Gillyflower, 1693).

de la Quintinie, Jean, *The Compleat Gard'ner*, 2nd edn, translated by George London and Henry Wise (London: M. Gillyflower, 1699).

Reynolds, Joshua, *The Works of Sir Joshua Reynolds, Knight*, Vol. 2 (London: T. Cadell, Jun. and W. Davies, 1798).

Salmon, Nathaniel, *The History of Hertfordshire* (London: s.n., 1728).

Salmon, Thomas, *The Present State of the Universities and of the Five Adjacent Counties* (London: Thomas Salmon, 1743).

Salmon, Thomas, *The Foreigner's Companion through the Universities of Cambridge and Oxford, and the Adjacent Counties* (London: William Owen, 1748).

Sarah, Duchess of Marlborough, *The Opinions of Sarah Duchess-Dowager of Marlborough. Published from original MSS.* (Edinburgh: s.n., 1788).

Spence, Joseph, *Observations, Anecdotes and Characters of Books and Men*, ed. James Osborn (Oxford: Clarendon Press, 1966).

Swift, Jonathan, *The History of Vanbrug's House (1706) in Miscellanies: The Last Volume* (London: B. Motte, C. Bathurst, 1736).

Swift, Jonathan, *Journal to Stella*, ed. Harold Williams, Vol. 1 (Oxford: Clarendon Press, 1948).

Switzer, Stephen, *The Nobleman, Gentleman, and Gardener's Recreation* (London: B. Barker and C. King, 1715).

Switzer, Stephen, *Ichnographia Rustica*, Vols 1, 2 and 3 (London: D. Browne, B. Barker, C. King, W. Mears and R. Gosling, 1718).

Switzer, Stephen, *An Introduction to a General System of Hydrostaticks and Hydraulicks*, Vols 1 and 2 (London: T. Astley, S. Austen, L. Gilliver, 1729).

Temple, Sir William, *Miscellanea. The Second Part in Four Essays*, 2nd edn, Vol. 2 (London: R. Simpson, 1690).

The Younger Pliny, *Les plans et les descriptions de deux des plus belles maisons de campagne de Pline le Consul*, Vol. 6, translated by Jean-François Félibien des Avaux (Paris: Florentin & Pierre Delanine, 1699).

The Younger Pliny, *The Letters of the Younger Pliny*, translated by Betty Radice (London: Penguin, 1969).

James Thomson, *Autumn* (Dublin: George Rise, 1730).

Vanbrugh, Sir John, *The Complete Works of Sir John Vanbrugh*, ed. Geoffrey Webb, Vol. 4 *The Letters* (London: Nonesuch Press, 1928).

Virgil, *The Works of Virgil: Containing his Pastorals, Georgics and Æneis*, translated by John Dryden, Vol. 1 (London: Jacob Tonson, 1709).

Walpole, Horace, *Anecdotes of Painting in England*, 1st edn, Vol. 3 (London: Horace Walpole, 1762).

Ward, Edward, *The Secret History of Clubs* (London: J. Bagnall, 1709).

Wentworth, Thomas, *The Wentworth Papers 1705–1739*, ed. J Cartwright (London: Wyman, 1883).

Wotton, Sir Henry, *The Elements of Architecture, Collected by Henry Wotton Knight, from the Best Authors and Examples* (London: John Bill, 1624).

Secondary sources: authored books

Ackerman, James, *Palladio* (London: Penguin, 1991).

Ackroyd, Peter, *Venice: Pure City* (London: Chatto & Windus, 2009).

Al-Khalili, Jim, *Pathfinders* (London: Allen Lane, 2010).

Askham, Francis, *The Gay Delavals* (London: Wyman, 1955).

Ayres, Philip, *Classical Culture and the Idea of Rome in Eighteenth-Century England* (Cambridge: Cambridge University Press, 1997).

Balen, Malcolm, *A Very English Deceit* (London: Fourth Estate, 2003).

Battestin, Martin C., *The Providence of Wit: Aspects of Form in Augustan Literature and the Arts* (Oxford: Oxford Clarendon Press, 1974).

Browning, Reed, *The Duke of Newcastle* (London: Yale University Press, 1975).

Carey, Daniel, *Locke, Shaftesbury and Hutcheson: Contesting Diversity in the Enlightenment* (Cambridge: Cambridge University Press, 2006).

Clark, J. C. D., *English Society 1660–1832*, 2nd edn (Cambridge: Cambridge University Press, 2000).

Clarke, G., *Descriptions of Lord Cobham's Gardens at Stowe* (Aylesbury: Buckingham Record Society, 1990).

Colvin, Howard, *Architecture and the Afterlife* (London: Yale University Press, 1991).

Dixon Hunt, John, *Garden and Grove: The Italian Renaissance Garden in the English Imagination: 1600–1750* (Philadelphia: University of Pennsylvania Press, 1996).

Downes, Kerry, *Vanbrugh* (London: A. Zwemmer, 1977).

Downes, Kerry, *Sir John Vanbrugh* (London: Sidgwick & Jackson, 1987).

Drake, Stillman, *Discoveries and Opinions of Galileo* (New York: Anchor Books, 1957).

Duffy, Christopher, *The Fortress in the Age of Vauban and Frederick the Great 1660–1789* (London: Routledge, 1985).

Erskine-Hill, Howard, *The Augustan Idea in English Literature* (London: Edward Arnold, 1983).

Everett, Nigel, *The Tory View of Landscape* (London: Yale University Press, 1994).

Garson, William, *Old Seaton Sluice and Seaton Delaval Hall* (North Shields: Private, 1930).

Grafton, Anthony, *Leon Battista Alberti* (New York: Hill & Wang, 2000).

Green, David, *Blenheim Palace* (London: Country Life, 1951).

Green, David, *Gardener to Queen Anne* (London: Oxford University Press, 1956).

Habermas, Jurgen, *The Structural Transformation of the Public Sphere* (Cambridge: Polity Press, 2008).

Harris, Eileen, *British Architectural Books and Writers 1556–1785* (Cambridge: Cambridge University Press, 1990).

Hart, Vaughan, *Sir John Vanbrugh: Storyteller in Stone* (London: Yale University Press, 2008).

Hayton, David, Eveline Cruickshanks and Stuart Handley, *The House of Commons, 1690–1715* (Cambridge: Cambridge University Press, 2002).

Hoskins, W. G., *The Making of the English Landscape* (London: Penguin, 1985).

Hussey, Christopher, *English Gardens and Landscapes 1700–1750* (London: Country Life, 1967).

Israel, Jonathan, *A Revolution of the Mind* (Woodstock: Princeton University Press, 2010).

Jacques, David, *Georgian Gardens: The Reign of Nature* (London: Batsford, 1988).

Kelch, Ray, *Newcastle, a Duke without Money: Thomas Pelham-Holles 1693–1768* (London: Routledge & Kegan Paul, 1974).

Kemp, Martin, *Leonardo da Vinci* (Oxford: Oxford University Press, 2006).

Kingsbury, Dorothy, *Bilton Hall: Its History and Literary Association* (London: Mitre Press, 1957).

Lazzaro, Claudia, *The Italian Renaissance Garden* (London: Yale University Press, 1990).

LeFaivre, Liane, *Leon Battista Alberti's Hypnerotomachia Poliphili: Recognizing the Architectural Body in the Early Italian Renaissance* (Cambridge, MA: MIT Press, 1997).

McCormick, Frank, *Sir John Vanbrugh: The Playwright as Architect* (University Park: Pennsylvania State University Press, 1991).

Mayhew, Robert, *Enlightenment Geography: The Political Languages of British Geography, 1650–1850* (Basingstoke: Macmillan, 2000).

Mazzini, Donata and Simone Martini, *Villa Medici a Fiesole: Leon Battista Alberti e il Prototipo di Villa Rinascimentale* (Firenze: Centro Di, 2004).

Mowl, Timothy, *Gentlemen and Players* (Stroud: Sutton, 2004).

Mowl, Timothy, *The Historic Gardens of England: Gloucestershire* (Stroud: Tempus, 2005).

Mowl, Timothy, *The Historic Gardens of England: Oxfordshire* (Stroud: Tempus, 2007).

Murray, Ciaran, *Sharawadgi: The Romantic Return to Nature* (London: International Scholars, 1999).

Opper, Thorsten, *Hadrian Empire and Conflict: Exhibition Catalogue* (London: British Museum Press, 2008).

Pincus, Stephen, *1688: The First Modern Revolution* (Yale: Yale University Press, 2009).

Pocock, J. G. A., *Barbarism and Religion*, Vol. 1 (Cambridge: Cambridge University Press, 2003).

Porter, Roy, *Enlightenment Britain and the Creation of the Modern World* (London: Penguin, 2001).

Richardson, Tim, *Arcadian Friends* (London: Transworld, 2007).

Saliba, George, *Islamic Science and the Making of the European Renaissance* (Cambridge, MA: MIT Press, 2007).

Saumarez Smith, Charles, *The Building of Castle Howard* (London: Pimlico, 1997).

Scott, Geoffrey, *The Architecture of Humanism: A Study in the History of Taste* (London: Constable, 1929).

Smithers, Peter, *The Life of Joseph Addison* (Oxford: Clarendon Press, 1954).

Steenbergen, Clemens and Wouter Reh, *Architecture and Landscape: The Design Experiment of the Great European Gardens and Landscapes* (Munich: Prestel, 1996).

Strong, Roy, *The Renaissance Garden in England* (London: Thames and Hudson, 1998).

Weinbrot, Howard, *Britannia's Issue: The Rise of British Literature from Dryden to Ossian* (Cambridge: Cambridge University Press, 1993).

Whistler, Laurence, *The Imagination of Vanbrugh and his Fellow Artists* (London: B. T. Batsford, 1954).

White, K. D., *Country Life in Classical Times* (London: Book Club Associates, 1978).

Williamson, Tom, *Polite Landscapes* (Stroud: Sutton, 1998).

Williamson, Tom and John Barnatt, *Chatsworth: A Landscape History* (Macclesfield: Windgather Press, 2005).

Willis, Peter, *Charles Bridgeman and the English Landscape Garden* (Newcastle upon Tyne: Elysium Press, 2002).

Wittkower, Rudolf, *Architectural Principles in the Age of Humanism* (London: Warburg Institute, 1949).

Secondary sources: edited books

Beltramini, Guido and Howard Burns (eds), *Palladio: Exhibition Catalogue* (London: Royal Academy of Arts, 2008).

Bond, Donald (ed.), *The Spectator* (Oxford: Clarendon Press, 1965).

Bond, James and Kate Tiller (eds), *Landscape for a Palace*, 2nd edn (Stroud: Sutton, 2000).

Chevalier, Tracy (ed.), *Encyclopedia of the Essay* (London: Taylor & Francis, 1997).

Colvin, Howard and John Harris (eds), *The Country Seat* (London: Allen Lane, 1970).

Cosgrove, Denis and Stephen Daniels (eds), *The Iconography of Landscape* (Cambridge: Cambridge University Press, 1988).

Crossley, Alan and C. R. Elrington (eds), *History of the County of Oxford: Volume 12* (London: Victoria County History of the Counties of England, 1990).

Daniele, Emilia (ed.), *Leon Battista Alberti Firenze e la Toscana: Exhibition Catalogue* (Firenze: Maschietto Editore, 2006).

Graham, Walter (ed.), *The Letters of Joseph Addison* (Oxford: Clarendon Press, 1941).

Harris, John (ed.), *The Palladian Revival: Exhibition Catalogue* (London: Royal Academy of Arts, 1994).

Hind, Charles (ed.), *The Rococo in England* (London: Victoria & Albert Museum, 1986).

Dixon Hunt, John and Peter Willis (eds), *The Genius of the Place* (Cambridge, MA: MIT Press, 1988).

Dixon Hunt, John (ed.), *Gardens and the Picturesque* (Cambridge, MA: MIT Press, 1992).

Gillespie, Stuart and David Hopkins (eds), *The Oxford History of Literary Translation in English. Vol. 3 1660–1790* (Oxford: Oxford University Press, 2005).

Millican, Peter (ed.), *David Hume: An Essay Concerning Human Understanding* (Oxford: Oxford University Press, 2008).

Porter, Roy and Mikulas Teich (eds), *The Renaissance in National Context* (Cambridge: Cambridge University Press, 1994).

Ridgway, Christopher and Robert Williams (eds), *Sir John Vanbrugh and Landscape Architecture in Baroque England* (Stroud: Sutton, 2000).

Rowe, Anne (ed.), *Garden Making and the Freman Family: A Memoir of Hamels 1713–33* (Hertford: Hertfordshire Record Society, 2001).

Schulman, Jana K. (ed.), *The Rise of the Medieval World, 500–1300: A Biographical Dictionary* (London: Greenwood Press, 2002).

Turnbull, H. W., J. F. Scott and A. R. Hall (eds), *The Correspondence of Isaac Newton* (Cambridge: Cambridge University Press, 1959).

Wenger, Mark (ed.), *The English Travels of Sir John Percival and William Byrd II: The Percival Diary of 1701* (Columbia: University of Missouri Press, 1989).

Secondary sources: journal articles

Barlow, Graham F., 'Vanbrugh's Queen's Theatre in the Haymarket, 1703–9', *Early Music* (1989), Vol. 17, No. 4, pp. 515–521.

Baron, Hans, 'The Querelle of the Ancients and Moderns as a Problem for Renaissance Scholarship', *Journal of the History of Ideas* (1959), Vol. 20, No. 1, pp. 3–22.

Batey, Mavis, 'The Pleasures of the Imagination: Joseph Addison's Influence on Early Garden Design', *Garden History* (2006), Vol. 33, No. 2, pp. 189–209.

Birkett, Stephen and William Jurgenson, 'Why Didn't Historical Makers Need Drawings? Part I – Practical Geometry and Proportion', *Galpin Society Journal* (2001), Vol. 54, pp. 242–284.

Black, Jeremy, 'Fragments from the Grand Tour', *Huntington Library Quarterly* (1990), Vol. 53, No. 4, pp. 337–341.

Boys, Richard C., 'The Architect Vanbrugh and the Wits', *College Art Journal* (1947), Vol. 6, No. 4, pp. 283–290.

Brownell, Morris R., 'The Gardens of Horatio and Pope's Twickenham: An Unnoticed Parallel', *Garden History* (1977), Vol. 5, No. 2, pp. 9–23.

Clarke, George, 'Sir Richard Temple's House and Gardens', *Stoic* (1968), Vol. 23, p. 70.

Cosgrove, Denis, 'Prospect, Perspective and the Evolution of the Landscape Idea', *Transactions of the Institute of British Geographers* (1985), Vol. 10, No. 1, pp. 45–62.

Downes, Kerry, 'The Kings Weston Book of Drawings', *Architectural History* (1967), Vol. 10, pp. 7+9–88.

Elmquist, Karl Erik, 'An Observation on Chaucer's Astrolabe', *Modern Language Notes* (1941), Vol. 56, No. 7, pp. 530–534.

Erickson, Bryce, 'Art and Geometry: Proportioning Devices in Pictorial Composition', *Leonardo* (1986), Vol. 19, No. 3, pp. 211–215.

Erskine-Hill, Howard, 'The Medal against Time: A Study of Pope's Epistle to Mr Addison', *Journal of the Warburg and Courtauld Institutes* (1965), Vol. 28, pp. 274–298.

Fraser, Nancy, 'Rethinking the Public Sphere: A Contribution to the Critique of Actually Existing Democracy', *Social Text* (1990), No. 25/26, pp. 56–80.

Gibbon, Michael, 'Stowe, Buckinghamshire: The House and Garden Buildings and Their Designers', *Architectural History* (1977), Vol. 20, pp. 31–44, 82–83.

Gray, John M., 'Memoirs of the Life of Sir John Clerk of Penicuik, Baronet . . . Extracted by himself from his own Journals', *Publications of the Scottish Historical Society* (1892), Vol. 13, pp. 236–240.

Harris, John, 'An English Neo-Palladian Episode and Its Connections with Visentini in Venice', *Architectural History* (1984), Vol. 27, pp. 231–240.

Harris, John, 'The Beginnings of Claremont: Sir John Vanbrugh's Garden at Chargate Surrey', *Apollo* (1993), Vol. 374, April, pp. 223–226.

Harris, John, 'Is Chiswick a "Palladian" Garden?', *Garden History* (2004), Vol. 32, No. 1, pp. 124–136.

Howard, Deborah, 'Four Centuries of Literature on Palladio', *Journal of the Society of Architectural Historians* (1980), Vol. 39, No. 3, pp. 224–241.

Howard, Deborah and Malcolm Longair, 'Harmonic Proportion and Palladio's "Quattro Libri"', *Journal of the Society of Architectural Historians* (1982), Vol. 41, No. 2, pp. 116–143.

Kellum, Barbara, 'The Construction of Landscape in Augustan Rome: The Garden Room at the Villa ad Gallinas', *Art Bulletin* (1994), Vol. 76, No. 2, pp. 211–224.

Lake, Peter and Steve Pincus, 'Rethinking the Public Sphere in Early Modern England', *Journal of British Studies* (2006), Vol. 45, April, pp. 270–292.

Lang, Susan, 'Vanbrugh's Theory and Hawksmoors Buildings', *Journal of the Society of Architectural Historians* (1965), Vol. 24, No. 2, pp. 127–151.

Leatherbarrow, David, 'Character, Geometry and Perspective: The Third Earl of Shaftesbury's Principles of Garden Design', *Journal of Garden History* (1984), Vol. 4, No. 4, pp. 332–358.

Levine, Neil, 'Castle Howard and the Emergence of the Modern Architectural Subject', *Journal of the Society of Architectural Historians* (2003), Vol. 62, No. 3, pp. 326–351.

Lord, John, 'Sir John Vanbrugh and the 1st Duke of Ancaster: Newly Discovered Documents', *Architectural History* (1991), Vol. 34, pp. 136–144.

McCormick, Frank, 'John Vanbrugh's Architecture: Some Sources of His Style', *Journal of the Society of Architectural Historians* (1987), Vol. 46, No. 2, pp. 135–144.

Markowsky, George, 'Misconceptions about the Golden Ratio', *College Mathematics Journal* (1992), Vol. 23, No. 1, pp. 2–19.

Mayhew, Robert, 'Was William Shakespeare an Eighteenth-Century Geographer? Constructing Histories of Geographical Knowledge', *Transactions of the Institute of British Geographers* (1998), Vol. 23, No. 1, pp. 21–37.

Milledge, Jenny, 'Sacombe Park Hertfordshire: An Early Bridgeman landscape', *Garden History* (2009), Vol. 37, No. 1, pp. 38–55.

Morgan, Luke, 'Isaac de Caus *invenit*', *Studies in the History of Gardens & Designed Landscapes* (2009), Vol. 29, No. 3, pp. 141–151.

Neckar, L. M., 'Castle Howard: An Original Landscape Architecture', *Landscape Journal, University of Wisconsin Press* (2000), Vol. 19, No. 1/2, pp. 21–45.

Phibbs, John, 'Projective Geometry', *Garden History* (2006), Vol. 34, No. 1, pp. 1–21.

Skinner, Quentin, 'Meaning and Understanding in the History of Ideas', *History and Theory* (1969), Vol. 8, No. 1, pp. 3–53.

Skinner, Quentin, 'Thomas Hobbes and the Nature of the Early Royal Society', *Historical Journal* (1969), Vol. 12, No. 2, pp. 217–230.

Saumarez Smith, Charles, 'Supply and Demand in English Country House Building 1660–1740', *Oxford Art Journal* (1988), Vol. 11, No. 2, pp. 3–9.

Shields, Steffie, 'The Magnificence of Grimsthorpe', *Lincolnshire Life* (2006), August, pp. 16–20.

Stapleford, Richard and John Potter, 'Velazquez' "Las Hilanderas"', *Artibus et Historiae* (1987), Vol. 8, No. 15, pp. 159–181.

Stasavage, David, 'Partisan Politics and Public Debt: The Importance of the "Whig Supremacy" for Britain's Financial Revolution', *European Review of Economic History* (2007), Vol. 2, pp. 123–153.

Stewering, Roswitha, 'Architectural Representations in the "Hypnerotomachia Poliphili" (Aldus Manutius, 1499)', *Journal of the Society of Architectural Historians* (2000), Vol. 59, No. 1, pp. 6–25.

Stratford, John, 'The Lost Gardens of Kimbolton Castle', *Kimbolton Local History Journal* (1998), Vol. 3, pp. 21–30.

Syson, Luke, 'Holes and Loops: The Display and Collection of Medals in Renaissance Italy', *Journal of Design History* (2002), Vol. 15, No. 4, pp. 229–244.

Townsend, Dabney, 'Shaftesbury's Aesthetic Theory', *Journal of Aesthetics and Art Criticism* (1982), Vol. 41, No. 2, pp. 205–213.

Willis, Peter, 'From Desert to Eden: Charles Bridgeman's "Capital Stroke"', *Burlington Magazine* (1973), Vol. 115, No. 840, pp. 150, 152–155, 157.

Worsley, Giles, 'Nicholas Hawksmoor: A Pioneer Neo-Palladian?', *Architectural History* (1990), Vol. 33, pp. 60–74.

Worsley, Giles, 'In the English Campagna', *Country Life* (2001), 27 September, pp. 118–123.

Conference papers, Historic Manuscripts Commission, unpublished papers

Brogden, William, *Stephen Switzer and Garden Design in the Early Eighteenth Century*, PhD thesis, University of Edinburgh (1973).

Flintshire, *Leeswood Hall Garden Site Report*, Royal Commission on the Ancient and Historical Monuments of Wales.

Historic Monuments Commission, *1st Report, Appendix, p. 13, and 8th Report, App., Pt. II, The Manuscripts of the Dukes of Manchester* (London: British Library, 1870 and 1881).

Historic Manuscripts Commission, *Calendar of the Manuscripts of the Marquis of Bath* (London: British Library, 1904).

Jacques, David and Jane Furse, *Report of the Historical Interest of the Gardens and Grounds at Leeswood Hall, Clwyd*, Garden History Society (1981).

Mowl, Tim, *Early Mediaevalism: 'To Have Built in Heaven High Towers' – The Castle as a Theme in English Architecture before the Gothic Revival*. A Gothick Symposium, Victoria & Albert Museum (London: The Georgian Group, 1983).

'The Landscape and Buildings of Stowe'. Symposium – An English Arcadia: Landscape and Architecture in Britain and America, Vol. 55 (California: Huntingdon Library Quarterly, 1992), pp. 477–500.

Online sources

Myers, K. Sarah, 'Representations of Gardens in Roman Literature', at http://www.virginia.edu/classics/Myerschapteruse.pdf, accessed on 17 February 2011.

Officer, Lawrence H., 'Purchasing Power of British Pounds from 1264 to Present', MeasuringWorth, 2011, at http://www.measuringworth.com/ppoweruk/, accessed on various dates.

Ovid, 'Metamorphoses', at http://oaks.nvg.org/eg6ra11.html, accessed on 1 May 2008.

Oxford English Dictionary (online edition), at http://dictionary.oed.com/, accessed on various dates.

Oxford Dictionary of National Biography (online edition), at http://www.oxforddnb.com, accessed on various dates: J. D. Davies, 'Temple, Sir William, Baronet (1628–99)'; Howard Erskine-Hill, 'Pope, Alexander (1688–1744)'; Stuart Handley, 'Charles Talbot, Duke of Shrewsbury'; A. Hanham, 'George Bubb Dodington, Baron Melcombe (1690/91–1762)'; D.W. Hayton, 'Edward Southwell (1671–1730)'; Calhoun Winton, 'Steele, Sir Richard (bap. 1672, d. 1729)'.

ILLUSTRATION CREDITS

FIGURE 0.1   Special Collections, University of Bristol.

FIGURE 0.2   © V&A Images, Victoria and Albert Museum, London E433.1951.

FIGURE 0.3   Photo: author, 2008.

FIGURE 1.1   Su concessione del Ministero per i Beni e le Attivita Culturali – Soprintendenza Speciale per i Beni Archeologici di Roma.

FIGURE 1.2   Drawing: author, 2011.

FIGURE 1.3   Annotations: author, 2009.

FIGURE 1.4   Author's copy.

FIGURE 1.5   Photo: author, 2008.

FIGURE 1.6   Bibliothèque nationale de France, NB-C-51006.

FIGURE 2.1   Special Collections, University of Bristol. The Bodleian Libraries, University of Oxford, Vet E4 f62 p126 Tabula III.

FIGURE 2.2   © V&A Images, Victoria and Albert Museum, London, 86.NN.2.

FIGURE 2.3   Special Collections, University of Bristol.

FIGURE 3.1   © National Portrait Gallery, London 3231.

FIGURE 4.1   © V&A Images, Victoria and Albert Museum, London E434.1951.

FIGURE 4.2   Castle Howard Archives P1/4.

FIGURE 4.3   Ordnance Survey 1891: © and database right 'Crown Copyright and Landmark Information Group Ltd.' (All rights reserved 2011). Castle Howard Archives P1/2.

FIGURE 4.4   Ordnance Survey 1891: © and database right 'Crown Copyright and Landmark Information Group Ltd.' (All rights reserved 2011). Annotation: author, 2009.

FIGURE 4.5   Castle Howard Archives P1/4. Annotation: author.

FIGURE 4.6   Castle Howard archives P1/11. Annotation: author.

FIGURE 4.7   Ordnance Survey 1891: © and database right 'Crown Copyright and Landmark Information Group Ltd.' (All rights reserved 2011). Annotation: author.

FIGURE 4.8   Ordnance Survey on behalf of HMSO © Crown copyright (2011). All rights reserved. Ordnance Survey Licence number 100050286. Layout taken from map P1/4 Castle Howard archives. 3D model: author 2010.

FIGURE 4.9	Photo and reconstruction: author.

FIGURE 4.9   Photo and reconstruction: author.
FIGURE 4.10   Huntingdonshire Archives M1B/3-1.
FIGURE 4.11   The Bodleian Libraries, University of Oxford MS. Top. Gen. D14 f38v.
FIGURE 4.12   Photo: author, 2008.
FIGURE 4.13   © The British Library Board Maps 7.TAB10, view 8.
FIGURE 4.14   Photo: author, 2007.
FIGURE 4.15   Photo and reconstruction: author, 2008.
FIGURE 4.16   Source unknown.
FIGURE 4.17   © The British Library Board CRACE PORT XIX 18.
FIGURE 4.18   The Bodleian Libraries, University of Oxford Gough Maps 30, fol. 58.
FIGURE 4.19   Photos: author, 2008. Bottom left: © The British Library Board Maps K.Top 40 19a.
FIGURE 4.20   The Bodleian Libraries, University of Oxford MS. Top. Gen. D14 f37v.
FIGURE 4.21   © The British Library Board Maps 7.TAB10, view 14.
FIGURE 4.22   Ordnance Survey 1872: © and database right 'Crown Copyright and Landmark Information Group Ltd.' (All rights reserved 2011). Annotation: author.
FIGURE 4.23   The Bodleian Libraries, University of Oxford Gough Maps 17, fol. 41b
FIGURE 5.1   Photo: author, 2008.
FIGURE 5.2   © V&A Images, Victoria and Albert Museum, London, E433.1951.
FIGURE 5.3   Drawing: author, 2007 based on Castle Howard Archives P1/4 and P1/16.
FIGURE 5.4   Mortham Estates (Trustees) Ltd. Reproduced by kind permission of Sir Andrew Morritt.
FIGURE 5.5   Photos: author, 2007.
FIGURE 5.6   Special Collections, University of Bristol.
FIGURE 5.7   Ordnance Survey on behalf of HMSO © Crown copyright (2011). All rights reserved. Ordnance Survey Licence number 100050286.
FIGURE 6.1   Plan: author; based on the Bodleian Libraries, University of Oxford MS. Top. Oxon. A.37★ first plan.
FIGURE 6.2   The Bodleian Libraries, University of Oxford MS. Top. Oxon. A.37★ first plan. Annotation: author.
FIGURE 6.3   The Bodleian Libraries, University of Oxford MS. Top. Oxon. A.37★ first plan (detail). Annotation: author.
FIGURE 6.4   The Bodleian Libraries, University of Oxford MS. Top. Oxon. A.37★ second plan (detail). Annotation: author.
FIGURE 6.5   Photo: author, 2007.
FIGURE 6.6   Blenheim Palace Archives, by kind permission of His Grace the Duke of Marlborough.
FIGURE 6.7   Photo: Richard Craggs, 2007, by kind permission of His Grace the Duke of Marlborough.
FIGURE 6.8   The Bodleian Libraries, University of Oxford MS. Top. Gen. D.14 fol. 14v.
FIGURE 6.9   Oxford County Council Historic Environment Record, Fairey Aviation Surveys 6125/8071-2 (1961). Annotation: author.
FIGURE 6.10   Special Collections, University of Bristol.
FIGURE 6.11   © V&A Images, Victoria and Albert Museum, London, 86.NN.2.
FIGURE 7.1   Photo: author, 2007.
FIGURE 7.2   Huntingdonshire Archives Map 83.
FIGURE 7.3   © V&A Images, Victoria and Albert Museum, London, 86.NN.2.

INDEX

Note that references to illustrations in the text are italicised.